D0848532

ENERGY EFFICIENT
DESIGN AND CONSTRUCTION
FOR COMMERCIAL BUILDINGS

ENERGY EFFICIENT DESIGN AND CONSTRUCTION FOR COMMERCIAL BUILDINGS

STEVEN WINTER ASSOCIATES, INC.

ADRIAN TULUCA

(LEAD AUTHOR)

McGraw-Hill

New York   San Francisco   Washington, D.C.
Auckland   Bogotá   Caracas   Lisbon   London
Madrid   Mexico City   Milan   Montreal   New Delhi
San Juan   Singapore   Sydney   Tokyo   Toronto

Library of Congress Cataloging-in-Publication Data
Tuluca, Adrian.
   Energy-efficient design and construction for commercial buildings
  / Adrian Tuluca.
      p.   cm.
   ISBN 0-07-071159-3
   1. Commercial buildings—Energy conservation. 2. Architecture and
energy conservation. I. Title.
TJ163.5.B84T85   1997
696—dc20   96-34522
                                              CIP

McGraw-Hill

*A Division of The **McGraw·Hill** Companies*

1 2 3 4 5 6 7 8 9 0 DOC/DOC 9 0 1 0 9 8 7 6

ISBN 0-07-071159-3

The sponsoring editor for this book was Wendy Lochner,
the editing supervisor was Penny Linskey, and the production supervisor
was Pamela Pelton. Interior design and composition: North Market Street Graphics

Printed and bound by Donnelley/Crawfordsville.

McGraw-Hill books are available at special quantity discounts to use as premiums and sales promotions,
or for use in corporate training programs. For more information, please write to the Director of Special
Sales, McGraw-Hill, 11 West 19th Street, New York, NY 10011. Or contact your local bookstore.

CONTENTS

INTRODUCTION

Energy Efficient Design and Construction for Commercial Buildings is a working guide to energy efficiency strategies. Sustainability, "green" materials and methods, and indoor air quality are related and important aspects of integrated designs. These aspects could only be occasionally mentioned here because of space limitations. Also the book only briefly addresses design philosophy issues. Its focus is on practical applications for typical designs.

Designers should command a working knowledge of *all* aspects of the building process, including the latest developments in energy efficiency. This is difficult, since *current* information on energy saving measures has to be assembled from a variety of sources, including scientific publications and engi-

neering journals, which often address the subject from a narrow technical perspective.

This book examines a selection of innovative, yet proven energy efficiency strategies, focusing on practical applications. It also highlights several established but underutilized techniques to reduce energy use, and mentions developments on the horizon.

Each chapter is designed as a self-contained unit which addresses a different building subsystem. All chapters start with highlights of technical advances in energy efficiency.

Next, a section on basic principles explains, in simple terms, the technical reasons behind the effectiveness of various efficiency strategies. Applications are then discussed, with the help of illustrations, case studies, and lists of practical considerations.

DEFINITIONS

Several terms are widely used throughout the book. This glossary presents a detailed explanation of the most important ones. For further technical information refer to the latest edition of the *ASHRAE Handbook of Fundamentals* and of the *IESNA Handbook*.

▶ THE BTU

Btu stands for British Thermal Unit and is a measure of heat. It takes 12,000 Btu to melt one ton of ice. A person doing office work gives off about 250 Btu every hour. A 100 watt bulb gives off 3,413 Btu every hour (3,413 Btu/hr).

If a double pane window is located in a house where the temperature is maintained at 70°F, and if outside the air is at 30°F (no wind), the window loses through every square foot about 20–25 Btu every hour.

If, instead of the window, we have a wood stud wall with 6" batt insulation, the wall loses through every square foot about 2–2.5 Btu every hour.

▶ THE U-VALUE

This book examines exterior walls and roofs. For such assemblies, the U-value measures the heat flow that occurs during one hour through one square foot of construction, when there is 1°F temperature differential between the inside and outside air temperatures. The units are Btu/(hr · °F · ft²). If an assembly has a higher U-value it means that it loses more heat.

A window with single pane glass and uninsulated metal frames could have U = 1.3. A window with double pane low-e glass and thermally broken metal frames could have U = 0.35. That means that the low-e window loses about 3.5 times less heat than the single pane window.

Note: The U-value is sometimes referred to as U-factor or thermal transmittance.

▶ THE R-VALUE

The R-value is the inverse of U-value. Instead of measuring how much heat flows through an assembly, it measures the resistance that the assembly poses to the flow of heat.

$$R = 1/U$$

The units of the R-value are $(hr \cdot °F \cdot ft^2)/$ Btu. They can be interpreted as the number of hours it takes for heat to flow across one square foot of assembly, when there is 1°F temperature differential between inside and outside temperatures. If an assembly has a higher R-value it means that it poses more resistance to the flow of heat, i.e., that it takes longer for a given amount of heat to flow across it.

▶ THE SHADING COEFFICIENT

The shading coefficient, sometimes abbreviated SC, is the ratio between the solar heat gain through a given glazing assembly and the solar heat gain through a single pane of clear, ⅛ in thick sheet glass, at predetermined conditions. These conditions are:

- indoor air temperature 75°F
- outdoor air temperature 89°F
- outdoor air velocity 7.5 mph
- solar radiation 248 Btu/$(hr \cdot ft^2)$

Accordingly, the shading coefficient of a clear, ⅛ in glass pane is 1.0. Glazings with lower shading coefficients allow less solar heat into the conditioned space. Two glazings can have the same shading coefficients yet admit different amounts of light (visible solar radiation) into a space.

▶ THE RELATIVE HEAT GAIN

The relative heat gain of a glazing assembly measures the amount of heat that crosses that assembly when the solar intensity is 200 Btu/$(hr \cdot ft^2)$ and when the outdoor temperature is 14°F higher than the indoor temperature.

The relative heat gain (RHG) is similar to the shading coefficient. The ratio between RHG of two glass types is usually very close to the ratio of the SC of these glass types. This means that, in general, one can compare glazings using either SC or RHG and reach the same conclusion.

▶ THE EMITTANCE

The emittance of a surface is defined as the ratio between the radiant flux emitted by that surface and that emitted by a *blackbody* at the same temperature.

A *blackbody* is an ideal construct that emits the maximum heat that the laws of physics allow, given a certain temperature.

Low-e coatings can only emit little heat via radiation. The better ones have an emittance of 0.1. Others have emittances up to 0.3.

Acknowledgments

Energy Efficient Design and Construction for Commercial Buildings was initially conceived as a practical guide that would catalog and describe energy efficient techniques for use by a non-technical audience. New York State Energy Office (NYSEO) selected Steven Winter Associates, Inc. (SWA) to perform the work. Tishman Research Corporation, Perkins and Will, and Cosentini Associates were also on the SWA team. During the course of the project the emphasis changed to include more explanation of the concepts that are behind the energy efficient application. The catalog was becoming a manual.

NYSEO ceased to exist in 1995 and most of its functions were transferred to New York State Energy Research and Development Authority (NYSERDA). The manual was not going to be published by the state, but McGraw-Hill expressed an interest. After reviews and revisions, this book is the final product.

Throughout the development of the NYSEO manual, Steven Winter Associates, Inc. had the prime role in developing the content and made final decisions on technical issues, in consultation with NYSEO personnel. Therefore, the contents of the book do not reflect all opinions of all participants. SWA has tried hard to make this book informative and accurate, but if there are any errors, omissions or problems with the book, they are entirely attributable to SWA and not to any of its collaborators.

SWA gratefully acknowledges the contribution of Tishman Research Corporation in setting the direction for the project, collecting background information on all energy efficient strategies, providing input into the overall book structure and reviewing the NYSEO version of chapter 1 on walls, roofs and floors. James Carpenter Design Associates contributed to data collection on glazings through Tishman Research Corporation.

Perkins and Will was helpful in collecting data and case studies for architectural and daylighting strategies. Cosentini Associates was involved in the very beginning, providing an overview of the areas of interest in

HVAC. SWA thanks the two firms for their valuable contribution.

Ned Nisson of Energy Design Associates collaborated in a substantial manner in the organization and writing of chapter 1 (walls, roofs and floors) and chapter 2 (windows ang glazing). His work made the NYSEO manual better.

The lead author of the book is Adrian Tuluca, R.A., principal with Steven Winter Associates, Inc. He oversaw the entire process, researched information, wrote and rewrote sections, edited and revised. He was supported by the work of many professionals in the company, with significant contributions from Deane Evans, AIA, Robert Erwin, R.A., AIA and Steven Winter, FAIA, president of SWA.

Serge Preston worked closely with SWA on the NYSEO version and reviewed all HVAC sections. An internal review was performed before publication by Robert Supon, P.E., formerly with SWA, on HVAC equipment and controls. Ian Graham of SWA checked and updated data in the HVAC chapter. Kimberly LeBel of SWA provided input into the lighting section. Lori R. Baker steered the book at SWA during the final phase and coordinated the interaction with McGraw-Hill.

We would like to mention organization and data gathering work by SWA current and former colleagues, including Ann-Marie Bars-ness, R.A., and Dinesh Kumar, computer analyses by Dennis O'Keefe, Jawad Zaidi, P.E., Ph.D., Devashish Lahiri, and drawings by Peter Stratton and Jonathan Tham, as well as guidance on passive solar issues by Helen English.

Mary Seymour deserves special thanks for her skill and patience typing and formatting the final versions of the book. Robin Geller typed the original versions of the NYSEO manual.

The Tishman Research Corporation (TRC) team was led by Barry Donaldson, AIA who was assisted by Kevin Taylor. Harvey Brickman, P.E., of Tishman Construction also offered his advice as part of the TRC team.

The Perkins and Will team included James Garretson, AIA and Cameron Rashti, AIA. Michael Maybaum, P.E., represented Cosentini Associates.

From NYSEO, Technical Services Bureau, SWA gratefully acknowledges the management and advice of Delaine Jones, FAIA, Clifford Wassell, and Floyd Barwig, AIA. David Abrey, Karen Kinzler, Mark Eggers, R.A., Eric Noble and Thomas Eapen reviewed the manual and made useful contributions.

Finally, the Energy User News is acknowledged for having provided searches in their archives for case studies, some of which are presented in this book.

CHAPTER 1

THE BUILDING ENVELOPE: WALLS, ROOFS, AND FOUNDATIONS

1.1 ▶ THE BUILDING ENVELOPE—INNOVATION THROUGH INTEGRATION

The pursuit of thermally efficient walls, roofs, and foundations has been a catalyst for innovation. Better materials and systems are now available. Better concepts on the role of the building envelope gain ground.

Increasingly, the building envelope is viewed not simply as protection from, but as connection to the environment. This connection is achieved by integration with the lighting, HVAC, and control systems. Within the envelope itself, the concept of integration is often applied to increase construction efficiency while reducing energy use. Envelope subsystems integrate several envelope functions (e.g., thermal protection, structural support, or water and weather protection) into a single, cost-effective component.

This chapter examines the performance of the building insulation system in interaction with the entire envelope, and then describes several innovative applications in detail. A dis-

cussion of air leakage and air retarders follows. Finally, two new technologies currently under development are presented: ultra-thin, high R-value panels and insulating structural concretes. A third technology is used in Europe but has not yet been introduced in the United States: a self-drying vapor retarder for roofs.

1.2 ▶ THE MEMBRANE ENVELOPE

As part of the design process, architects and engineers create a shape, defined by an envelope, that responds to functional, structural and aesthetic considerations. The envelope encloses distinct spaces and provides controlled access to them. It facilitates and blocks views. It makes aesthetic and symbolic statements. It contributes to the structural integrity of the building and protects it against weather. The last function is of specific interest for this discussion, since in traditional design the envelope is viewed as a cocoon which decouples the building interior from the environment. Mechanical and electrical systems then take over to maintain comfort.

▶ 1

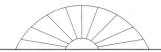

INNOVATION THROUGH INTEGRATION

- An insulating technique for metal roof systems not only increases thermal efficiency, but also reduces condensation potential on interior surfaces.
- Plastic ties between the two faces of concrete panels with core insulation eliminate thermal bridging and moisture condensation.
- Insulating concrete masonry units combine thermal insulation and structural support into a single element.
- A foundation insulation system combines ground water control and thermal insulation into a single component.
- A membrane system serves as air retarder and weather protection for exterior walls.
- A metal panel under development combines very low weight with high R-value.
- A roof vapor retarder, not yet in use in the US, allows trapped water to vent back into the conditioned space. This keeps the roof dry and allows for early detection of major leaks.

This approach results in buildings that are expensive to operate. If, for instance, all windows in an office building use reflective glass, the solar heat gain will be cut not only in summer but also in winter, increasing the heating load. Further, the amount of daylight will be reduced year-round, foregoing opportunities to dim or turn off the lamps.

A much more attractive approach is to replace the cocoon concept with a membrane concept. An envelope functioning as a membrane is coupled to the environment so that, over the year, the interaction between interior and environment (heat, air, and solar radiation exchanges) results in low-energy use and improved comfort. Returning to the example with reflective windows, north-facing areas could receive only a light tint. If nothing else were done, the slight increase in cooling energy use would be more than offset by a decrease in heating energy use. However, a good design will take advantage of the opportunity to dim or turn off the lamps during daytime. Lower electricity use for lighting will result in lower cooling loads. Lower cooling loads can result in smaller fans, ducts, and chillers.

This example introduces the concept of integration. The envelope can successfully function as a membrane only if it is integrated with lighting, HVAC, and controls. The means to achieve integration are specific to the function of the building and to the climate. Obviously, a combination of strategies that excel for an office located in the sunny warm Washington, D.C. area will yield disappointing results for a school located in the cloudy, cool Seattle, Washington climate.

The integration concept that brings together the envelope, lighting, HVAC, and controls also applies to the envelope itself, since the envelope is a system. A wall needs structural support, exterior and interior finishes, thermal insulation, and protection of the insulation from moisture and air intrusion. These functions are usually, but not necessarily, accom-

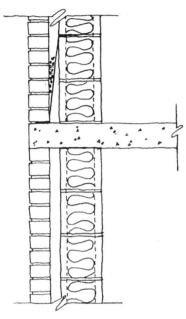

Figure 1.1 ▶ Typical wall detail where floor slab directly supports exterior finish.

plished by different components or even by different subsystems. Too often each component is designed independently of the others.

A typical example is the wall detail shown schematically in Fig. 1.1, encountered in schools and dormitories, nursing homes and treatment centers, etc. The floor slab sustains the exterior brick wythe and the concrete masonry unit (CMU) backup wythe. The insulation is located inside the CMU cores. The backup wythe does not receive parging on the exterior surface. The slab edge remains exposed and allows heat to easily flow from the conditioned space to the outside.

When wind blows, the exterior brick wythe bears some of the air pressure. Some pressure is also borne by the concrete blocks. Since the blocks are not parged, they are not likely to pose much higher resistance to the air than the bricks. The pressure differential created across the exterior finish forces the rain into bricks and mortar. During late fall, winter, and early spring this moisture freezes and thaws, engendering spalling. As the finish deteriorates, the water penetrates more easily into the brick wythe accelerating the destructive process.

As air pushes onto one facade, it creates suction on another. Air moves out of the building (exfiltrates) through the leeward wall. Likely entry areas are created by cracks in the mortar joints between blocks and slab. The junction area between wall and windows can also be vulnerable. In its path, the exfiltrating air encounters the exterior shell of the CMU, the slab underside, and brick ties. If the air has significant moisture content (e.g., as in a nursing home with humidification or in a kitchen/cafeteria), that moisture condenses. Condensed moisture reduces the R-value of fill-type insulation, such as perlite and vermiculite. If the core insulation is made of polystyrene inserts, the moisture will probably not affect the R-value, but may accumulate at a higher rate on the exterior shell. In either case, if this shell becomes moist, it deteriorates just like the exterior brick. The ties embedded in mortar rust.

For buildings with winter humidification (be it intentional or as a result of usage), walls with the detail of Fig. 1.1 will tend to have higher repair and maintenance costs over their useful life. Just as important, these walls are not very forgiving to flaws in design or execution. Details that contain significant thermal bridging, or areas where the insulation is left out can result in relatively fast and severe deterioration of the construction. Finally, the energy use of buildings with these walls is higher.

Of course, the air intrusion phenomena described above cannot occur unless there are some pathways of air penetration into the concrete block wythe, such as mortar with cracks. Very good site supervision can result in superior performance, even for the walls of Fig. 1.1. However, from a statistical standpoint, very good supervision is not possible in all projects. Furthermore, even perfect execution cannot confer the intrinsic advantages given by the design described below.

An integrated approach to wall design is presented in Fig 1.2. The insulation protects the structure and backup wall, which are now at a temperature close to that of the room. Condensation is highly unlikely. A continuous air retarder is placed behind the insulation.

The air retarder is effective in stopping most air infiltration and exfiltration (see Sec. 1.4 for further information). This air retarder bears almost all wind pressure. The brick wythe is intentionally left air-permeable. The wind creates only a small difference in pressure between the exterior and interior surfaces of the brick wythe. As a result, rain is less likely to be pushed into the brick and the probability of spalling is significantly reduced.

This approach works because it integrates all functions of the envelope.

A successful envelope is a membrane, allowing the passage of heat and solar radiation according to season and climate. A successful envelope also integrates its subsystems. Also, a successful envelope preserves the integrity of each subsystem, protecting it from degradation due to air

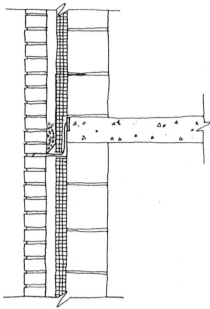

Figure 1.2 ▶ **Typical wall detail where the slab edge is covered by insulation and exterior finish.**

intrusion, moisture intrusion, and thermal short circuiting. Chapters 1 through 3 are structured as practical examples of these themes.

Finally, in a broader context, energy efficiency is part of sustainability. The selection of environmentally-benign materials and systems, with low embodied energy and without adverse effects on indoor air quality is becoming more and more a part of the vocabulary of the modern designer. Space considerations did not permit addressing these important issues in the book. Yet "green" needs to be merged with energy efficiency just as energy efficiency can only be considered in the context of structure and function.

1.3 ▶ INSULATION SYSTEMS

1.3.1 ▶ *Thermal Integrity and Multifunctionality*

The primary role of the thermal insulation system is to maintain comfort within occupied spaces. Additionally, thermal insulation protects construction elements (e.g., interior finishes, vapor retarders) from large variations in temperature. The thermal insulation system itself needs to be protected from air and moisture intrusion. To be effective, thermal insulation must also be relatively free of interruptions by construction elements with high conductivity, i.e., thermal bridges. Air intrusion, moisture intrusion, and thermal bridging can degrade the effectiveness of a wall or roof until the energy use becomes excessive and the construction deteriorates.

The energy use is termed excessive given the amount of insulation in the envelope. Assume, for instance, a 6 in steel stud wall with R-21 fibrous insulation but *without insulating sheathing*. The total R-value of the wall, averaged over its entire surface, could be in the R-10 to R-13 range, depending on stud spacing, types of interior and exterior finishes, etc. This range could be acceptable for code-compliance purposes or even for energy use, but is low when considering that R-21 insulation was used to achieve it. Further, if the conditioned space maintains a high humidity level during winter, as is often the case with computer rooms, restaurants, or housing for the elderly, moisture could condense on the steel studs. This example shows that it is quite feasible to specify a wall that is not particularly wasteful of energy but that creates maintenance and repair problems.

Thermal degradation is the primary focus of this chapter. Integration of several functions is the secondary focus. If the insulation system performs functions in addition to thermal protection, it integrates better in the envelope and becomes more cost effective.

For example, a concrete masonry unit made of insulating concrete is a single physical component which serves as both insulation and structural support. Another example is the foundation insulation which also provides protection from ground water.

Protection from thermal degradation and integration of several functions is often achieved simultaneously. In the example of the concrete masonry unit, the insulating concrete not only increases the R-value of the CMU but also reduces the thermal bridging created by the webs.

1.3.2 ▶ *Principles of Thermal Degradation*

Some of the most effective methods to reduce heat loss through the building envelope involve the *entire* insulation system. These methods protect the performance of insulation materials by reducing or eliminating on-site thermal degradation.

The severity of thermal degradation depends on both system design and construction quality. Research on air intrusion, moisture intrusion, and thermal bridging suggests that the insulation system can lose from less than 5% to more than 60% of its calculated R-value.

PRINCIPLES OF AIR AND MOISTURE INTRUSION

Air circulation in and around the insulation material creates thermal short-circuits which decrease the effective R-value of the system.

This occurs even when the outside air does not cross into the conditioned space, but rather, it simply enters and exits the insulation system. The amount of outside air that does enter the conditioned space (infiltration) is counterbalanced by indoor air which leaves the space (exfiltration). Humid air which exfiltrates from conditioned spaces deposits moisture within the insulation system, damaging both the physical and thermal integrity of the building envelope.

Fibrous Insulation

Batts and blankets made of fiberglass and mineral wool can be affected by air circulation both within and around the insulation. Air convection *within* the insulation (Fig. 1.3) occurs only with substantial temperature differential across the assembly, but air convection *around* the insulation (Fig. 1.4) occurs readily if the batt or blanket is installed with air gaps on either side. This happens, for instance, when batts intended for wood stud installation are placed in the wider cavity created by steel studs.

To prevent thermal degradation from air convection, all six sides of the insulation material should be in contact with a solid surface to the greatest practical extent.

Rigid Foam Insulation

Rigid insulation foam boards are impermeable to air currents and thus not degraded by

Figure 1.3 ▶ Air convection within fibrous insulation.

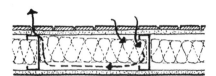

Figure 1.4 ▶ Air convection around fibrous insulation.

air convection within the insulation material. However, insulation systems using rigid foam insulation can suffer from air convection *around* the boards. This situation can occur, for example, in cavity walls with concrete masonry backup and brick finish, when the CMU substrate is irregular (Fig. 1.5).

To prevent air convection within rigid foam insulation systems, the boards should be tightly sealed at all four edges. The substrate should be as smooth as possible. The CMU backup wythe, for instance, should be parged. The parging has the additional benefit of sealing discontinuities in the mortar between blocks.

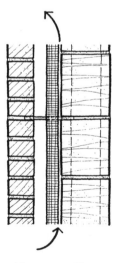

Figure 1.5 ▶ Air convection around rigid insulation.

Air diffusion in rigid foam Most types of plastic foam insulation are subject to air diffusion. Currently, most polyurethane, polyisocyanurate, and phenolic foams as well as extruded polystyrene foams are manufactured with HCFCs or HFCs as the blowing/expansion agents. While the ozone-depleting effect of these gases is much less marked than that of previously used CFCs, there are questions, not yet fully resolved, on the adverse effect of HCFC and HFC on the environment. Other alternatives are under development.

The gas in unfaced foam boards made of urethane, polyisocyanurate, and phenolic materials can be replaced by air over time. Air has lower insulating capability. Water can also penetrate into the cell matrix, causing further decrease in R-value, and even destroying the insulation.

Unfaced phenolic insulation boards degrade over several years from about R-8/in, which is the manufacturer-listed R-value for 6-month-old stock, to about R-4.5/in. Unfaced polyisocyanurate boards decrease from R-7.2/in to about R-6.0/in. Fiberglass-faced products also can age, but to a much lesser extent.

The aging problem can be largely avoided through material selection. Foil-faced boards are only slightly affected by aging, since outgassing can occur only at the edges.

Extruded polystyrene foam has not been shown to significantly decrease its R-value below the nominal R-5/in through either air or moisture intrusion. Expanded polystyrene is not affected by air intrusion either, although if it has low density it can lose part of its effectiveness by soaking with water (e.g., in a damaged roof with ponding water or in a subsurface installation). However, one advantage of the expanded polystyrene is that it does not contain gas in its cells, and is therefore more benign for the environment than its extruded counterpart.

New foam types A Canadian manufacturer has been producing for several years a version of urethane foam, called polyicynene, which uses CO_2 as the blowing agent and has an R-value of about 4.0/in. This foam does not outgas and therefore is expected to maintain its R-value over time.

PRINCIPLES OF THERMAL BRIDGING

A thermal bridge is a highly conductive construction element of the building envelope; this element penetrates or bypasses the insulation and acts as a thermal short circuit. See Figs. 1.6 and 1.7 for two examples of wall thermal bridges.

In general, thermal bridging can occur in the following situations:

- structural elements which penetrate the insulation system, such as columns, mullions, or balconies
- attachments to and penetrations of the envelope by nonstructural elements, such as piping and railing
- component connections, such as the connection between insulated metal panels
- system connections such as the juncture between wall and roof, wall and floors

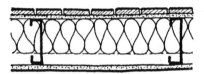

Figure 1.6 ▶ Thermal bridging at steel studs.

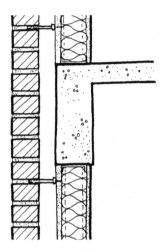

Figure 1.7 ► Thermal bridging at slab edge.

• geometry effects such as exterior angles and corners

Laboratory tests have shown that the R-value of wall areas with thermal bridging are 10 to 50% lower than the R-value of adjacent areas without thermal bridging.

Computer studies on poor construction practices have indicated a reduction in thermal resistance of over 80%. Most compelling, however, are the results of field investigations of office buildings, which demonstrated 10 to 20% increases in the *overall* envelope heat loss due to thermal bridging. (The areas affected by thermal bridging had their thermal resistance degraded by 25 to 50%.)

Effects of Thermal Bridging
In addition to excessive heat loss through the envelope, thermal bridges cause moisture condensation via two mechanisms:

1. Because thermal bridges lower the temperature of interior surfaces, the condensation potential on and within interior finishes is increased. Excessive condensation can readily occur in spaces with high indoor relative humidity (40% or above).
2. Because most thermal bridges penetrate the envelope, they are often accompanied by air infiltration and exfiltration. Exfiltrating air reaches cold thermal bridge surfaces, and deposits moisture *within* the building envelope.

Consequently, thermal bridging can cause costly maintenance and repair problems. At a minimum, damp and moldy interior spaces lose rental value. In severe cases hidden moisture condensation engenders staining, rusting, rotting, disintegration, and even complete failure of the affected envelope systems.

Thermal Bridges and Vapor Retarders
Since moisture is more likely to condense on thermal bridges than on other surfaces, it is important to confer protection against such occurrences. In cold climates the vapor retarder should be placed on the winter-warm surface of the insulation, i.e., at the interior surface. For example, a steel stud wall with glass fiber insulation has the vapor retarder placed between the steel studs and the interior gypsum board. In hot and humid climates the vapor retarder, if any, should be placed on the summer-warm surface of the insulation, i.e., at the exterior surface. This distinction is important since in Florida, Texas, and similar locations, moisture tends to migrate from the hot and humid environment into the cool and dry interior space.

Assume a typical CMU construction. If the insulation is placed onto the summer-warm surface of the CMU, the concrete blocks will be kept relatively cool by the air-conditioned interior space. The concrete of the CMU is a fairly effective vapor retarder. Water vapor contained in the warm outside air will condense on the exterior surface of the CMU wythe, especially at the shell/web joints, since webs act as thermal bridges, creating cooler lines on the exterior shell. To avoid such problems, the CMU wall should be furred and insulated to the interior. The concrete is now in the summer-warm zone of the wall. Since the CMU is warm, moisture from the outside air cannot condense on it.

However, an important point must be made on the furred-in insulation. This insulation should not be foil-faced and the finish should not be vapor-impermeable (e.g., vinyl), to avoid creating a second vapor retarder plane. If such a plane were created, moisture could be trapped inside the wall, between the exterior vapor retarder (the CMU shell) and the interior vapor retarder (the foil facing or the vinyl finish). This moisture generates stains and creates conditions for mold and mildew growth.

Recent Developments

The knowledge base on thermal bridges has grown substantially during the past few years and now allows building designers to make thermal improvements within any construction system. Of particular relevance are tests performed by Oak Ridge National Laboratory; National Research Council of Canada; and the American Society of Heating, Refrigerating and Air Conditioning Engineers, Inc. on commercial construction.

Sec. 1.3.3 presents four specific building systems that are designed to overcome the deleterious effects of thermal bridges.

1.3.3 ▶ Walls and Roofs with Reduced Thermal Bridging

EXAMPLES

Thermal bridging is usually caused by highly conductive structural components within walls and roofs, such as corner columns, eave beams, and roof supports. Figures 1.8 through 1.10 show examples of thermal bridges. As discussed, thermal bridging not only leads to increased energy consumption, but to greater moisture condensation potential as well.

DATA INTERPRETATION

The following sections present four techniques for reducing thermal bridging in walls and roofs. When developing specific designs, architects might employ materials and methods of construction that are different from those assumed here. Consequently, the *exact* figures on heat loss and moisture condensation will vary. However, the problems created by the four types of thermal bridges will be similar in all cases, and the benefits obtained through energy-efficient alternates will be of the same order of magnitude.

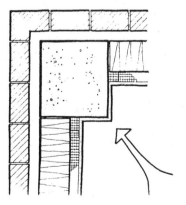

Figure 1.8 ▶ Thermal bridging at corner column.

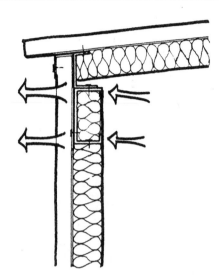

Figure 1.9 ▶ **Thermal bridging at metal building eave.**

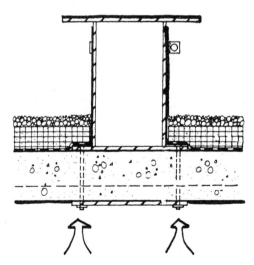

Figure 1.10 ▶ **Thermal bridging at HVAC equipment support.**

Technical articles from ASHRAE Conference Proceedings provide additional guidance on principles of design without thermal bridges. One source used in this book is the *Catalog of Thermal Bridges in Commercial and Multi-Family Residential Construction*, developed by Steven Winter Associates, Inc., in collaboration with and under subcontract to Oak Ridge National Laboratory.

STEEL STUD WALLS WITH REDUCED THERMAL BRIDGING

Typical steel stud walls are composed of steel studs, placed at 16 in or 24 in o.c., with fibrous insulation in-between gypsum board is generally used for exterior sheathing and interior finish. Exterior finishes include brick, glass, metal, vinyl, or wood.

The thermal conductivity of steel is 1000 times higher than that of fibrous insulation. Because of thermal bridging, a wall with 4 in steel studs at 16 in o.c. and R-11 insulation (Fig. 1.11) has an overall R-value of only 7.75 (See Table 1.1.). This R-value includes the exterior ceramic finish, two layers of ⅝ in gypsum board, the air films, plus the insulation/stud layer. The R-value of this layer is about 40% below the R-value of the insulation.

The steel studs cause a 60% degradation in the performance of R-19 insulation (Fig. 1.12), reducing the overall R-value of the wall to 12.25.

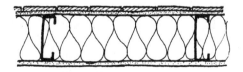

Figure 1.11 ▶ **Wall with R-11 cavity insulation.**

Insulative sheathing reduces the thermal bridging effect of steel studs (Fig. 1.13). The overall R-value of a 4 in steel stud wall with R-11 insulation and R-5 sheathing is about R-13.70.

Case Study: Low-Rise Office Building

A four-story, 58,000 ft² office building has walls with 4 in steel studs at 16 in o.c. and R-11 insulation. The interior finish and exterior sheathing are ⅝ in gypsum board. The exterior finish is 4 in face brick positioned 2 in from the gypsum board sheathing. The tinted glazing is 15% of the gross wall area, has a U-value of 0.49, and a shading coefficient of 0.50. Lighting and office equipment use 3 watts/ft², characteristic of many code-complying, but not particularly energy-efficient buildings. Each floor is served by an AHU with inlet vanes, which delivers air via VAV boxes with reheat coils. An air economizer supplies "free" cooling to 62°F. Temperatures are maintained at 72°F with 65°F setback during winter, and at 76°F with 90°F setup during summer. The two boilers have 85% AFUE. The chillers are electric-driven with air-cooled condensers.

If the R-11 steel stud wall of Fig. 1.11 receives 1 in of extruded polystyrene sheathing, the thermal bridging, moisture condensation, and energy use are reduced (Fig. 1.13).

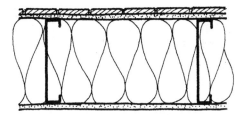

Figure 1.12 ▶ **Wall with R-19 cavity insulation.**

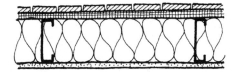

Figure 1.13 ▶ **Wall with R-11 cavity insulation and R-5 sheathing.**

Moisture condensation At 20°F outdoor temperature and 40% indoor relative humidity, each 100 linear ft of the R-11 unsheathed wall creates roughly 260 ft² moisture condensation on the interior surface of the wall. The exterior foam sheathing eliminates the condensation potential.

Energy savings With just R-11 insulation, the annual gas consumption for this building, if

Table 1.1 ▶ U-values of Steel Stud Walls

Wall Construction with Studs at 16" o.c.	Wall Overall R-value Including Finishes and Air Films	Wall U-value	Percent Decrease in U-value
R-11 steel stud	7.75	0.129	N/A
R-19 steel stud	12.25	0.089	31
R-11 steel stud and R-5 insulating sheathing	13.70	0.073	43

located in White Plains, NY, just north of New York City, is 20,435 ccf (hundreds of cubic feet). Adding the R-5 insulative sheathing reduces the annual gas consumption by 10%, to 18,410 ccf.

CONCRETE SLAB EDGE WITH REDUCED THERMAL BRIDGING

Most brick-clad walls have steel stud or concrete masonry backup (Figs. 1.14 and 1.15). The concrete slab edge, if unprotected, may create an area of significant thermal bridging.

Both wall systems shown in Figs. 1.14 and 1.15 suffer from thermal bridging through the concrete slab edge. The facade strip defined by the top of the slab and the brick shelf angle in Fig. 1.14 has an overall R-value of only about 2.2.

Adding R-5 rigid foam insulation (Fig. 1.16) more than doubles the thermal resistance of the affected area. Although the shelf angle still short circuits the insulation, both heat loss and moisture condensation potential are substantially reduced.

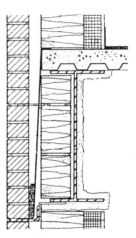

Figure 1.15 ▶ Uninsulated slab edge at masonry wall.

Case Study: Low-Rise Office Building

A four-story, 58,000 ft² office building has walls with 4 in steel studs at 16 in o.c. and R-11 insulation. The interior finish and exterior sheathing are ⅝ in gypsum board. The brick cladding is positioned 2 in from the exte-

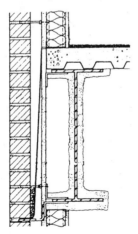

Figure 1.14 ▶ Uninsulated slab edge at steel stud wall.

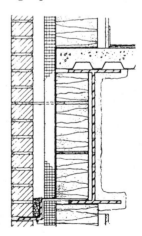

Figure 1.16 ▶ Insulated slab edge at masonry wall.

rior sheathing. The tinted glazing accounts for 15% of the gross wall area, has a U-value of 0.49, and a shading coefficient of 0.50 (Table 1.2). Lighting and office equipment use 3 watts/ft^2.

Each floor is served by an AHU with inlet vanes, which delivers air via VAV boxes with reheat coils. An air economizer supplies "free" cooling up to 62°F. Temperatures are maintained at 72°F with 65°F setback during winter, and at 76°F with 90°F setup during summer. The two boilers have 85% AFUE. The chillers are electric-driven with air-cooled condensers.

The steel studs can be sheathed with 1 in of extruded polystyrene or 1¾ in expanded polystyrene to reduce thermal bridging. If the polystyrene is positioned to cover the slab edge (Fig. 1.16), additional benefits occur.

Moisture condensation At 20°F outdoor temperature and 40% indoor relative humidity, each 100 lineal ft of uninsulated slab edge can create roughly 66 ft^2 of condensation area on the steel beam and slab underside. With insulated slab edge, no interior surface is subject to moisture condensation.

Energy savings With uninsulated slab edge, the annual gas consumption of this building, if located in White Plains, NY, just north of New York City, is 20,435 ccf. Addition of R-5 rigid foam sheathing in the wall cavity reduces annual consumption to 15,920 ccf (hundreds of cubic feet), a 22% savings. The insulation at slab edge accounts for 12% savings.

PREINSULATED, PRECAST CONCRETE PANELS WITH REDUCED THERMAL BRIDGING

Preinsulated, precast concrete panels are used in offices, hospitals, schools, and shopping malls. Many of these panels have an internal layer of foam insulation fully encased in concrete (Fig. 1.17).

Rigid insulation in precast concrete panels has a conductivity of 0.125 to 0.26. The top and bottom beams are made of concrete with a conductivity of 10 to 15. Because of thermal bridging at the connecting concrete beams, a 5 ft high panel containing R-15 insulation has an overall R-value of only 5.4.

By eliminating the concrete beams and instead using either metal ties (Fig. 1.18) or plastic ties (Fig. 1.19) to structurally bond the

Table 1.2 ▶ U-Values of Brick-Clad Walls at Slab Edge

Wall Construction	Slab Edge Overall R-value Including Finishes and Air Films	Slab Edge U-value	Percent Decrease in U-value
Steel stud backup with fibrous insulation	2.20	0.454	N/A
CMU backup with insulation in steel stud furring	2.26	0.443	2
CMU backup and R-5 rigid insulation in cavity	5.10	0.196	57

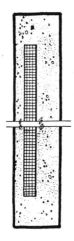

Figure 1.17 ► Fully encased precast concrete panel.

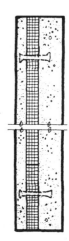

Figure 1.19 ► Precast concrete panel with plastic ties.

two concrete wythes, the overall R-value of the system increases from 5.4 to 15 and 16.75, respectively.

Case Study: Low-Rise Office Building
A four-story, 58,000 ft^2 office building has precast concrete panel walls with 3 in extruded

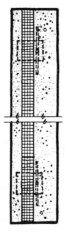

Figure 1.18 ► Precast concrete panel with metal ties.

polystyrene insulation (R-5/in) or 4 in expanded polystyrene insulation (R-3.75/in). The tinted glazing (15% of the gross wall area) has a U-value of 0.49 and a shading coefficient of 0.50. Fluorescent lights and office equipment use 3 watts/ft^2. Each floor is served by a separate AHU with inlet vanes, which delivers air via VAV boxes with reheat coils. An air economizer supplies "free" cooling up to 62°F. Temperatures maintained in the office are 72°F with setback to 65°F during the heating season, and 76°F with setup to 90°F during the cooling season. The two boilers have 85% AFUE. The chillers are electric-driven with air-cooled condensers.

If the concrete wall panels are changed from a fully encased configuration (Fig. 1.17) to one with metal connectors, as shown in Fig. 1.18, thermal bridging is reduced with beneficial effects for both moisture condensation and energy use.

Moisture condensation At 20°F outdoor temperature and 40% indoor relative humid-

Table 1.3 ▶ U-values of Preinsulated, Precast Concrete Panels

Wall Construction	Panel Overall R-Value Including Finishes and Air Films	Panel U-value	Percent Decrease in U-value
Panel with continuous casing	5.40	0.186	N/A
Panel with metal ties	15.00	0.666	65
Panel with plastic ties	16.75	0.060	68

ity, the fully encased panels could produce roughly 125 ft^2 of moisture condensation on interior finishes for every 100 linear ft of facade. For panels built with either metal or plastic ties, no moisture condenses on interior surfaces.

Energy savings With fully encased precast panels, a building located in White Plains, NY, just north of New York City, will have the annual gas consumption of about 22,960 ccf (hundreds of cubic feet). If replaced with panels built with metal ties, the annual gas consumption drops to 18,950 ccf—a significant reduction of 18%.

METAL ROOFS WITH REDUCED THERMAL BRIDGING

Conventional insulation techniques for metal roofs use fiberglass or mineral wool batts and blankets, which are compressed between purlins and roofing (Fig. 1.20).

When fibrous insulation is compressed at purlin, it loses R-value in the entire zone from the point of maximum compression to the point where it regains full thickness. The roof in Fig. 1.20 with R-19 fiberglass insulation has an overall R-value of only 9.9 for the 4-ft-wide strip centered on the purlin.

By inserting a ½ in extruded polystyrene spacer between purlin and roofing (Fig. 1.21),

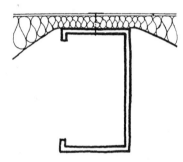

Figure 1.20 ▶ Compressed insulation at metal roof purlin.

the overall R-value of the 4-ft strip around the purlin is raised from 9.9 to 16.2.

Performance is further enhanced using 2 in polystyrene inserts plus wire insulation hangers, which allow the insulation to be installed without any compression (Fig. 1.22). The R-value of the 4-ft-wide strip around the purlin now increases to 17.2.

Case Study: Warehouse

This 32,000 ft^2 one-story building has several administrative offices and a large electronics storage area. The construction uses brick-faced walls with a U-value of 0.11 for the office area and metal-clad walls with a U-value of 0.12 for the storage area. Clear

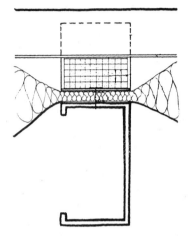

Figure 1.21 ▶ Spacer and compressed insulation at metal roof purlin.

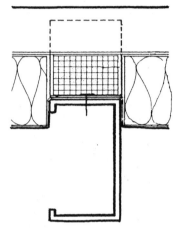

Figure 1.22 ▶ Spacer and uncompressed insulation at metal roof purlin.

glass in thermally broken aluminum frames (U = 0.50) accounts for 5% of the gross wall area. The roof uses compressed fiberglass insulation at metal purlins.

Rooftop units (AFUE = 0.80, EER = 7.8) maintain 70°F in the office area during the heating season, with 65°F setback. A constant-volume heating and ventilation system maintains 60°F in the storage area during the heating season. The warehouse has a metal

roof insulated with R-19 fiberglass, both with and without polystyrene spacers at purlins.

Moisture condensation At 20°F outdoor temperature and 30% indoor relative humidity, the unprotected system could create roughly 40 ft^2 of moisture condensation surface per 100 linear ft of purlin. The moist surface area is reduced to practically zero with the polystyrene inserts.

Table 1.4 ▶ Insulated Metal Roofs

Roof Construction	Panel Overall R-value Including Air Films	Panel U-value	Percent Decrease in U-value
Insulation compressed at purlins	9.9	0.101	N/A
Insulation compressed at purlins and ½ in spacer	16.2	0.062	39
Uncompressed insulation and 2-in spacer	17.2	0.058	42

Energy consumption Without polystyrene spacers, the annual gas consumption of this building, located in White Plains, NY, just north of New York City, is 9300 ccf (hundreds of cubic feet). With the addition of ½ in polystyrene spacers the gas consumption drops to 8800 ccf, a 5% reduction.

PRACTICAL CONSIDERATIONS FOR WALLS AND ROOFS WITH REDUCED THERMAL BRIDGING

Design
- During the schematic design phase, reduce or eliminate thermal bridging when selecting wall and roof types. These decisions may affect the aesthetic of the building.
- Plan on small changes during design development. Any attempt to redress major thermal bridging problems could add extra expense to your already established budget.
- Avoid specifying highly conductive materials for those building components which extend across the envelope.
- Focus on the envelope areas with lowest R-value.
- Focus on spaces and buildings that may experience interior relative humidities of 40% and above during winter.
- When thermal bridging is unavoidable, provide a path to eliminate the water formed through moisture condensation.
- Do not attempt to obtain high R-values by increasing the insulation levels between thermal bridge members (e.g., R-30 insulation between steel joists). Such use of resources is ineffective and can actually increase the likelihood of

moisture condensation. Instead specify exterior insulating sheathing.
- Provide air retarders for walls with thermal bridges. (See also Sec. 1.4.) Moist air that exfiltrates through walls can cause extensive damage through condensation on cold thermal bridges.

Construction
- In construction types with high potential for thermal bridging (e.g., steel stud walls) ensure that all specified exterior insulating sheathing is actually installed.
- Thermal bridging may be created because of construction defects, such as missing insulation. Consider troubleshooting new buildings with *infrared thermography* before occupancy. The test provides a quick and relatively inexpensive method of detecting thermal bridging problems.
- Thermography methods have evolved considerably during the past few years and are no longer restricted to scientific applications.

Operation/Maintenance
- Maintain tight joints in the area of thermal bridges. Air exfiltration can exacerbate moisture condensation problems.
- Maintain low relative humidities in buildings with thermal bridges.

1.3.4 ▶ *Walls with Insulating Concrete Masonry Units*

THE INSULATING CMU
Insulating concrete masonry units can achieve R-values ranging from R-5 to R-15 (Figs. 1.23 and 1.24). This range is many times

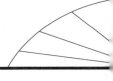

Figure 1.23 ▶ Single-wythe masonry wall.

BUILDINGS WITH REDUCED THERMAL BRIDG-
ING ARE CONSTRUCTED THROUGHOUT
THE UNITED STATES

Steel Stud Walls with Insulating Sheathing
- Columbia Presbyterian Hospital, New York, NY
- The Waterside Apartments, New York, NY
- Nehemiah Housing Development, Brooklyn, NY

Insulated Slab Edge in Brick-Clad Walls
- Battery Park City, New York, NY
- Columbia Presbyterian Hospital, New York, NY
- Police Athletic League, New York, NY
- Consolidated Edison Energy Training Center, New York, NY

Preinsulated, Precast Concrete Panels with Plastic Ties
- Mid-rise Condominium, Rochester, MN
- Office Building, Ames, IA
- Factory Building, Columbus, OH

Metal Roofs with Fibrous Insulation and Polystyrene Spacers
- LILCO Cogeneration Plant, Shoreham, NY
- Hofstra University Recreation Center, New York, NY
- Altobello Children's Hospital, Middletown, CT

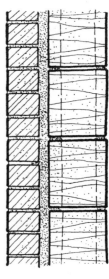

Figure 1.24 ▶ Composite masonry wall.

higher than that obtained with conventional, uninsulated CMUs, which typically attain R-values of R-1.0 to R-2.5. Such good thermal performance is obtained with modified geometry, lightweight concrete, and core insulation.

Insulating CMUs are less likely to suffer from thermal degradation than their conventional counterparts. Core insulation reduces not only conduction but also convection, because it obstructs the air spaces. The webs, made of lightweight concrete with density below 105 pcf, are no longer fast conduits for the heat. In normal weight masonry (over 125 pcf), core insulation is easily short circuited by heat flowing through webs. In lightweight masonry the webs have higher R-value and pose similar resistance to the heat flow as the core insulation.

These advances have significantly narrowed the gap in thermal performance between the group formed by *single-wythe and composite walls*, which can now incorporate the high-R CMUs, and *cavity walls*, which were always better insulated and therefore do not benefit as much from the newer technologies. (See Figs. 1.23, 1.24, and 1.25.)

INSULATING CMU WALL VS. CAVITY WALL

Integrated Functions
By integrating thermal insulation with structural support, insulating CMUs offer a labor-saving alternative to the masonry cavity wall. Insulating CMUs can be used in single wythe or in composite masonry walls. Either insulating CMU configuration decreases construction time by comparison to masonry cavity wall construction, which requires three separate, field-installed functional

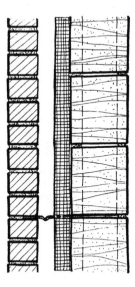

Figure 1.25 ▶ Cavity masonry wall.

components—block, exterior rigid insulation, and brick veneer.

Lower Cost
Insulating CMU systems tend to cost less than typical cavity masonry walls not only because they reduce the amount of field work, but also because they permit the use of less expensive finishes.

Less Protection to Water Penetration
Because the insulating CMU construction lacks the air space of the cavity configuration, wind-driven water can more easily penetrate into the wall. The exterior air retarder, which practically eliminates air and water intrusion, can only be specified for cavity construction (see Sec. 1.4). For multistory construction the slab edge is always exposed in the single-wythe wall, but can be covered by insulation in the cavity wall.

For these reasons cavity masonry walls present advantages that are important in climates with significant rain and high wind, especially when freeze/thaw cycles are present. In many instances, however, the single-wythe system has become competitive in both thermal performance and durability.

Three Levels of Performance Improvement vs. Conventional CMUs

From a thermal standpoint, a concrete masonry unit consists of two components—concrete webs and shells, and hollow cores. In a typical normal weight block with two hollow cores, the predominant heat path is through the concrete webs, which act as thermal bridges around the air spaces. The R-value of a typical 8 in, hollow-core, normal weight CMU (with concrete density above 125 pcf) is about R-1.

The R-value of a CMU can be increased by modifying the web configuration, by using higher R-value concrete, or by insulating the cores; some enhancements are significantly more effective than others. The following examples demonstrate that high R-value concrete is always essential to obtain a high R-value CMU.

In general, concrete with lower density has higher R-value. There are exceptions. Higher R-value can also be obtained by reducing the amount of sand in the concrete, or by using aggregates with lower conductivity.

1. *Normal weight CMUs with insulated cores—R-2.5 to R-3.5.* A CMU core has an R-value of about 1 due to the airspace it creates. This core can be filled with perlite or vermiculite, can be foamed in place, or can be fitted with rigid insulation inserts. The core R-value can increase to 6 or 7; however, webs of CMUs made with normal weight concrete still have R-values much lower than 1. Heat flows around the insulated cores through the conductive concrete webs, which in effect act as thermal bridges. The overall R-value of normal weight CMUs with insulation in the cores rarely surpasses 3.5.

2. *Lightweight CMUs with insulating fill or rigid foam inserts—R-5 to R-7.* Lightweight concrete (80 pcf to 125 pcf) reduces the heat flow through the webs of the concrete blocks by 50 to 70%. In turn, core insulation becomes more effective, since it is no longer short ciruited by highly conductive webs. As a result, the overall R-value of 8 in lightweight CMUs with core insulation ranges from 5 to 7. Higher R-values can be obtained with even lower density concrete (See Figs 1.26 and 1.27).

3. *Ultra-light, multicore CMUs—R-8 to R-14.* The highest performance of insulating CMUs is achieved by using very light (50 to 70 pcf) low-conductivity aggregate combined with a multicore design which drastically reduces thermal bridging through the webs (Fig. 1.28). The CMUs can reach R-8 without any core insulation, and R-14 when the cores are filled with polystyrene.

The thermal improvements of this design over that in example 2 consists mainly in the multicore configuration. The heat flow path around the cores is significantly lengthened, increasing the R-value of the solid portion of the CMU. The cores, too, have better R-value when empty because they are narrower, impeding air convection.

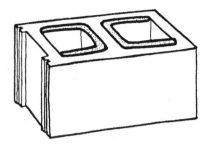

Figure 1.26 ▶ CMU with C-shaped insulating inserts.

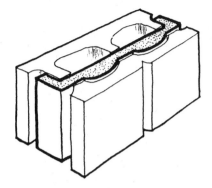

Figure 1.27 ▶ CMU with straight insulating inserts.

LIGHTWEIGHT CMUs WITH RIGID FOAM INSERTS

Two-core CMUs can be manufactured with lightweight aggregates such as (a) expanded shale, clay, and slate, (b) slag and scoria, or (c) cinders and fly ash. The density of concrete obtained with these aggregates ranges typically from 80 to 125 pcf. By contrast, normal weight concretes manufactured with gravel have densities of 125 to 140 pcf.

Several configurations of foam insulation for CMUs are available. Figure 1.26 depicts a C-shaped insert which fits into cores of conventionally configured blocks. Another system, shown in Fig. 1.27, uses straight inserts which extend across notched webs; the notches reduce thermal bridging effects.

The core insulation boosts the R-value of the CMU in the 5 to 7 range. C-shaped inserts, shown in Fig. 1.26, yield R-values toward the bottom of this range.

Straight inserts reduce thermal bridging at webs (Fig. 1.27); additionally, one manufacturer positions the insert to create two air spaces in each core. This method is more effective. The highest R-value measured to date (R-7) was obtained with straight, foil-faced inserts which create two reflective air spaces.

ULTRALIGHT, MULTICORE CMUs

This innovative CMU uses very low density concrete (50 to 70 pcf) made with polystyrene beads, perlite, vermiculite, or with expanded glass aggregate.

The concrete has an R-value of about 0.5/in, which is 5 to 10 times higher than that of normal weight concretes.

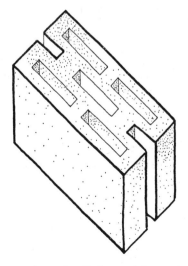

Figure 1.28 ▶ Ultralight multicore CMU.

The block geometry consists of three rows of narrow cores that are arranged in a staggered pattern (Fig. 1.28). This configuration significantly lengthens the heat pathway by comparison to conventional two- or three-core design. As a result, thermal bridging at webs is reduced.

The combination of high R-value concrete and extended heat pathway gives these polystyrene CMUs exceptional thermal performance characteristics. An 8 in block made of polystyrene concrete has an R-value of about 8. Adding polystyrene foam inserts to the cores raises the R-value to 14. Consequently, a single-wythe wall built with these blocks has a thermal resistance similar to:

- brick/CMU cavity walls with R-10 to R-12 rigid insulation in the cavity
- brick/CMU cavity walls with R-5 to R-7 rigid insulation in the cavity, and R-11 batt insulation in steel stud furring
- steel stud wall with R-11 batt insulation and R-5 rigid insulation sheathing

Limitations
Multicore CMUs cannot be gripped with one hand as can the two-core CMUs, and may therefore increase labor costs to some extent. Also, polystyrene concretes have relatively low structural resistance and cannot be used in load-bearing walls higher than two to three stories. The polystyrene CMU soaks water and must be protected from prolonged exposure to moisture.

Case Study: Low-Rise Office Building
A four-story, 56,000 ft² office building has a 590 ft perimeter. The building has concrete block walls with furred-in gypsum board interior finish and brick exterior finish. The glazing, which accounts for 15% of the gross wall area, has a U-value of 0.50 and a shading coefficient of 0.50. Fluorescent lights and typical office equipment use 3 watts/ft². Each floor is served by a separate air-handling unit with inlet vanes, which delivers air via VAV boxes with reheat coils. An air economizer supplies "free" cooling up to 62°F.

Temperatures maintained in the office are 72°F with setback to 65°F during the heating season, and 76°F with setup to 90°F during the cooling season. The two boilers have 85% AFUE. The chillers are electric driven with air-cooled condensers. Table 1.5 compares the annual energy consumption for three wall systems if the building is located in White Plains, NY, just north of New York City.

1. Steel studs with R-11 insulation and exterior gypsum sheathing
2. R-6 lightweight CMU with rigid insulation inserts
3. Uninsulated 8 in polystyrene CMU

The polystyrene CMU results in lower energy use and comparable first cost. Production of these CMUs has been recently discontinued, but the concept proved viable and could be revived in the near future.

PRACTICAL CONSIDERATIONS FOR WALLS WITH INSULATING CMUs

Design
- Polystyrene CMUs (50–70 pcf) have lower compressive strength than CMUs made with typical lightweight concrete (80–105 pcf). For this reason they are not used in load-bearing walls higher than three stories.
- Core insulation is ineffective in CMUs made of normal weight concrete.

Table 1.5 ▶ CMU Walls

Wall System	Annual Gas Consumption (ccf)	Percent Savings (%)	Annual Electricity Consumption (kwh)
R-11 steel studs	20,436	N/A	1,110,000
R-6 CMU with foam inserts	20,130	2	1,105,000
Polystyrene CMU	19,315	5	1,103,000

- Extruded polystyrene inserts retain R-value over time because they do not outgas and do not absorb water. However, polystyrene is more flammable than polyisocyanurate foams.
- Polyicynene foam is a type of urethane which is CO_2-based and therefore does not outgas. Because it contains no CFCs or HCFCs, this foam is also more benign to the environment.
- Protect lightweight CMUs against bulk water intrusion with a waterproof finish (e.g., paint, ceramic tiles, brick, normal weight concrete). Lightweight CMUs could absorb more water than normal weight CMUs and could be damaged by freeze/thaw cycles if permanently exposed to weather.
- CMU R-values derived from ASTM tests of full-scale walls are reliable. Two- and three-dimensional computer analyses (e.g., using FRAME, HEATING or CFD-2000) also yield accurate results. Calculated CMU R-values are acceptable if obtained with the ASHRAE Parallel Series method, also called the Isothermal Planes method. The ASHRAE Parallel Path method predicts *unrealistically high R-values* for insulating CMUs.
- If the R-value of a wall with insulating CMUs must be increased, it is best to provide insulation on the *exterior* (winter-cold) of the CMU wythe, such as in an EIFS application. If insulation is located in the interior (winter-warm) surface of the CMU, perform calculations to ensure that water vapor does not condense on the CMU shell.

Construction
- Protect the top of walls built with insulating CMUs against water intrusion even when the walls are erected during the cooling season. The lightweight concrete can absorb water, which can then stain interior and exterior finishes.
- Check for missing rigid insulation inserts. If possible, check for voids using thermography when perlite or vermiculite is used.
- If polyicynene is used as core insulation (on-site foaming), it will probably fill most spaces around mortar deposits, mortar gaps, and misaligned blocks, because it has an expansion factor higher than 60. When expansion is completed, the foam solidifies, developing "skins" at the contact with other materials.
- Give special attention to polystyrene CMUs during shipping, storage, and handling. These CMUs are more easily chipped than the higher density units.

Operation/Maintenance
- Maintain masonry joints in good condition to prevent air penetration in CMU cores.
- Maintain roof/wall connections in good condition. Water accumulation in CMU cores reduces the R-value of the lower section of the wall and promotes deterioration of concrete.

1.3.5 ▶ *Foundation Insulation*

TYPES OF FOUNDATION INSULATION

Foundation insulation is usually placed on the exterior of a footing or basement wall (Fig. 1.29), under a slab (Fig. 1.30), within a basement wall (Fig. 1.31), or on the interior surface of a basement wall (Fig. 1.32).

Exterior insulation is typically made of extruded polystyrene boards. Integral insulation can be made of rigid inserts, fills (e.g., perlite, vermiculite), or can be foamed in place. Interior insulation is usually fibrous.

Figure 1.29 ▶ Exterior foundation insulation.

LIGHTWEIGHT, INSULATING CMUs ARE USED IN BUILDINGS THROUGHOUT THE NORTHERN UNITED STATES

Lightweight CMUs with Rigid Insulation Inserts
- Sullivan County Health Care Facilities, Monticello, NY
- Middle and Junior High Schools, Albany, NY
- Federal Express Distribution Center, Rochester, NY
- Sears Distribution Center, Utica, NY
- Binghamton Regional Maintenance Facility, Binghamton, NY
- Multiplex Cinema, Medford, NY
- Heartland Business Center, Edgewood, NY
- Proctor & Gamble Office/Lab, Norwich, CT
- Municipal Maintenance Building, Niagara Falls, NY
- Fordham University Dormitories, Bronx, NY
- The Brickyard Restaurant, Kingston, NY

Polystyrene Multicore CMUs
- Center Islip Congregation of Jehova, Islip, NY
- The Brickyard Restaurant, Kingston, NY
- Shopping Center, Epping, NH
- Stone Machine Co., Chester, NH

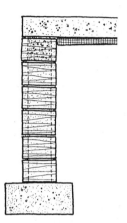

Figure 1.30 ▶ Under-slab foundation insulation.

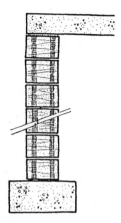

Figure 1.31 ▶ Foundation insulation within the basement wall.

DESIGN OF FOUNDATION INSULATION SYSTEMS

Calculation Methods for Ground Heat Loss
Foundation heat loss is considerably more complex and more difficult to calculate than heat loss from the above-grade portions of buildings. Foundations lose heat in two directions: upward toward the ground surface and downward toward deep ground zones. Near the surface, soil temperature tracks air temperature closely. The amplitude of soil temperature swings decreases with depth.

Until recently, only mainframe computer programs could accurately model ground thermal dynamics and its effect on building energy use and electric demand. Most designers necessarily relied on the simplified heat loss estimation methods presented in the *ASHRAE Handbook of Fundamentals.*

Recent and near-future developments simplify the task. Oak Ridge National Laboratory has developed guidelines for ground insulation. The schematic design software,

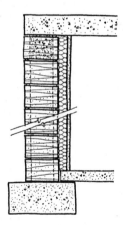

Figure 1.32 ▶ Interior foundation insulation.

ENERGY-10, developed by National Renewable Energy Laboratory, will soon incorporate credible ground heat transfer algorithms.

Cost-Effective Foundation Insulation
Using dynamic foundation heat loss calculation techniques, the designer is able to specify

foundation insulation and mechanical equipment with increased confidence.

Dynamic computer simulations show that, in moderate and cold climates, foundation insulation is cost-effective when applied to heating dominated buildings. Such buildings usually have a long foundation perimeter and relatively small internal heat gains from lights and equipment.

Moisture Protection

The R-value of the foundation insulation system can be compromised if ground water (a) permeates the insulation material, as in insulating fills, or (b) circulates around the insulation board, as in exterior insulation applications. Moisture protection can be achieved by relieving the static pressure of groundwater.

One innovative product, presented below, integrates the insulation and drainage functions.

INSULATION AND DRAINAGE SYSTEM FOR FOUNDATIONS

This product consists of a rigid foam foundation insulation with vertical and horizontal grooves that act as groundwater drainage channels. The grooves are covered with a spun-bonded filter fabric which protects the channels from clogging (Fig. 1.33). The insulated drainage panels have a specified drainage capacity of 5 gpm/linear ft.

By combining both thermal insulation and foundation drainage into one component, this system reduces the amount of site labor and the need for site supervision. Drainage rates are more predictable, and the insulation performance is more reliable. R-values of 6.9 and 10.6 are achieved.

Case Study: Low-Rise Office Building

The following analysis examines the advantages of increased foundation insulation in a four-story, 58,000 ft^2 office building located in White Plains, NY, just north of New York City. The calculations were performed using the DOE-2.1 computer program.

Two foundation insulation systems are compared—R-5 perimeter insulation, two-ft deep (code required), with gravel drain, and R-6.9 insulation-and-drainage system carried full depth to the footings.

The basecase building, described in greater detail in section 1.3.3, uses 20,435 ccf gas. The R-6.9 insulation saves 420 ccf of gas annually, but has no effect on cooling electricity consumption. At 45 cents per ccf, the annual savings is about $190. More important, the R-6.9 insulation-and-drainage system will provide a more reliable protection against moisture intrusion.

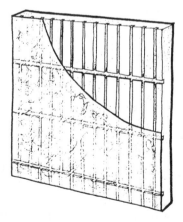

Figure 1.33 ► Insulation and drainage system for foundations (*courtesy of Dow Styrofoam® Brand Products*).

PRACTICAL CONSIDERATIONS FOR INSULATION AND DRAINAGE SYSTEMS FOR FOUNDATIONS

Design
- The insulated drainage panels have standard 2 ft by 8 ft sizes.
- The cost is about 50% higher than for drainage-only panels. However, the insulated drainage panels can achieve cost savings when compared with drainage-only panels that are installed in conjunction with separate boards of polystyrene.

Construction
- The rigid insulated drainage panels conform less easily with irregular foundation surfaces than aggregate fill or wire core drainage products.

Operation/Maintenance
- These panels are less likely to clog than aggregate fill.
- Because basement walls are kept warm and dry, mold and mildew is unlikely to form.

1.4 ► AIR RETARDERS

1.4.1 ► *Air Retarder Types*

An air retarder system (AR) consists of one or more air-impermeable components which are sealed at all seams and penetrations to form a continuous wrap around the building walls.

In some AR systems the function of the air-tight component is assumed by an existing construction element. In steel stud walls, for example, the exterior gypsum board sheathing can also serve as the air-impermeable component of the air retarder (Fig. 1.34). In curtain walls, the airtight component may be steel sheet (Fig. 1.35) or glass (Fig. 1.36). In either situation, all joints between airtight components must be sealed. In the case of the gypsum board AR, for instance, the joints between boards must be taped and the penetration of the brick ties must be sealed with a bituminous mastic.

However, most AR systems use membranes that serve the specific purpose of impeding air leakage into conditioned spaces. In most large commercial buildings the membranes are liquid-applied bituminous, liquid-applied rubber, sheet bituminous, and sheet plastic. These membranes impede the passage of *both* air and vapor. In

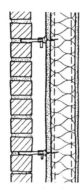

Figure 1.34 ▶ Exterior gypsum sheathing as air retarder component.

Figure 1.35 ▶ Steel cladding as air retarder component.

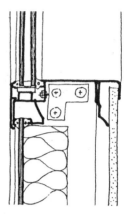

Figure 1.36 ▶ Glass and glass-spandrel panel as air retarder component.

never reaches the low temperatures at which moisture could condense.

Small commercial buildings with steel or wood stud walls can employ residential-type air retarders. These membranes are not vapor retarders. They prevent air penetration but allow the interior moisture to escape to the outside. For this reason they are typically placed on the winter-cold side of the insulation. Products include spun-bonded poly-olefin sheet on wood substrate; thin paper-backed polystyrene delivered in long strips folded in accordion fashion; and pressed wood or paper products with or without punched aluminum foil. (This foil is punched to allow water vapor diffusion.)

1.4.2 ▶ Air Leakage

Measurements in eight U.S. office buildings found average air leakage rates of 0.1 to 0.5 air changes per hour, which account for an esti-mated 10 to 25% of the peak heating load.

cold climates the membranes must be posi-tioned on the winter-warm side of the insula-tion to avoid moisture condensation. A typical detail positions the membrane AR on the exterior surface of the CMU wythe. Both membrane and CMU are protected by rigid insulation. The exterior shell of the CMU

These air leakage rates are higher than those assumed by most engineers when performing calculations for pressurized buildings. Excessive air leakage has the following effects:

- *Increased energy use* Not only must infiltrating air be heated or cooled, humidified or dehumidified, but air intrusion into the building envelope degrades the effectiveness of the insulation system (see Sec. 1.3).
- *Discomfort* Localized under-heating and drafts reduce occupant productivity during the winter.
- *Damage* Infiltrating air can carry rain water into exterior finishes and into backup elements, causing brick spalling and other problems. Exfiltrating air carries indoor humidity which may condense in the building envelope, causing rusting and rotting (see Sec. 1.3).

DIFFUSE VERSUS CHANNEL AIRFLOW

Air leakage through a building envelope occurs via two types of airflow. "Diffuse" airflow is air movement *through* a layer of the envelope, such as wind through loosely-woven cloth or through a masonry wall (Fig. 1.37).

"Channel" airflow is air movement *around* a solid retarder, through holes, seams, or joints, as shown in Fig. 1.38. Channel airflow commonly occurs at thermal bridges, where structural components penetrate the building envelope. (See "Principles of Thermal Bridging" in Sec. 1.3.2.) The long airflow pathways often result in intense cooling of exfiltration air, which, in turn, releases its moisture inside building components.

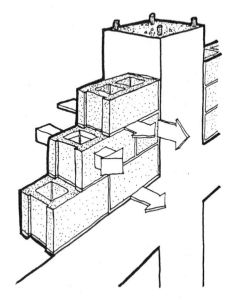

Figure 1.37 ▶ Diffuse airflow through a masonry wall (*courtesy Bakcor*).

Both diffuse and channel airflow occur in most wall types. Although diffuse airflow typically accounts for most air leakage, channel airflow creates most problems. Diffuse airflow is controlled by selecting air-impermeable air retarder materials such as bituminous or plastic membranes. Channel airflow is controlled by sealing the air retarder at all seams and joints and by protecting the air retarder system from damage.

RECENT ADVANCES

During the past decade, membrane ARs have experienced the fastest pace of development. Types and applications have diversified and the field experience has increased. With a

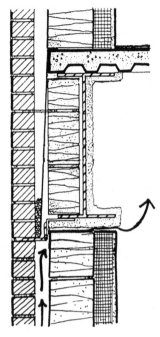

**Figure 1.38 ▶ Channel airflow at joint
in a masonry wall.**

solid track record in Canada, membrane air
retarders are increasingly specified in buildings in the United States. The following section presents two membranes in common
use and a new entry in the marketplace.

1.4.3 ▶ *Membrane Air Retarder Systems*

Most membrane air retarder systems used
today in larger commercial buildings are
bituminous or rubber, and are delivered to
the building site either in liquid state, for
trowel and brush application, or in sheets,
which are glued or heat-fused to the walls.
One new membrane AR is made of plastic,
and is mechanically attached to the substrate.

LIQUID-APPLIED BITUMINOUS MEMBRANE

Liquid-applied membranes consist of compounds which are trowelled or sprayed in
place. When cured, they form a flexible, continuous film over the building exterior. The
most common compounds are bituminous or
rubber-type.

Liquid-applied membranes can be used in
any construction type, regardless of geometry, number of penetrations through the envelope, or number of materials. This flexibility
has a price. Because liquid membranes are
applied on site, they require supervision and
quality control.

Specifically, the liquid membranes should
not be applied to surfaces that are wet, oily,
dusted, or frosted. This includes surfaces that
get moist from internal sources, such as cast-
in-place concrete that has been cured for less
than two weeks.

Further, although liquid membranes can
span hairline cracks, they should be supported by a reinforcing fabric, mesh, or by
sheet membrane when they span wider joints.

All these requirements can be easily met by
construction teams which have experience in
applying bituminous compounds to walls for
waterproofing purposes. The training period
is brief.

Case Study: Hospital in New York City

The new Mount Sinai Hospital, designed by
Pei, Cobb, Freed and Partners (Fig. 1.39), was
completed in 1989. The building has exterior
cavity walls, with the following layers: brick
veneer, air space, rigid insulation, concrete
masonry units, steel stud furring, and gypsum wall board.

To protect the building against New York's
winds and frequent freeze/thaw cycles, the

Figure 1.39 ▶ The Mount Sinai Hospital in New York City uses liquid-applied, bituminous air retarder (*photo courtesy Paul Warchol*).

architects wrapped the concrete masonry backup wall in a bituminous air retarder. A trowel-applied membrane was selected because brick tie perforations would have required extensive patching for a bituminous sheet membrane.

Because of the air retarder, the brick cladding does not pose a significant resistance to the wind, and the air pressure inside the wall cavity is not very different from the outside air pressure. Consequently, it is less likely that rain will be entrained into the

brick. The air retarder also minimizes air leakage into the building.

BITUMINOUS SHEET MEMBRANE

Bituminous sheet-applied membranes consist of bitumen impregnated fabrics which are either heat-fused or adhered to the wall. All joints are lapped and sealed.

Bituminous sheet membranes are best suited for walls without many perforations. Penetrations and joints must be sealed with liquid-applied membranes. If liquid-membrane patching is extensive, the advantage gained through the quick application of the bituminous membrane is lost.

Case Study: Library

The Wessell Library of the Tufts University was built in 1964, into the south side of "The Hill," a steep slope that marks the historic center of the suburban Boston campus. The original building had 184,000 ft² and was clad with limestone panels.

The new addition, designed by Shepley Bulfinch Richardson and Abbott of Boston nearly doubles the size of the building. Energy efficiency and moisture control were among the design goals (see Fig. 1.40).

The addition expands the building on two of the three original floor levels and adds a smaller lower level down the slope of the hill on the south and east sides. New construction also partially infills the existing entry courtyard to create a new clerestory lit entry. Large windows on the new facades along with clerestories and skylights bring natural light into study and administrative areas. The windows use low-e glazing.

New bookstack areas are kept toward the interior and are efficiently lit with indirect fluorescent fixtures running perpendicular to the shelving.

The original flat-slab concrete structural system is continued in most portions of the

Figure 1.40 ▶ The Wessel Library at Tufts University (*courtesy Grace Construction Products*).

addition. Lighter weight steel infill is used where additional weight on the existing structure is constrained by footing sizes.

The steel stud walls are sheathed with gypsum board surfaced with glass fiber. All exterior wall surfaces are then completely covered with a 40 mil membrane made of cross-laminated rubberized asphalt and polyethylene.

This membrane creates an air retarder. By impeding air movement into the building, the air retarder also reduces the moisture transport. For a library, the ability to control the moisture of the air is essential.

The air retarder is covered by 2½ in of extruded polystyrene board. The exterior finish, composed of granite and limestone masonry veneer, is anchored to either the concrete structure or to the 6 in metal stud infill walls.

SNAP-ON PVC MEMBRANE

One innovative sheet membrane AR is mechanically attached to the wall. This system consists of a PVC sheet with special PVC profiles, which accommodate the brick ties without compromising the integrity of the air retarder (Fig. 1.41).

The brick ties arrive at the job site already attached to long, extruded PVC profiles. These profiles are positioned in the horizontal joints of the CMUs. Next, strips of membrane are stretched between and fastened to each row of PVC members. Finally, a second set of PVC profiles snaps over the extrusions already in place, covering the top and bottom of each membrane strip and creating airtight seals.

This mechanically-attached membrane was introduced to the market a few years ago. Should it withstand the test of time, it will pro-

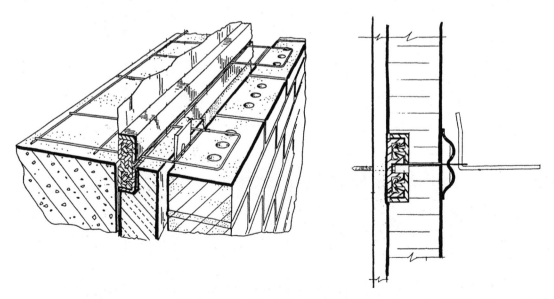

Figure 1.41 ▶ **Perspective and vertical section through PVC sheet, mechanically-fastened air retarder system (*courtesy Kap-Shor Technology, Ltd.*).**

vide a compelling alternative to both liquid-applied and bituminous membrane ARs for brick and stone-clad facades. Mechanically attached ARs can be quickly applied to the wall just like bituminous membrane ARs, but require no additional patching.

Case Study—University of Guelph, Canada
Robbie, Young and Wright Associates designed a large complex at the University of Guelph, in Guelph Ontario (Fig. 1.42). Although all facades are brick clad, some of the backup walls use steel studs and others use CMUs. Both wall types are protected with the PVC snap-on air retarder system.

PRACTICAL CONSIDERATIONS FOR AIR RETARDERS

Design
- Typically, air retarders for commercial buildings are impermeable to water vapor. In cold climates, to avoid vapor condensation on the inside surface of the membrane, the air retarder should be located on the winter-warm side of the insulation.

  Dew point temperature calculations are required to determine how much insulation, if any, can be placed between the vapor-impermeable AR and the conditioned space.

Figure 1.42 ► The University of Guelph, in Guelph, Ontario, uses a mechanically-fastened air retarder system (*courtesy Kap-Shor Technology, Ltd.*).

- Small buildings may use fibrous insulation in conjunction with air retarders that are permeable to water vapor. These ARs can be made of spun-bonded polyolefin, of thin, paper-backed polystyrene, or of other materials with a perm rating higher than 5. A vapor retarder (e.g., polyethylene sheet) is sometimes installed on the winter-warm side of the insulation if the building is located in a cold climate. Because the ARs are permeable to water vapor, they can be located on the exterior side of the insulation, to protect it from air convection.
- Bituminous sheet membranes must be patched at penetrations. For this reason, sheet membranes are most effective for applications with few penetrations through the envelope, such as panelized construction.
- For air-conditioned buildings located in hot, humid climates, if a vapor-impermeable AR is specified, it should be placed on the summer-warm side of the insulation. The construction must avoid creating two vapor retarder planes.

  Case-by-case analyses should be undertaken for buildings located in climates with both cold and hot, humid periods.
- Masonry walls have many steel ties that puncture the air retarder membrane. For these construction types bituminous liquid-applied membranes have been generally used.

  However, the mechanically-fastened PVC membrane system constitutes an interesting option for walls with brick and stone veneer.

EXAMPLES OF AIR RETARDER APPLICATIONS

Liquid Membrane
- Mt. Sinai Hospital, New York, NY
- St. Luke's Hospital, New York, NY
- Mississagua Central Library, Mississagua, Ontario
- University of Toronto, Toronto, Ontario
- Notre Dame High School, Burlington, Ontario
- Resurrection School, Kitchener, Ontario
- Ontario College of Nurses, Toronto, Ontario
- Regional Headquarters for Ottawa-Carleton, Ottawa, Ontario
- Museum of Civilization, Hull, Ontario

Bituminous Sheet Membrane
- Rowes Wharf Shops and Housing, Boston, MA
- 1700 West Park Drive, Westboro, MA
- Brampton City Hall, Brampton, Ontario
- Laurentian University, Sudbury, Ontario
- Holocaust Museum, Washington, DC

Snap-on Sheet Membrane
- University of Guelph, Guelph, Ontario
- Simcoe & Erie Insurance Office Building, Burlington, Ontario

Construction
- Quality control on site is important to maintain AR system integrity. All penetrations must be sealed.

- A pressurization test, performed with a colored gas, can be used to visualize gaps and to implement low cost remedial measures for defects. The method of applying a liquid membrane is very similar to that used to waterproof walls. However, if the contractor has not performed such an installation before, it may be advisable to have a small portion of the wall built first. This portion is pressure-tested. Any installation problems are corrected before the entire building is erected.

Operation/Maintenance
- If a membrane sheet air retarder has detached from its substrate, it must be repaired to avoid bypassing by air convection.
- Slashes and holes in the air retarder that may be caused by building renovation must be thoroughly repaired. Discontinuities in the air retarder can have a detrimental effect, especially if they allow "channel airflow."

1.5 ► DEVELOPMENTS ON THE HORIZON

This section introduces a U.S. invention ready for commercialization; one promising, but long-term development in a high-tech field; and one energy conservation measure in use in Europe but not yet applied in the U.S.

1.5.1 ► *Evacuated Panels*

Scientists at the National Renewable Energy Laboratory in Golden, Colorado (formerly called SERI) are developing a process to pro-

duce thin evacuated metal panels with impressively high R-values (Fig. 1.43). The panels are made of two layers of sheet steel that are laser-welded and separated by spacers to prevent collapse. Ultimately, researchers hope to achieve an R-value of 10 with a thickness of only 1/10 in.

Two manufacturers have already made prototypes for building panels. The cost of the panels is more than twice the price of rigid insulation, but the expense may be justifiable in applications where space is limited or at a premium. Possible uses include standing seam roofs, preengineered metal panel structures, and new or retrofit cladding.

In 1991 the scientists discovered how to switch on and off the R-value of the panels, converting them from insulating to conductive and vice-versa. Practical applications are years away, but might eventually include walls and roofs which allow the building either to cool off or to retain the internal heat needed.

Similar work is being carried at the Oak Ridge National Laboratory on powder-filled evacuated panels. These panels use particles of clay, fly ash, or gypsum and are intended for appliances; should this first application be economically feasible, it will be possible to extend the panels' use to building envelopes.

1.5.2 ► *Lightweight Insulating Structural Concrete*

In cooperation with a major manufacturing company, engineers at Construction Technology Laboratories in Skokie, Illinois, have developed a low-density, high-compressive-strength insulating concrete which uses a synthetic aggregate in place of stone. The R-value of the new material is R-8/ft, roughly

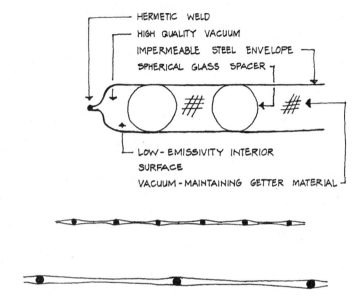

HERMETIC WELD
HIGH QUALITY VACUUM
IMPERMEABLE STEEL ENVELOPE
SPHERICAL GLASS SPACER
LOW-EMISSIVITY INTERIOR SURFACE
VACUUM-MAINTAINING GETTER MATERIAL

Figure 1.43 ▶ Thin, high-R metal evacuated panels.

ten times the R-value of conventional 125 pcf concrete.

The new concrete is intended for use in columns, beams, slabs, and balconies of low-rise commercial buildings.

Currently, columns, beams, and slab edges can be insulated to the outside, but no satisfactory method exists to prevent thermal bridging through balconies. Insulation placed above and/or below the floor slab that adjoins a balcony is ineffective; normal weight concrete simply conducts the heat from the next uninsulated floor slab area to the cold balcony slab. The high-R structural concrete offers a practical solution.

Production capabilities for the high R-concrete exist, and demand may be stimulated by building codes which increasingly take into account the detrimental effect of thermal bridging. The high-R concrete is less expensive

than normal weight concrete wrapped with insulation.

1.5.3 ▶ Self-Drying Vapor Retarder for Low-Slope Roofs

Energy efficiency, long-term performance and sustainability of roofs are topics investigated at Oak Ridge National Laboratory (ORNL). The following section draws on work and writings of Desjarlais and Christian of ORNL.

The basic components of a low-slope roof assembly are a membrane for waterproofing, insulation for thermal protection, and a deck for support of the entire system. Additional components may be added for specific reasons. For example an air/vapor retarder may be needed to impede vapor transport into the roof from conditioned spaces.

Moisture in low-slope roof systems has been a long-standing issue for the roofing industry for a number of reasons. Leaks into interior spaces are always unacceptable. Dimensional instability, corrosion, and material disintegration can lead to early failure. Also, wet insulation can lose much of its R-value. A more recent concern relates to the investment in roof insulation made during the past ten to twenty years. The waterproofing membranes on these roofs are aging, leaks are developing, and repair or replacement is required. The choices are to apply a new roofing membrane over the entire old roof, preserve only the undamaged part of the old roof, or remove and replace both insulation and roofing membrane. Basic questions about reroofing include whether or not recovered wet insulation dries and, if so, how rapidly. (Moisture Effects in Low-Slope Roofs, ORNL/CON-308, 1992.)

To control moisture within a flat or low-slope roof assembly, two approaches have been used in the United States (excluding IRMA):

1. Provide only a waterproofing membrane above the insulation. No air/vapor retarder is specified on the winter-warm surface of the roof.
2. Provide a waterproofing membrane above the insulation and a vapor retarder membrane on the winter-warm surface of the roof. Typically, this vapor retarder is polyethylene.

In Europe, a third option has been used during the past decade:

3. Provide a self-drying membrane on the winter-warm surface of the roof.

The three options are described below.

No Vapor Retarder

This option relies on the integrity of the waterproofing membrane to prevent moisture from entering the insulation. If the integrity of this membrane is breached, moisture accumulates in the insulation. This moisture can be ventilated to some extent by vents below the roofing membrane. However, due to small driving forces, this type of ventilation is often ineffective. Further, a membrane perforated with a field of breather vents may allow external moisture to enter the system through these vents.

If the rate of moisture accumulation is high, water will seep into the structure. Often, this structure is metal decking, or metal decking with concrete on top. The decking collects the water, which could be ponding. This water eventually finds its way into the conditioned space below at joints.

Moist insulation loses much of its R-value. Further, freeze-thaw cycles can actually destroy some insulation types. Either or both phenomena raise energy costs and decrease ceiling temperatures, with the associated effect of higher rate of moisture condensation.

If the space is humidified, moisture may migrate from the space into the roof (since there is no *continuous* vapor retarder), condensing and entering the cycle described above.

Vapor Retarder

A vapor retarder is sometimes installed between the supporting deck and the insulation. This construction significantly reduces the moisture condensation problems, but increases the risk of water entrapment within the roof. Any water leaking through the roofing membrane, or already present during construction, is trapped between the two water-impermeable layers. This water reduces the

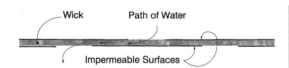

**Figure 1.44 ▶ Self-drying vapor retarder
(*courtesy of Vagn Korsgaard*).**

insulation R-value, and can even destroy some types of insulation during freeze-thaw cycles, leading to increased energy use and lower ceiling temperatures. This, in turn, can lead to moisture condensation on the ceiling surface.

Self-Drying
According to the self-drying concept, heat energy from spring and summer sun will evaporate winter-accumulated liquid moisture and will drive it downward through a water-permeable deck into the building interior, where it is then evacuated.

A water permeable vapor retarder (WPVR), as shown in Fig. 1.44, consists of a synthetic fabric with good capillary suction properties sandwiched between strips of diffusion-tight plastic film. The strips are staggered with an overlap. The size of the overlap and the thickness of the fabric, together with the permeance of the plastic film, determine the permeance of the WPVR. Consequently, the WPVR can be designed as a vapor retarder.

The WPVR membrane stops moisture in the form of water vapor (usually coming from below), but allows passage of moisture in the form of construction water, leaked water, or condensed water. Construction water, leaked water, or condensed water wicks through the WPVR membrane into the space, where it evaporates. In principle, small amounts of water (such as construction water) evaporate unnoticeably. However, if a serious roofing leak were to develop, the moisture will show up almost immediately and near the point of entry. This allows for prompt repair of the roofing damage, before the insulation is irretrievably damaged.

The permeance of the WPVR can be tailored to different climate zones by varying the width of the plastic film strips, the overlapping, and the thickness of the wicking fabric.

Applications
The WPVR concept is used in Europe, especially Denmark. Laboratory studies have been performed in the U.S. by Oak Ridge National Laboratory and are also currently under way under the aegis of the American Society of Heating, Refrigerating and Air Conditioning Engineers, Inc. It is probable that the new roof vapor retarder will soon have installations in North America.

CHAPTER 2

GLASS, GLAZING, AND SOLAR CONTROL

2.1 ▶ FENESTRATION— HIGHER COMFORT, LOWER ENERGY USE

Many commercial fenestration products use films and coatings to reduce heating and cooling loads while admitting high levels of daylight. Cooling loads are also reduced by innovative exterior shading devices.

Energy-efficient glazed surfaces create comfortable environments, with evenly distributed temperatures and quality lighting.

The energy efficiency of fenestration is greatly enhanced by design concepts which integrate fenestration with lighting, HVAC, and control systems.

Chapter 2 presents technological advances in films, coatings, insulating spacers, and inert gases, and exemplifies their applications for fenestration.

Chapter 2 also covers shading devices which automatically control the amount and direction of solar radiation.

Techniques under development include glazings that can be switched from opaque to transparent, and those that direct the light deep into the building using holographic films.

2.2 ▶ INTEGRATION OF GLAZING AND FENESTRATION

A fenestration assembly is composed of glazing, frame, shading devices, and attachments to the envelope (Fig. 2.1).

All components of an energy-efficient fenestration assembly should be integrated to reduce heat flow and to control solar radiation. Their roles are as follows:

- Insulating spacers between glass panes impede heat conduction.
- Multiple glass and film layers reduce heat gain/loss through convection and radiation.
- Argon and krypton gas in the interpane space further decrease the heat transfer through convection.

FENESTRATION—HIGHER COMFORT, LOWER ENERGY USE

- Low-e coatings are widely used for double pane glazings, providing U-values in the 0.29 to 0.35 range.
- Single low-e films in the interpane space improve the U-values of glazings to the 0.21 to 0.27 range.
- Glazings with double low-e films in the interpane space achieve U-values as low as 0.12, comparable to those of insulated, opaque walls.
- Inert gas in the interpane space can reduce the U-value of the glazing by 15 to 30%.
- The U-value of the entire fenestration unit can be 10 to 30% higher than the U-value of the glazing. Thermal breaks and plastic spacers keep this increase in the low range.
- Selective low-e coatings can achieve a daylight transmittance which is twice as high as the total solar transmittance.
- Movable shades are more effective due to improved hardware and controls.
- Glazings under development will allow the occupants to better control the amount of solar radiation that reaches the conditioned space.

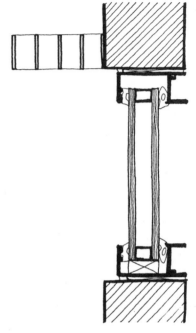

Figure 2.1 ▶ **Fenestration components. The glazing is made of one or several transparent layers (glass, plastic sheet, or plastic film), and of spacers between these layers. The frame can be composed of sash and jamb, as in small buildings, or of mullions, as in curtain wall construction. Shading devices can be fixed or mobile, and exterior or interior.**

- Low emittance coatings on glass and film reduce heat gain/loss through long-wave radiation.
- Reflective coatings, low-emittance (low-e) coatings, and tints protect against the full spectrum of solar radiation. Some coatings are formulated to also admit a high level of daylight.
- Exterior shading devices deflect solar radiation before it reaches occupied spaces.

Integration of Fenestration Components

High performance fenestrations have U-values that are 1.5 to 4 times lower than those of inefficient units. A low U-value is beneficial in all climates with extended periods of cold or hot weather (e.g., Pittsburgh, PA, or Phoenix, AZ). However, the effectiveness of the entire fenestration assembly can be significantly reduced if any of the components underperforms.

For example, double-pane glass with two suspended low-e films may have a U-value as low as 0.12 at center, and 0.14 when the effect of plastic spacers is included. If the plastic spacers are replaced by tradi-tional, high-conductivity aluminum spacers, the U-value of the assembly could increase by another 20%.

Integration of Fenestration, Wall, and Roof

Just as energy-efficient components integrate into an energy-efficient fenestration assembly, the fenestration in turn must integrate within the building envelope. For example, windows can now attain R-values of 6, comparable to those of opaque walls (e.g., R-11 steel stud wall).

However, the thermal performance of both fenestration and wall can be compromised if the junction between vision and opaque elements is not protected against air infiltration. (See also the discussion on air retarders in Chap. 1.)

In passive solar applications both the thermal and spatial relationship between fenestration and other building elements is essential, since it determines the effectiveness of thermal mass storage.

Integration of Fenestration, Lighting, and HVAC Systems

Of the entire envelope, glazed surfaces have the largest effect on lighting, heating, and cooling. A good space-conditioning strategy must always consider the interaction between fenestration, lighting, HVAC systems, and controls. The need for coordination is acute in buildings that use daylighting strategies.

For example, a glass with shading coefficient below 0.3 drastically reduces both the cooling load and the effectiveness of daylighting systems. Conversely, clear glass offers high opportunity for daylight savings, but results in high cooling costs and perhaps glare. A well designed building optimizes the energy use for cooling and lighting by coordinating its fenestration with the selection of lamps, ballasts, and lighting controls, as well as with the type and size of HVAC systems.

Quite often, energy-efficient features are simply pasted on a traditional building design. This happens late into the design development phase, after the window geometry has been defined, after the lighting and HVAC systems have been detailed, and after the heating and cooling plant has been sized.

At this juncture the economic analyses show, almost without exception, that it is most advantageous to reduce lighting loads by using efficient lamps and ballasts. Lighting controls, such as occupancy sensors, and efficient motors follow closely. More efficient boilers and chillers are also justifiable in most instances. As for high-performance windows and daylighting, these strategies perform in a mediocre way when applied to a building that is already reasonably efficient.

This type of design procedure works through *juxtaposition* rather than integration. Its architectural equivalent is to design a load-bearing masonry building and then simply remove some brick every 15 ft and place instead steel columns. The steel columns will not be cost effective, but the lack of cost effectiveness is due to the misapplication of steel-building techniques.

When a design uses high-performance fenestration, it is possible, even necessary, to *integrate* the fenestration with lighting and HVAC. The design of the three systems should be simultaneous, since each presents advantages for the others. High-performance fenestration reduces glare and direct sun on occupants, making daylighting strategies easier to implement.

First, glazings with low shading coefficients and high daylight transmittance reduce or eliminate the discomfort caused by intense solar radiation on occupants. This makes it less likely that louvers will be pulled down. Second, daylight transmittance needs to be high in relation with the shading coefficient, but not necessarily high in absolute terms. In most climates clear glass allows much more daylight than needed. The windows form bright areas on the darker wall. The occupants tend to turn on the lights to reduce the visual contrast between window and wall. High-performance fenestration can be selected to admit sufficient, rather than excessive, daylight.

There is no need for dimmable electronic ballasts and continuous dimming controls *if* natural light satisfies all requirements of a space for most of the workday, during most seasons. A simple on-off switch suffices.

High-performance fenestration also has a simplifying effect on the heating system. There is no need for perimeter heating *if* the fenestration approaches the R-value of the wall, since the drafts have been eliminated.

In cooling, the high-performance fenestration results in a low solar gain. The internal load from electric lighting is also decreased, since the daylight allowed by fenestration is sufficient to keep the lights off for most of the time. As a result, the amount of air needed to cool perimeter spaces is significantly reduced. Ducts can be smaller. Sometimes it is even possible for the outside air required for ventilation to be equal to or higher than the air required for cooling. In this particular application, the system becomes 100% outside air, with constant volume, fan-powered boxes at zone level, to ensure sufficient air movement. This system is significantly less expensive than a full-blown VAV system. Furthermore, the 100% outside air distribution makes it possible to perform air-to-air heat recovery.

Regardless of the distribution system selected, there is no longer the need for a large heating and cooling plant. Actually, chillers can be further reduced in size by using desiccant dehumidification. The *combined* action of energy-efficient systems create a new building type, which may not be more expensive than a traditional one. This, however, cannot be achieved with incremental changes; only integration and synergy achieve the goal.

For this reason, the fenestration lighting techniques discussed in Chap. 2 are closely related to topics presented in Chap. 3, Secs. 3.4 and 3.5. In this book the description of hardware had to be separate. However, the design needs to be integrated.

2.3 ► HIGH-PERFORMANCE GLAZINGS AND FRAMES

High-performance fenestrations have moved from the laboratory to the marketplace dur-

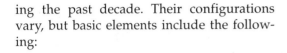

ing the past decade. Their configurations vary, but basic elements include the following:

- multiple air layers with plastic spacers between panes
- inert gas instead of air in the interpane space
- low-e coatings on glazings and films
- coatings with low shading coefficient and high daylight transmittance
- glazings with low shading coefficient yet clear-glass appearance
- ceramic deposits on the glass surface, which shade and redirect the light

These developments aim at reducing heat transfer through the windows, reducing glare, and maintaining a relatively high level of daylight penetration into the space. A brief discussion of the underlying physical phenomena can help the understanding and application of the high-performance fenestration.

Section 2.3.1 notes principles of heat transfer through glazings and frames, and describes several effective methods of reducing the energy use in buildings.

2.3.1 ▶ *Principles of Reducing Heat Gain/Loss through Fenestration*

Heat crosses a glazing assembly through conduction, convection, and radiation. Energy-efficient fenestrations reduce and/or control all three transmission modes.

CONDUCTION
The glazing frame and the interpane spacers represent the only significant conduction paths in a fenestration system (Fig. 2.2).

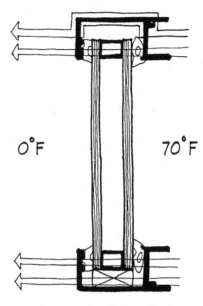

Figure 2.2 ▶ Conduction paths in fenestration systems.

In commercial applications both frame and spacers are usually metallic. Typically, the heat flow through the frame is slowed by thermal breaks. However, metal spacers create highly conductive paths around the frame. Plastic spacers can improve the U-value of the entire assembly by 5 to 20%. This is due to the low conductivity of plastics used in fenestration; about 60 times lower than steel, and 200 to 300 times lower than aluminum.

High R-value glazings benefit more from insulating spacers than their less efficient counterparts. While a metal spacer conducts just as much heat whether it is placed in an R-3 or an R-8 glazing, the R-8 window loses a higher *percentage* of its insulating value due to thermal short circuiting.

CONVECTION

The air between two glass panes moves in a convective loop: it rises along the warm surface, accumulating heat, and descends along the cold surface, releasing the heat. Convection, an important heat gain/loss mechanism for fenestration, can be reduced using three methods: create multiple air spaces, replace the interpane air with an inert gas, or evacuate the interpane space.

Multiple Air Spaces

Energy-efficient fenestrations create multiple air spaces by interposing one or two transparent plastic films between the glass panes. These additional plastic films and air spaces reduce both convection and radiation heat transfer. Overall, glazings with two air spaces lose 10 to 30% less heat than glazings with one air space.

Convection is fueled by the temperature difference between the warm and cold pane. If this temperature difference decreases, the ability of the convection loop to transport heat decreases too. When multiple air spaces are created, each air space is enclosed by glass panes or plastic films with a relatively small temperature differential (Figs. 2.3 and 2.4). Heat transfer caused by convection decreases by about 20 to 30%.

For this reduction to be possible, each new air space must have at least the same width as the original one. For example, convective heat loss can be reduced by up to 30% if a ½ in air space is replaced by *two* air spaces also ½ in wide. If the ½ in air space is replaced by two ¼ in wide air spaces, the U-value reduction is in the range of only 5 to 10%.

Note: Most air spaces in commercial fenestration are between ¼ in to ½ in thick. Under identical conditions a ¼ in air space has a

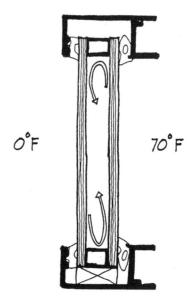

Figure 2.3 ▶ Air convection in double-pane glazing.

higher (worse) U-value than a ½ in air space. The reason: Randomly moving air molecules in the ¼ in air space can bounce more easily between the warm and the cold glass panes.

Inert Gases

Inert gases such as argon and krypton store, and therefore transport, less heat than the air. As a result, glazing units filled with inert gases lose less heat through convection and random molecular movement. Units filled with argon gas improve their U-values by about 10 to 30%. Krypton gas is more insulating than argon, but is not yet widely available. The reduction in U-value due to krypton can be in the 40 to 50% range. The highest effect of inert gases occurs in fenestrations with multiple interpane space, such as double-pane glass with one or two plastic films.

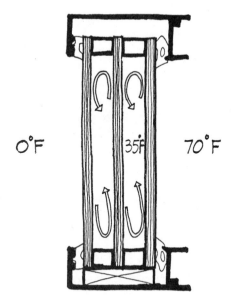

0°F   35°F   70°F

Figure 2.4 ▶ Air convection in multiple pane glazing.

Since heat loss through inert gas is lower than heat loss through air, the width of the interpane space has a smaller effect on the U-value of gas-filled fenestration than on the U-value of air-filled. Gas-filled fenestrations can be thinner without incurring a significant increase in energy use.

Evacuated Interpane Spaces
Convection and random molecular heat transfer can be eliminated if all gases are evacuated from the interpane space. Low-e glazings with argon gas can reach U-values around 0.25. If the interpane space is evacuated instead, a U-value as low as 0.16 can be obtained. Thus, vacuum glazing can yield the same or lower U-values than gas-filled glazing. This is to be expected, since convection is eliminated, not

just reduced. No practical applications exist yet, because it is expensive to manufacture a fully sealed glazing unit which would not deflect under the outside air pressure.

RADIATION

Solar Radiation
Short-wave solar radiation passes almost unobstructed through clear glass and film. This radiation is emitted by a hot source (the sun) and incorporates both visible and infrared/ultraviolet portions of the spectrum.

The relative intensity of solar heat admitted into a building through glazing is usually measured with the shading coefficient. The relative heat gain (see definitions) is a similar method of comparing the solar heat gain through different windows. Table 2.1 exemplifies two methods of reducing the shading coefficient and the relative heat gain:

1. By coating the outer pane with a reflective film, which rejects a large portion of the solar radiation
2. By tinting (coloring) the outer pane, which absorbs a portion of the solar radiation, warms up, and releases much of the heat back to the outside

These conventional approaches decrease all wavelengths that compose the solar radiation: infrared (about 50% of solar radiation), visible (about 47% of solar radiation), and ultraviolet (about 3% of solar radiation).

The reduction in infrared is beneficial since it directly diminishes the heat gain; the reduction in ultraviolet (UV) can also have positive effects, since UV exposure causes fading of furniture and carpets.

The glazings presented in Table 2.1 and Fig. 2.5 do not cover the entire range of glazings

Table 2.1 ► Examples of Conventional Methods to Reduce Solar Gain Based on 1-in Glazing Assembly with Double-Pane, ¼ in Glass and ½ in Air Space

Insulating Glazing Assembly			Total Solar Energy				
Type	Outer Pane	Outer Pane Surface #2	Solar Transmittance (Percentage)	Solar Reflectance (Percentage)	Absorptance (Percentage)	Daylight Transmittance (Percentage)	Shading Coefficient
Clear	Clear	Uncoated	64–77	8–12	15–29	78–80	0.81–0.84
	Green	Uncoated	38–45	6–7	49–55	66–76	0.56–0.68
	Gray	Uncoated	35–41	6–7	42–59	38–45	0.53–0.65
Tinted	Bronze	Uncoated	37–48	6–7	46–56	46–52	0.57–0.70
	Blue-Gray	Uncoated	30–41	5–8	52–65	63–71	0.48–0.60
	Dark Gray	Uncoated	25–36	5–6	59–69	58–67	0.43–0.61
	Clear	Silver	13–17	16–21	65–70	18–20	0.26–0.32
Reflective	Clear	Blue	8–11	14–22	67–78	14–19	0.20–0.24
	Clear	Bronze	8–16	11–20	70–81	15–19	0.23–0.31

Note: The ranges are based on several glazings. For this reason, the lowest and highest values for solar transmittance, reflectance, and absorptance may not add to 100%.

commercially available. There are reflective glazings with even lower shading coefficients; there are also tinted/reflective glazings; and there are many more colors offered for both tinted and reflective types. However, Table 2.1 and Fig. 2.5 illustrate two important facts:

1. Clear, tinted, and reflective glazings have distinct ranges of shading coefficient and daylight transmittance. There is little or no overlap.
2. The range for daylight transmittance closely follows that of the shading coefficient.

As the visible portion of the solar spectrum is reduced, *both* heat gain and daylight decrease. Consequently, the use of electricity for lighting of perimeter zones may increase. At a minimum, daylighting control systems become less effective.

Some glazing types control both the amount and the spectrum of solar radiation admitted in a space. Selective coatings reject the nonvisible portion of the radiation, but allow most of the visible light through, resulting in glazings with low shading coefficients

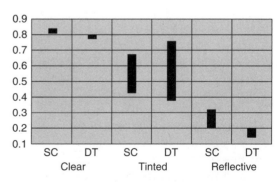

Figure 2.5 ► Examples of clear, tinted, and reflective glazings.

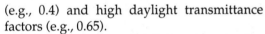

(e.g., 0.4) and high daylight transmittance factors (e.g., 0.65).

The ratio between daylight transmittance and shading coefficient is called *efficacy factor* or *coolness index* and is discussed in the following section. At this juncture it is worth noting that glazings with high efficacy factors are usually desirable. Such factors can reach in the 1.3 to 1.5 range, which means that roughly 30 to 50% more daylight is admitted than solar heat. A few of the low-e coatings applied on clear glass, as well as many combinations of low-e tinted and low-e reflective glass yield superior daylight performance.

Long-wave Radiation

The glass also exchanges radiation with the building interior and the environment. This radiation, emitted by sources at low temperature (e.g., furniture, walls, pavement), is long wave and therefore invisible. By contrast the sun emits both long-wave and short-wave, visible radiation.

The glazing allows most of the visible solar radiation to pass through; this radiation is absorbed by the building interior, which increases its temperature. The building interior radiates back toward the glass in the long-wave spectrum. However, glass is practically opaque to long-wave radiation. For this reason, solar heat gets "trapped" in a glazed enclosure.

Although long-wave radiation is not transmitted through glass, it is absorbed by it. During the heating season the inner pane of a window becomes warmer than the outer pane by absorbing long-wave radiation from warm interior surfaces and also through convection of the indoor air. The inner pane, in turn, loses heat through long-wave radiation to the cold outer pane, and through convec-

tion in the interpane space. Long-wave radiation is present in each step of this heat transfer mechanism and contributes to an increase in the energy use for heating.

Conversely, during warm, sunny days the outer pane of a window is heated by the sun and by the hot outside air. The outer pane then transfers heat to the cooler, interior pane by long-wave radiation as well as convection. The inner pane, in turn, radiates to the building interior, and also transfers heat to the conditioned air through convection, thereby increasing the cooling load. Long-wave radiation contributes in every step of this process that results in higher cooling energy use.

There are times, however, when long-wave radiation reduces the cooling load. During cool and sunny days the building interior can overheat. The inner pane is warm; the outer pane has lower temperature, since it is cooled by the outside air. The radiation exchange between the warm inner pane and the cool outer pane is now beneficial.

Low-emittance (low-e) coatings reduce the heat transfer, both in heating and cooling, by impeding the long-wave radiation by the glass panes which they cover. In heating, the effect of low-e glass is always beneficial. In cooling, low-e glass may or may not be effective, depending on climate and building use.

2.3.2 ▶ Low-e Glazings

Low-emittance glass is coated with layers of metal or metal oxide a few atoms thick. The coating emits very little radiation in the long-wave (infrared) spectrum. The net effect is to diminish heat loss from the building interior in winter, and to reduce heat gain in summer.

A low-e coating on surface 3 of the glazing (Fig. 2.6) reduces the ability of the inner pane

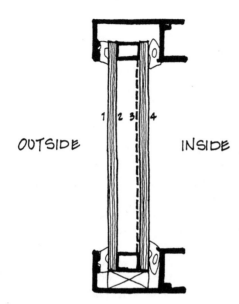

Figure 2.6 ► **Low-e coating on surface 3.**

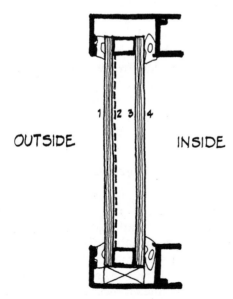

Figure 2.7 ► **Low-e coating on surface 2.**

to radiate outside, and is most effective in heating-dominated buildings. A low-e coating on surface 2 of the glazing (Fig. 2.7) reduces the ability of the outer pane to radiate toward the conditioned space, and is therefore used more often in cooling applications.

Although the low-e coating on surface 3 usually results in a lower U-value and a higher shading coefficient (i.e., more solar heat admitted), the difference is not major. Other considerations, including color, reflectivity, and cost may play a decisive role in the selection. (See Table 2.2).

Some manufacturers also offer low-e coatings on both surface 2 and surface 3. These glazings have a somewhat lower U-value (by about 5 to 10%), and also a lower shading coefficient (i.e., less solar heat admitted) than their single-coating counterparts.

Depending on the location of the coating and on fenestration configuration (e.g., number of air spaces), low-e coatings can achieve a U-value improvement of 10 to 50%.

Another important characteristic is the decrease in shading coefficient of low-e glass vs. uncoated glass. Low-e glass can maintain a clear appearance while reducing the shading coefficient by up to 50%. The tinted or reflective glass types need to vary their color to achieve such performance, while the low-e glazings do not; the same color glass can have different performance characteristics depending on the coating composition. Consequently, a building can have low-e glass with different solar characteristics on west vs. north, for instance, yet the glass would show no discernable difference in color.

According to the manufacturing process, low-e coatings are "soft" or "hard" (Table 2.2). Soft coatings are sputtered on the glass

Table 2.2 ▶ **Ranges for Two Types of Low-e Coatings Based on 1-in Insulating Assembly with Double-Pane, ¼ in Glass and ½ in Air Space**

Coating Type	Emittance Range of Coating (Percentage)	U-value Range		U-value Reduction over Uncoated Glass (0.5) (Percentage)		Shading Coefficient
		Air	Argon	Air	Argon	Clear Glass
Uncoated glass	N/A	0.48–0.55	0.40–0.45	N/A	N/A	0.81–0.94
Sputter (soft)	3–10	0.29–0.32	0.24–0.27	40–36	52–46	0.44–0.77
Pyrolitic (hard)	20	0.35	0.30	30	40	0.79–0.81

surface. As their name implies, these coatings can be more easily scratched or marred. For this reason, the coating is always applied to the inner surface of glass or film in multipane applications.

Hard coatings are applied using a pyrolitic process. These coatings can be used on any glass surface, and have by now overcome the sometimes objectionable blue-green tints of earlier products.

The emittance of soft coatings is very low. As a result, these coatings also achieve the lowest U-values, 10 to 20% lower than those of hard coatings.

The most important recent advances in low-e glazings have occurred in three areas: the development of low-e glazings with low shading coefficients and high daylight transmittance, the applications of low-e coatings in multiple pane fenestrations, and the wide availability of argon gas units.

GLAZINGS WITH LOW SHADING COEFFICIENT AND HIGH DAYLIGHT TRANSMITTANCE

Commercial buildings expend much electricity for lighting, sometimes as much as 40 to 50% of the entire annual use, so daylight strategies tend to be cost effective. However, increased daylight can bring increased solar heat and therefore increased cooling loads. Most of the larger commercial buildings are cooling-dominated. For this reason, it is usually desirable that glazings for commercial buildings allow into conditioned spaces a higher portion of the visible radiation than of the total solar radiation, i.e., that they allow more daylight and less heat. To achieve this goal, the ratio between daylight transmittance and shading coefficient factor should be maximized.

For example, a clear, uncoated, double-pane glass (Table 2.3, row 1) transmits about 78 to 80% of the outdoor daylight. The glass has a shading coefficient of 0.81–0.84. This means that the glass allows into the conditioned space about 80 to 84% as much solar heat as a single pane of clear glass. The range is not precise, as can be seen by examining the definition of the shading coefficient, but for the purpose of this example it is adequate. Since clear glass, in turn, allows about 95% of the solar heat into the space, (again, roughly), one can say that the double-pane, clear,

Table 2.3 ► **Coolness Index for Several Double-Pane Glass Types Based on 1-in Glazing Assembly with Double-Pane ¼ in Glass and ½ in Air Space***

	Insulating Glass Type	Daylight Transmittance (Percentage) (DT)	Shading Coefficient (SC)	Efficacy Factor (Coolness Index)	Color
1	Clear, uncoated	78–80	0.81–0.84	0.95–0.96	Clear
2	Tinted, uncoated	38–76	0.43–0.58	0.73–1.40	Varies
3	Reflective coating, clear	18–20	0.24–0.32	0.58–0.75	Varies
4	Reflective coating, tinted	9–17	0.21–0.25	0.44–0.73	Varies
5	Low-e, clear	70–76	0.44–0.81	0.90–1.59	Clear
6	Low-e, tinted	19–62	0.26–0.55	0.70–1.71	Varies
7	Low-e, reflective coating, clear	8–47	0.13–0.52	0.62–1.33	Varies
8	Low-e, reflective coating, tinted	8–28	0.15–0.33	0.47–1.43	Varies
9	Clear, low-e coating on film in interpane space	54–70	0.41–0.62	1.13–1.44	Clear
10	Tinted, low-e coating on film in interpane space	14–60	0.17–0.43	0.82–1.56	Varies
11	Clear, low-e coatings on two films in 3 in interpane space	37–58	0.28–0.50	1.16–1.32	Clear with light-brown reflections
12	Tinted, low-e coatings on two films in 3 in interpane space	14–60	0.19–0.29	1.0–1.65	Varies

* ½ in air space unless otherwise noted

uncoated glass allows into space about 76 to 80% of the solar heat. The range is comparable to the 78 to 80% portion of the daylight admitted into the space.

Because uncoated clear glass admits about the same fraction of solar heat as of solar daylight, it is not ideal for most daylight applications. Additionally, in most locations clear glass may be admitting too much daylight in absolute terms. A vision panel that is too bright causes glare. In general, the glazings most appropriate for daylighting of commercial buildings have lower daylight transmittance and *much* lower shading coefficient. Several types of low-e glass meet this criterion.

Daylighting versus Solar Gain

Most low-e coatings on clear glass reduce the daylight transmittance to the 70 to 75% range; the shading coefficients typically decrease in the 0.65 to 0.75 range. One manufacturer provides clear low-e glass with a low shading coefficient, comparable with that of tinted glass or glass/film combination (DT = 0.70, SC = 0.44). Another produces a very high SC glass, with good application for heating-dominated buildings (DT = 0.73, SC = 0.81).

To facilitate the comparison between different glazings, the ratio between natural light transmittance and shading coefficient can be used. This ratio is called the *efficacy factor* or the *coolness index* (CI).

A high coolness index indicates that the glazing is effective in admitting daylight and in stopping solar heat. Such glazings are well-suited for energy-saving daylight strategies. For a typical clear, ¼ in-thick, double-pane glazing the coolness index is 0.80/0.82 = 0.98. Most types of clear, double-pane, low-e glass have similar coolness indices: from 0.90 to 1.10. However, one low-e glass described above (DT = 0.70 and SC = 0.44) has very advantageous characteristics, with a CI greater than 1.5.

By examining Table 2.3 it is evident that, in general, reflective glass cannot be used for daylighting strategies. Clear uncoated glass and most of clear low-e glass types admit high levels of daylight, but also high levels of solar heat. For most applications these glazings will require shading devices. Finally, some of the tinted and low-e tinted glazings (with or without supplement of reflective films) satisfy the requirements for daylight applications without shading devices: they offer daylight transmittance factors above 20% and coolness indices above 1.0.

The above discussion demonstrates that the range of CI for any glass type is wide. Selection of low-e or tinted low-e glass does not automatically ensure good performance. The designer needs to decide on a particular product within the low-e range.

Effective Glazings for Daylighting Applications

Several low-e glazings are especially successful in selectively admitting the visible light spectrum. (See Table 2.4.) They transmit 33 to 76% of natural light, and they admit less than 23 to 64% of solar heat. As a result, their coolness index is in the range of 1.2 to 1.7. By com-

Table 2.4 ▶ Ranges for Low-e Glazings with Superior Daylighting Characteristics Based on 1 in Glazing Assembly, Double-Pane ¼ in Glass, ½ in Air Space

	Glass Type	A Daylight Transmission (Percentage)	B Shading Coefficient	C Efficacy Factor (Coolness Index) A/B	D U-value center-of-glass (air)
1	Clear, low-e	70–76	0.44–0.64	1.17–1.59	0.29–0.31
2	Tinted, low-e	54–63	0.35–0.46	1.30–1.71	0.31
3	Reflective (silver), low-e	40–46	0.30–0.37	1.19–1.33	0.30–0.32
4	Reflective, low-e, on tinted (green)	33–38	0.23–0.27	1.24–1.43	0.30–0.31
5	Clear, low-e, with one film	54–62	0.41–0.49	1.26–1.44	0.21–0.23
6	Tinted, low-e, with one film	40–60	0.27–0.43	1.40–1.56	0.21–0.23
7	Reflective, low-e, with one film	47	0.35	1.34	0.21
8	Clear, low-e, with two films	37–58	0.28–0.50	1.16–1.32	0.12–0.14
9	Tinted, low-e, with two films	38	0.23	1.65	0.13

Note: Glazings noted in this table have a coolness index of 1.15 or higher and a daylight transmittance of 30% or higher.

parison, the best of tinted uncoated glass achieves a coolness index of about 1.4, and clear, uncoated glass reaches only 0.95.

Most double-pane glazings with high daylight transmittance/low shading coefficient are clear or with a light green/light blue tint. One reflective glass in Table 2.4 has a silver tone. The cost of high CI glazings can be slightly higher than that of other low-e tinted products, but as the following case study shows, the additional expense can be easily recovered through energy savings.

The glazings can also be grouped by their center-of-glass U-value. For those with two panes of glass the U-value is about 0.3. If one plastic film is located in the interpane space, the U-value is about 0.22. A second plastic film in the interpane space further decreases the U-value to about 0.13.

It is apparent that the group with plastic films in the interpane space has very good daylighting properties as well as low U-values. However, the cost of such glazings is also considerably higher than that of double-pane, low-e glass. Integration with HVAC and lighting systems is important to create a

cost-effective application of this highly efficient glass type.

Case Study: Office Building

DOE-2.1 simulations were performed on a four-story, 58,000 ft² office building located in White Plains, just north of New York City. Fifteen percent of the wall area is composed of vision panels, with ¼ in double-pane glass and ½ in air space between panes. Interior blinds can be pulled to avoid glare. Space lighting is achieved with fluorescent lamps activated by electronic ballasts. On perimeter zones the lamps can be dimmed to 20% of output as part of daylighting strategies.

Centrifugal chillers serve a VAV system with perimeter baseboards. The electricity consumed for lighting, cooling, fans, and pumps is estimated at 1,070,000 kwh/year.

The glazing types examined are presented in Table 2.5.

- Glass one, the base case, is a typical clear glass.
- Glass two is a typical clear glass with low-e coating.

Table 2.5 ▶ Properties of Glass Analyzed for Office Building

Glass	Glass Type	A Daylight Transmittance (Percentage)	B Shading Coefficient	C Coolness Index A/B	U-value Center-of-Glass
1	Clear	78	0.81	0.96	0.50
2	Low-e clear A	73	0.73	1.00	0.31
3	Low-e clear B	70	0.44	1.59	0.31
4	Tinted green	65	0.56	1.16	0.50
5	Low-e green A	65	0.44	1.47	0.31
6	Low-e green B	60	0.35	1.71	0.31

- The third clear glass has an unusually low shading coefficient while maintaining a high daylight transmittance.
- The fourth glass is a typical green-tinted, uncoated glass.
- The fifth and sixth glasses are high performance, tinted with low-e coatings.

Although clear glass has the highest daylight transmittance and would theoretically result in more opportunities for dimming, the opposite is true. The high daylight transmittance often results in glare and excessive visual contrast. The shades are drawn more often than in the case of low-e glass. Occupants also need slightly higher footcandle levels to reduce visual contrast between glass and surrounding wall areas. As a result, Table 2.6 shows that, by decreasing the daylight transmittance in glazings, the lighting energy use remains relatively constant. Savings are achieved in cooling, fans, and pumps. Those glazings with higher coolness indices also attain high cost reductions in fuel use.

Additionally, the chiller plant decreases from 140 tons for clear glass to 120 tons for clear low-e B and for the two tinted low-e glazings. The boiler plant also decreases, from 130 MBtu for the uncoated glazings to 120 MBtu for all low-e glazings.

Note: In this example a decrease in daylight transmittance did not materially affect the lighting energy use, since any of the glass types analyzed have DT greater than 60%. In the New York City climate the daylight transmittance needs to decrease below the 30 to 50% range to significantly increase the lighting use. In southern climates the daylight transmittance could go even below 30%, with good results. These values are only useful to start a lighting analysis. The actual design is based on software analyses (e.g., RADIANCE, DOE-2) and/or physical models.

MULTIPLE GLASS AND FILM LAYERS WITH LOW-E COATINGS

Low-emittance coatings are also applied to flexible membranes, usually thin polyester films suspended between glass panes, to create two or more air spaces (Fig. 2.8). This results in performance that is superior to double-pane, low-e coated, or even to triple-pane glazings.

Table 2.7 compares daylight transmittances, shading coefficients, and center-of-glass U-

Table 2.6 ▶ Energy Savings for Office Building with Daylighting

Glass	Glass Type	Lighting kwh	Cooling kwh	Pumps and Fans kwh	Demand kw	Gas Use ccf	Energy $
1	Clear (base case): total energy use	318,832	228,915	250,081	281	19,075	119,708
2	Low-e clear A: change in energy use	−255	−7,251	−8,383	−3	−1,457	−2,200
3	Low-e clear B: change in energy use	17	−28,932	−25,210	−10	−887	−4,907
4	Tinted green: change in energy use	−266	−20,070	−20,231	−8	187	−3,245
5	Low-e green A: change in energy use	−266	−28,824	−25,161	−10	−879	−4,914
6	Low-e green B: change in energy use	262	−33,044	−27,403	−11	−516	−5,144

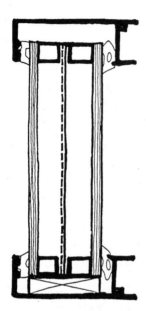

Figure 2.8 ▶ Low-e coating on film suspended in interpane space.

values, for several insulating glazings with ¼ in glass.

The double-pane, single-film unit (item no. 4, column D in the table) attains a center-of-glass U-value of 0.27–0.31, similar with the range of clear, soft-coat, low-e units with argon (0.25–0.30 in the cell above). Since it is less expensive to fill the interpane space with argon than to provide a low-e coated plastic film, the ½ in single-film unit has only the advantage of a lower shading coefficient. The real benefit of the film is obtained by increasing the interpane width from ½ in to 1 in. This step improves the U-value by over 30%, to a range of 0.21–0.23 (item no. 7, column D in the table).

An even better U-value is achieved by utilizing two films in the interpane space. For a

3 in width the center-of-glass U-value can be as low as 0.12.

It is clear that multiple glass and film units are most effective in wider configurations.

The U-value of ultimate importance, however, is that of the *entire* fenestration assembly. This overall U-value is determined by glazings, frames, and spacers. Typically, 1 ft² of metal frames and spacers loses more heat than 1 ft² of double-pane, low-e glass. For example, thermally-broken metal frames with aluminum spacers increase the heat flow through the glazed area of double-pane, low-e glass by approximately 5 to 30%. (Refer to Table 2.7, column F.)

The importance of thermal breaks in frames is well recognized and the technique is widely applied. Insulating spacers were developed to further reduce the edge heat loss.

Insulating Spacers

The least expensive, traditional spacers are manufactured of steel or aluminum. Better spacers, designed for use in low-U glazings, are typically made of plastic.

Research has shown that insulating spacers can improve the U-value of aluminum frames with thermal breaks by 10 to 20%, by replacing the aluminum spacers. The entire fenestration unit with insulating spacers can achieve U-value reductions ranging from 5 to over 15%.

The highest savings is obtained for glazings with low U-values. Careful frame and spacer design, for example, allows the fenestration unit 8 in Table 2.7 to attain a very low, and therefore very advantageous, U-value of 0.14–0.15—see column E.

This U-value is about 20% higher than the U-value measured at center-of-glass (column D). Although the increase may appear to be

Table 2.7 ▶ Ranges for Several Double-Pane, Clear, Low-e Glazing Types (¼-in Glass)

		A	B	C	D	E	F
				Efficacy Factor	U-value	U-value	
		Daylight		(Coolness	Center-of-	Unit	
		Transmittance	Shading	Index)	Glass	(approx)	
Unit	Glass Type	(Percentage)	Coefficient				E/D
1	Uncoated, ½ in air space	78–80	0.81–0.94	0.93–0.95	0.48–0.55	0.52–0.59	1.07–1.08
2	Low-e, soft-coat ½ in air space	70–76	0.44–0.81	0.90–1.60	0.29–0.32	0.36–0.39	1.24–1.27
3	Low-e, ½ in interpane space with argon gas	70–76	0.44–0.81	0.90–1.60	0.25–0.30	0.31–0.37	1.24–1.27
4	Low-e with film within ½ in interpane air space	59–70	0.41–0.62	1.14–1.44	0.27–0.31	0.34–0.37	1.26
5	Low-e, with film within ½ in interpane space and argon gas	51–59	0.39–0.47	1.26–1.31	0.20	0.25	1.26–1.31
6	Low-e, with film within ½ in interpane space and krypton gas	51–59	0.39–0.47	1.26–1.31	0.13	0.16	1.26–1.31
7	Low-e, with film within 1 in interpane air space	54–70	0.41–0.62	1.13–1.32	0.21–0.23	0.26–0.29	1.24–1.26
8	Low-e, with two films within 3 in interpane air space	37–58	0.28–0.50	1.16–1.32	0.12–0.14	0.14–0.15	1.07–1.17

* The units have thermally broken metal frames and aluminum spacers, except for unit 8, which has insulating spacers.

large, it represents in fact an achievement, as shown by a comparison between units 8 and 3.

Unit 3 uses a glazing with a much higher U-value than unit 8 (U = 0.25–0.30 versus U = 0.12–0.14). Despite this, the U-value of the entire assembly for unit 8 is only 20% higher than the U-value measured at center-of-glass, while the U-value of the entire assembly for unit 3 is almost 25% higher than the center-of-glass U-value.

Since glazings with lower U-value are more affected by heat loss at the edge, the reverse should have happened. Unit 8 should have experienced a *higher* increase in U-value than unit 3. However, the superior frame and spacer detail of unit 8 results in better performance.

INERT GASES IN INTERPANE SPACE

The interpane spaces of fenestration units can be filled with nontoxic inert gases that are less conductive than air, such as argon (combined with sulphur hexafluoride) or krypton. Argon gas windows have U-values that are 5 to 30% better than those of air-filled windows. Krypton gas can reduce the U-value by up to 50% (see Table 2.7, items 4 and 6, column E).

The use of inert gases has led to concern about the long-term efficiency of the fenestration, in the event that the gas escapes. However, indications are that only 10 to 20% of the gas may be lost over a 20-year period.

Figure 2.9 ▶ GTE telephone operations headquarters, Irving, TX (*courtesy HKS, Dallas, TX*).

Case Study: Office Building

GTE used innovative glazing systems to enhance the quality of its 1.2 million ft² telephone operations headquarters in Irving, Texas (Fig. 2.9). To accommodate the hot Texas sun and still provide adequate amounts of daylight, the architect specified glazings that could offer energy and solar control with high light transmission. A low emissivity coating on green glass was selected because of its 65% visible light transmission, shading coefficient of 0.44, and U-value of 0.32. Horizontal shading devices in the curved rotunda and subcore areas of the building further reduce the incidence of direct solar radiation on occupants and glare. The office sections are protected by vertical glass sunshades.

Case Study: Office Building

At the seven-story Ogden Regional Office in Utah, built in 1987, the architects Scott, Louie & Browning specified glazings with one low-e coated film. The glazings of the south and west windows provide solar protection with a 0.26 shading coefficient, while the glazed areas on the east and north admit higher levels of daylight (35%), with a shading

Figure 2.10 ▶ Engineering Office Building, University of Victoria, B.C. (*courtesy The Wade Williams Corporation*).

coefficient of 0.34. However, the appearance of lightly tinted bronze, nonreflective glass is the same on all four sides.

The U-value of the glass is 0.31 in winter and 0.36 in summer. Perimeter offices experience even temperature conditions and heating loads are reduced.

Case Study: University

In the 32,000 ft² Engineering Office Building, University of Victoria, British Columbia, architects Wade Williams Corp. used a glazing system with two low-e coated films (Fig. 2.10). The framing system thermally separates the inside and outside aluminum elements. A quick-refill desiccant system maintains interior pane surfaces free of condensation. The U-value of the glazings is 0.13 and that of the assembly 0.17.

The windows transmit a relatively low percentage of natural light (20%) with an even lower shading coefficient (0.13), to reduce cooling loads and eliminate glare. The building has exceptionally low heating energy use—only 9500 Btu/ft²/year in the 5700 degree day climate.

Figure 2.11 shows the Engineering Laboratory Wing designed by Wade Williams Corp. and Young + Wright Architects, and completed in 1995. This four-story, 127,800 ft²

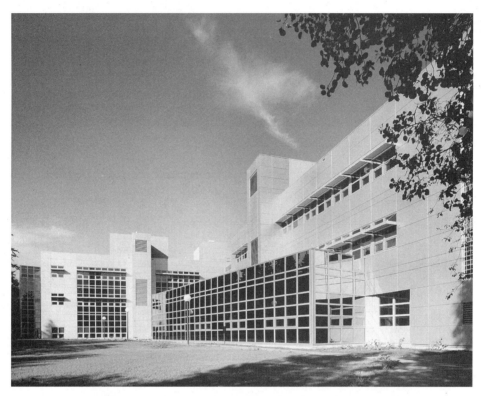

Figure 2.11 ▶ **Engineering Laboratory Wing, University of Victoria, B.C. (***courtesy The Wade Williams Corporation***).**

addition uses the same fenestration system with two low-e coated films. The high R-value envelope and the low solar gains made it possible to eliminate all perimeter heating *and* all mechanical cooling. Cooling is performed with outside air, even though the building has a high rate of internal heat gain from computer equipment. However, the lighting load is low, due to efficient fluorescent lamps, electronic ballasts, task lighting, direct-indirect luminaries and daylighting strategies. The latter include exterior *and* interior light shelves which direct daylight deep into the laboratories, dimming with photo-cells, and occupancy sensors. Local cooling is also achieved by opening windows. Other energy-efficient concepts include (a) low velocity air system; (b) modulation of air with branch dampers which require lower air pressure, and therefore lower fan energy, than VAV boxes; (c) fan tracking to ensure synchronization between return and supply rates; (d) thermostat setback based on occupancy sensors; (e) heat recovery and others.

Case Study: Convention Center
Architects HOK and Plus 4 specified 33,000 ft² of high-performance glazing and curtain

Figure 2.12(a) ▶ **Indiana Convention Center, addition to Indiana Hoosier Dome, Indianapolis, IN** (*courtesy Hellmuth, Obata, Kassabaum Inc.*).

wall systems for the Indiana Convention Center addition to the Indiana Hoosier Dome in Indianapolis (Fig. 2.12a and 2.12b), to respond to the energy and comfort concerns associated with large expanses of north-facing glass. The interior and exterior aluminum frame members are separated by 3-in-deep insulative spacers to eliminate thermal bridging and condensation at edges. The four-element glazing units are constructed using clear or green tinted outer pane, two internal biaxially suspended low-emittance coated films, and clear glass inner pane.

The overall window U-value is 0.14, shading coefficients vary from 0.29 to 0.53, and the visible light transmission varies from 44 to 54%. The high temperature of the inner glass pane surface eliminates almost all cold weather downdraft problems as well as excessive occupant radiant heat transfer. Even though the building uses 35-ft-tall glass walls, perimeter heating is not required.

The high ratio between visible light and shading coefficient ensures a good day and night visual appearance and good use of daylighting, while at the same time reducing the space cooling load.

Case Study: Emergency Services Building
The Emergency Services Building in Valmeyer, Illinois, is part of the National Renewable Energy Laboratory's Exemplary

Figure 2.12(b) ► **Indiana Convention Center, addition to Indiana Hoosier Dome, Indianapolis, IN** *(Continued)* *(courtesy Hellmuth, Obata, Kassabaum Inc.).*

Buildings program (Fig. 2.13). The architect, ARTEC Architecture, of Belleville, Illinois, was assisted by ENSAR Group, Inc., of Boulder, Colorado, to design a building that demonstrates energy efficiency. This building houses the city's police, fire, and rescue services in a climate that is typically hot and humid in the summer and cool and humid in the winter.

The 9000 ft² building has approximately 1300 ft² of south-facing glazing utilizing both walls and roof clerestories. High-performance, low-e windows with an argon fill have been chosen as the glazing system. Total energy savings are projected to be approximately $9000 per year with a simple payback for energy efficiency measures of just less than two years.

Case Study: Showroom
The Cochran Infiniti auto showroom in Monroeville, Pennsylvania, employs a clear low-e glass with the coating deposited on surface 2 to reduce summer heat gain. The interpane space is filled with argon gas. The glazing achieves a 73% daylight transmittance, a 0.81

Figure 2.13 ▶ Emergency Services Building, Valmeyer, IL (*courtesy ARTEC Architecture*).

shading coefficient, and a center-of-glass U-value of 0.30.

PRACTICAL CONSIDERATIONS FOR LOW-E GLAZINGS

Design
- When comparing the cost effectiveness of several glazing types, always consider the possibility of reducing the size, and therefore the cost, of the HVAC system.
- Always compare and use U-values of the entire fenestration units rather than U-values of center-of-glass areas. The former can be over 30% higher than the latter.

- If possible, perform hourly computer simulations to select an optimum combination of glazing, lighting, and HVAC systems. DOE-2.1 is state-of-the-art software for energy-use analysis. RADIANCE is best for examination of light distribution and visual comfort.
- When analyzing the effectiveness of glass types with daylighting strategies, consider whether the occupants will be subject to glare. If glare exists, occupants will pull shades or even paste paper on windows. Daylighting strategies will yield mediocre results. For this reason buildings with large areas of clear or lightly tinted glass require special attention to avoid excessive direct solar radia-

tion and glare in work spaces. Exterior shading devices and light shelves can help toward this goal.

- Not all glazing manufacturers offer insulating spacers as part of their standard line of double-glass units; however, if the glazing units are assembled by the window manufacturer, insulating spacers can be provided at little or no extra cost. Further, for large enough orders even the manufacturers are usually willing to insert other spacers. Finally, as more manufacturers include insulating spacers as part of their standard lines it is to be expected that availability problems will disappear.

- Glare is not the only undesirable consequence of high daylight transmittance glazings. If such glazings are too bright by comparison to the surrounding walls and ceilings, the contrast becomes uncomfortable. Occupants will tend to turn the lights on in order to reduce this contrast. Thus, beyond a certain point of visual comfort, more daylight through the windows can actually translate into higher electricity use for lighting.

Construction

- If glass types vary by orientation, clearly mark the fenestration units and check the installation.
- Ensure that the glass is mounted in the frame as specified. For example, tinted panes must be located on the exterior. Low-e coatings could be meant for either surface 2 or 3, and the insulating glass must be oriented to observe this important requirement.

Buildings with high-performance glazings and frames are becoming common

Low-e Glass with High Coolness Index
- 75 State Street, Boston, MA
- Citicorp Building at Court Square, New York, NY
- GTE Headquarters, Irving, TX
- Dupont Offices at 101 Basch Street, Wilmington, DE
- AAA Headquarters, Orlando, FL
- Northeast Point Offices, Hartford, CT
- Landsdowne Executive Center & Hotel, Leesburg, VA
- Rock-n-Roll Hall of Fame, Cleveland, OH
- Four Times Square Tower, New York, NY

Low-e Glass with One Film
- National Audubon Society, New York, NY
- Natural Resource Defense Council, New York, NY
- McDonald's Corp., Denver, CO
- Western Savings Bank, Waco, TX
- Sheraton World Tower, Flushing, NY
- Spokane City Hall, Spokane, WA
- MIT Roach Library, Cambridge, MA

Low-e Glass with Two Films
- Reimer Tower, Burlington, Ontario
- Indiana Convention Center, Indianapolis, IN
- Engineering Office Building, University of Victoria, British Columbia
- Pinebush Business Centre, Cambridge, Ontario

Operations/Maintenance
- Regularly clean glass surface, especially for daylighting applications.
- Regularly refill the desiccant in fenestration units that require this type of maintenance.

2.3.3 ▶ *Ceramic Frit Glazings*

Ceramic frit glazings achieve solar control, high strength, and interesting aesthetic effects by fusing a ceramic layer to glass.

The "frit" is basically finely ground, colored glass. This glass powder is deposited on a pane of float glass, either uniformly to obtain a solid color, or with a silk screen, to achieve practically any design, from geometric patterns to artistic delineations.

Once the preparation is finished, the fritted glass is heated in a furnace, where the frit melts and adheres to the glass surface.

The heat process strengthens the glass and increases resistance to wind loads and thermal stress. However, because of this process the glass cannot be cut again.

Solid frit, which covers the entire surface of the glass, is typically used for decorative purposes in spandrel panels or for translucent effects in vision panels. The silk screen frit has applications for both visions and spandrel panels.

SILK SCREEN FRIT GLASS

Silk screening can create designs that have a primary aesthetic function, achieve a low shading coefficient without a mirrorlike effect, or block high-angle sunlight.

Applications for Solar Control
The artistic designs can extend to nearly any combination of shapes and hues using color

separation techniques. As a result the same pane of glass can be made opaque or part transparent. The limitations to this application are primarily related to the cost of custom artwork and of small production series.

The low shading coefficient designs use regular patterns of semiopaque, ceramic dots, lines, or surfaces with holes (Fig. 2.14). These frit patterns can achieve shading coefficients of 0.36 to 0.60 on clear insulating glass, depending on the density of the ceramic pattern and on its color.

While the dots and lines of the frit pattern superimpose themselves on any view, they do allow an observer on the street to see the shapes in the building interior. Reflective glazings with similar low transmittance

DZigns® Ceramic-Pattern Coated Glass

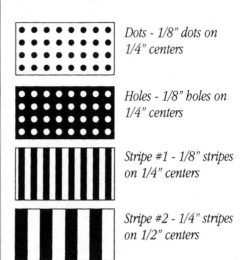

Dots - 1/8" dots on 1/4" centers

Holes - 1/8" holes on 1/4" centers

Stripe #1 - 1/8" stripes on 1/4" centers

Stripe #2 - 1/4" stripes on 1/2" centers

Figure 2.14 ▶ Regular patterns with ceramic frit glass (*courtesy Interpane*).

present a mirrorlike image. The transparent look may be important for public spaces, which otherwise might employ clear glass and incur high cooling costs.

Finally, a frit glass can vary its horizontal line pattern (Fig. 2.15) from narrow at the top of the fenestration unit to widely spaced at the bottom. As a result, high-angle direct radiation is blocked, while direct vision remains unimpeded.

A similar but stronger effect can be obtained by staggering the horizontal frits in two panes of glass (Fig. 2.16), to selectively admit light at certain angles and to block it at others.

Low U-value Frit Glazings

Any ceramic frit glass can receive a transparent low-e coating to reduce its U-value from about 0.50 to approximately 0.29–0.35. Low-e ceramic frit glass also benefits from a lower shading coefficient (0.27 to 0.48) with only a small change in appearance.

Relatively High Cost

Ceramic frit coating currently costs about twice as much as a highly reflective film and three to four times as much as a low-e coating. This relatively high cost could decrease as the application becomes more widespread.

Case Study: Office Building

At the Steelcase Corporate Development Center in Grand Rapids, MI (Fig. 2.17), the designer, Beta Group (formerly WBDC), used ceramic frit glass to limit glare from daylight and yet maintain views to the outside. The windows employ alternate strips on sloped surfaces to block direct sunlight. Vertical surfaces use dark ceramic lines, which start thick and narrowly spaced at the top, and end thin

CERAMIC FRIT GLASS WAS INSTALLED FOR VISION PANELS IN MANY U.S. BUILDINGS

- Abraham & Strauss Plaza, New York, NY
- Aquarium of the Americas, New Orleans, LA
- 1585 Broadway Offices, New York, NY
- Steelcase Corporate Development Center, Grand Rapids, MI
- Litton Federal Credit Union, Chatsworth, CA
- Barcorp Building, Rockville, MD
- Baltimore Gas & Electric Offices, Baltimore, MD
- Cabot Plaza, Bellevue, WA
- National Air & Space Museum Restaurant, Washington, DC
- Orlando Airport Terminal, Orlando, FL
- United Airlines Terminal, O'Hare Airport, Chicago, IL
- Convention Center, San Diego, CA
- UCSD, Clinical Sciences Building, La Jolla, CA
- N.I.U. Engineering Building, Chicago, IL
- AT&T Promenade, Atlanta, GA
- North Decatur Building, Decatur, GA

and widely spaced above eye level. The lines prevent glare from high altitude sun.

Case Study: Airport Terminal

In the United Terminal at Chicago's O'Hare Airport the architects selected ceramic frit for skylights and vertical surfaces. In addition to

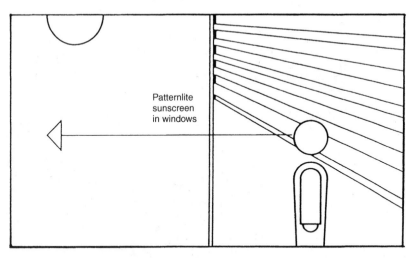

Figure 2.15 ▶ Horizontal pattern on ceramic frit glass at the Steelcase Development Center (*courtesy PPG*).

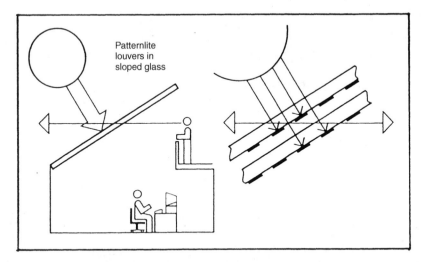

Figure 2.16 ▶ Alternating horizontal patterns on laminated, double-pane, sloped glass at the Steelcase Development Center (*courtesy PPG*).

Figure 2.17 ▶ Steelcase Corporate Development Center, Grand Rapids, Michigan (*courtesy the Beta Group*).

the decorative effect, the frit reduces solar heat gain while allowing relatively high levels of natural light. Because of the large areas of skylight, considerable energy savings in cooling is achieved.

PRACTICAL CONSIDERATIONS FOR CERAMIC FRIT GLAZINGS

Design

- The use of ceramic frit does not preclude other solar control and U-value reduction techniques for insulating glazings such as reflective coatings, tinted glass, low-e coatings, multiple glazings and films, inert gas fill.
- Frit designs on vision panels can be complemented by similar treatments on spandrel panels.
- Light-color frit treatments diffuse the light. For this reason they are not indicated when a transparent look is desired. However, diffuse light might be actually sought when the view is objectionable or nonessential (e.g., overhead glazing).
- Large surfaces that diffuse light can also produce glare. For this reason light-color

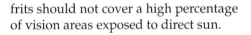

frits should not cover a high percentage of vision areas exposed to direct sun.

Construction
• Since frit glass is heat strengthened, it cannot be further cut on site.

Operations/Maintenance
• Ceramic frits can be very resistant to weather and other abuse, such as graffiti. However, clean according to manufacturers instructions.

2.4 ▶ SHADING DEVICES

A fenestration assembly is composed of glazing, frame, shading devices, and attachments to the envelope. (See Sec. 2.2.) Shading devices can be designed to exclude most solar heat during the cooling season, yet to allow appropriate levels of natural light into the building throughout the year. These devices can also be optimized for other purposes, such as glare reduction.

Because solar radiation varies considerably in both intensity and direction, no single control technique based on fixed shades can closely respond to the needs of a building. Movable shading devices track changes in weather, yet they bring an increased level of complexity and higher costs.

Section 2.4.1 touches upon the mechanisms through which shading devices accomplish their role in an energy-efficient building. Examples and applications follow.

2.4.1 ▶ Principles of Effective Shading

Solar radiation can be intercepted before it reaches the fenestration, within the fenestration unit, or within the conditioned space. The latter method has low effectiveness, since solar heat is absorbed by the shading assembly and by the interior pane of the glass, and then released into the space. Shading devices positioned in the interpane space achieve better performance, yet part of the heat collected within that space eventually becomes a cooling load. Both methods have valid applications. However, this manual discusses only the most effective technique for rejecting and modulating solar heat: exterior shading.

The type and operation of exterior shading devices responds to the mechanisms through which solar radiation penetrates into the building as heat and light. A review of these mechanisms follows.

FACTORS AFFECTING THE SIZE OF SHADING DEVICES

The size and shape of shading devices is affected by the amount of diffuse vs. direct radiation transmitted through a glazing assembly. Some of the sun beams entering the atmosphere are scattered by dust and water vapor, and reach the fenestration as background, diffuse radiation. The fraction of diffuse radiation increases in humid, cloudy days, or, in technical terms, in days with high *atmospheric turbidity.*

Most locations have more diffuse radiation in summer than in winter. The protection afforded by a shading device against diffuse radiation is roughly proportional to the part of the sky vault it obstructs (Fig. 2.18).

Of the direct radiation striking a glazed surface, some is reflected, some absorbed, and some transmitted (Fig. 2.19). During summer, direct sun beams fall on vertical surfaces at a very sharp angle; as a result, much of this direct light is reflected even by a clear

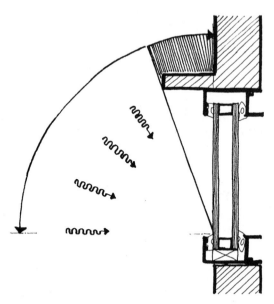

Figure 2.18 ▶ Protection from diffuse radiation.

pane of glass (Fig. 2.20). In winter the angle is closer to 90° (Fig. 2.19) and the amount of reflected light decreases; however, glare can be a problem.

Shading devices are dimensioned to block direct sunrays as shown in Fig. 2.18. Because glazings reflect a high percentage of direct radiation in summer, most of the solar radiation transmitted *through* clear, insulating glass is diffuse. In New York City, for example, about 80% of the August solar heat gain *through* double-pane clear glass originates from diffuse radiation.

This preponderance of heat gain from diffuse radiation persists for all glass types, albeit to different degrees. As a result, in most locations except dry, arid ones, design schemes based solely on blocking direct radiation are insufficient. Shading devices that

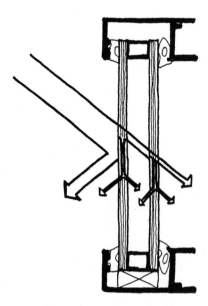

Figure 2.19 ▶ Solar radiation through glass.

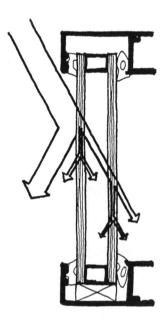

Figure 2.20 ▶ Summer light reflection off glass.

only block the direct radiation can have little effect on the much more important diffuse component.

The practical consequences of this observation are significant: Effective summer shading can only be achieved with relatively wide shades, or with combinations of vertical/horizontal shades which obstruct much of the sky vault. *The belief that south-facing facades can be protected with narrow horizontal shades is wrong for most locations in the United States.*

FACTORS AFFECTING THE SHAPE OF SHADING DEVICES

The ideal shape of a shading device depends on window orientation. For example, a horizontal shade could be intended to reduce summer heat gain and to increase winter heat gain. Fig. 2.21 depicts theoretical shapes of horizontal shading devices that accomplish this goal for a 3 ft by 5 ft window in New York City. The devices are assumed to be continuous to the left of the diagram. Similar geometries can be obtained for vertical fins.

Under most circumstances the shading devices cannot follow such irregular contours; however, the calculated shapes can offer a basis for interesting geometrical patterns on the facade, serving both aesthetic and energy conservation purposes. If, for instance, a building has small balconies under each window, the shape of the balconies on different facades could be justifiably different.

FACTORS AFFECTING THE SELECTION OF SHADING DEVICES

The complexity of solar heat gain makes it impossible to fully meet competing goals while using fixed shading devices. Inevitably, a high degree of summer shading will result in reduced daylight in winter. Problems also

occur with the spring and fall months that have the same amount of solar radiation. A fixed shading device that blocks some of the undesirable solar radiation in fall also blocks

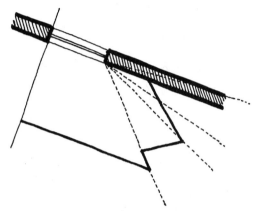

BEARING ANGLE : 18°W OF S AUGUST

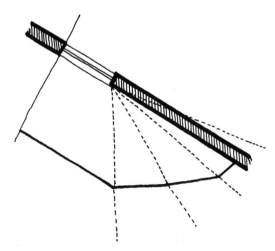

BEARING ANGLE : 30° W OF S AUGUST

Figure 2.21 ▶ Ideal shapes of horizontal shading devices in New York City.

the same beneficial solar radiation in spring. Movable shading devices can, theoretically, solve this problem. The following section presents applications of both shading techniques, with comments on feasibility and practicality.

2.4.2 ▶ *Exterior Shading Devices*

Traditional exterior shading devices are fixed. Movable types, such as exterior louvers, blinds, and awnings, have been employed to modulate solar gains for a long time, but operation difficulties prevented their widespread use.

A renewed interest in both energy conservation and daylighting has revitalized the use of all shading devices. Additionally, better sensors, controls, and mechanical parts have solved many of the reliability problems which marred the early movable devices.

MOVABLE LOUVERS AND BLINDS

Louvers installed on the exterior of buildings have been utilized for sun control in commercial buildings for decades. The louvers can reduce or eliminate glare; restrict solar heat gain; reflect light deeply into the building interior; and, when closed, reduce energy loss from the building.

Louvers can be installed both vertically and horizontally; they can be installed adjacent to glazing or can extend out over it like an awning; and, they can consist of large or small blades. The exterior appearance of the building is a major driving force in the selections. However, practical considerations are also important: small vertical louvers are closer together and can impair views; awning-type arrays can offer minimal view restriction.

Exterior venetian blinds and rolling shutters are also used, but this use is more fre-

quent in Europe than in the United States. When solar protection is not required, they can be opened entirely for an unrestricted view. Shutters can play the additional role of security devices.

Exterior louvers or blinds which open at 45 degrees can offer some exterior visibility, yet can reach a shading coefficient as low as 0.15.

Control Systems

Most louvers are adjustable to accommodate changing sun angle, weather, and building use. Controls range from manual to automatic. Some automatic systems are highly sophisticated, with computer-controlled operating profiles that respond to input from photocells. The best of the automated systems are connected to building energy management or daylight dimming systems for maximum efficiency. Louvers are even available with hail detectors, which close the louvers in the event of hail to prevent damage.

Case Study: University

The University of Colorado Health Service Center in Denver, Colorado, has large vertical louvers encapsulating its facade, as shown in Fig. 2.22. The 81,000 ft^2 of louvers are automatically adjusted; they have been operating continuously since the building was completed in 1964.

RETRACTABLE AWNINGS

Retractable awnings protect the fenestration from direct sun, and allow maximum daylight when glare and heat gain is no longer a problem.

The awnings are made of canvas or other flexible fabrics, and can be opaque or translucent, to admit more light. While the fabrics are less durable and require more mainte-

Figure 2.22 ▶ **University of Colorado Health Service Center** (*courtesy University of Colorado*).

nance than solid building materials, they are typically less heavy and less costly.

Controls

Retraction of awnings can be manual or automatic, and can be controlled with photocell systems. Wind sensors are also available; the awning retracts automatically if wind speed reaches dangerous levels.

Energy Savings

The fabrics of retractable awnings have solar transmittances ranging from 30 to 70%. Their effectiveness is threefold:

- They eliminate occupant exposure to direct sun, and they reduce heat gain from direct radiation.

- They shield the fenestration from a large portion of diffuse radiation, by obstructing the sky vault.
- They admit natural light and solar heat only when advantageous.

By comparison to fixed overhangs, fabric awnings have an additional benefit in buildings with extended operation hours. The fabrics cool rapidly after sundown, and therefore they contribute less to cooling loads.

2.4.3 ▶ Fixed Overhangs and Fins

Fixed shading devices offer similar benefits to louvers but do not have the same flexibility or performance as the adjustable types.

Overhangs (horizontal projections) are generally effective on facades with southern orientation, because the summer sun is high when these facades receive direct radiation. To block the lower afternoon sun on eastern or western facades, the overhangs need to be very deep—in effect to become porches and porticoes. This strategy is not feasible on multistory buildings. Instead, fins (vertical projections) are used. Fins cast deep shadows as soon as the sunrays are not perpendicular to the window.

A combination of overhangs and fins is often used in "grille" format. The openings in the grille can be large or quite small, a few inches even, resulting in a latticelike appearance of the building.

Materials are generally concrete and metal, but small commercial buildings sometimes use wood.

Energy Savings

Fixed shading devices decrease the cooling loads and increase the heating loads. While fuel savings is always achieved, the cost benefits vary with each particular design and are not always large enough to justify the devices. However, the overhangs and fins can be simultaneously used to enhance daylighting, protect from glare, and create aesthetic effects.

Case Study: Office

The 21,000 ft² Blue Cross/Blue Shield Building in New Haven, Connecticut (Fig. 2.23), has deep overhangs on the south facade to protect from direct solar radiation in summer and to reduce cooling loads. An atrium divides the building into two sectors. Light shelves on facades and in the atrium project natural light deep into the space.

Ellenzweig Associates, Inc., were the architects for the project, which was completed in 1990.

PRACTICAL CONSIDERATIONS FOR EXTERIOR SHADING DEVICES

Design

- Most simplified design tools, including nomographs and many computer programs, size the shading devices to protect from direct radiation incident on the glazing surface. This approach can be used to avoid direct sun on the occupants. *Do not* use such rough methods to optimize the size, shape, or operation of a shading device for energy efficiency or for daylighting.

  Since the efficiency of a shading device is determined by the amount of solar radiation that *crosses* the glazing as heat, energy use or daylighting optimization should only be performed with computer programs which contain algorithms that account for the effect of the shade on diffuse radiation. DOE-2.1 is an example of such a program, applicable to complex buildings. ENERGY-10 is an example of a program well-suited for simpler buildings, in the schematic design stage. However, DOE-2.1 and ENERGY-10 do not perform accurate calculations on the effect of exterior and interior shading devices on daylight distribution.

  RADIANCE is state-of-the-art software for examining glare and light effects. RADIANCE is combined with other programs into a lighting design and analysis set called ADELINE.

- When designing a shading device, examine both solar gain and glare. One

Figure 2.23 ▶ **Blue Cross/Blue Shield Building, New Haven, CT (***photo courtesy Steven Rosenthal***).**

building, for example, was designed with horizontal shading devices made of reflective glass. The devices reduced the solar heat gain as intended, but created unacceptable glare for occupants.

- Always consider the effect of shading devices on building maintenance (e.g., possibility of dirt streaks).
- When specifying movable shading devices inquire about the track record of the manufacturer and investigate the performance of previous installations.

Construction

- Protect surfaces of shading devices from stains and rips.
- Clean debris and dust deposits from shading devices.

Operations/Maintenance

- Remove the grime that may form at building angles to avoid streaking on the facade.
- Regularly maintain the moving parts of the mobile shading devices.

- Periodically verify the calibration of photocells which operate mobile shading devices.

2.5 ► DEVELOPMENTS ON THE HORIZON

The highest rate of technological advances in construction materials is occurring with glazings. Some innovations, such as krypton gas glazings, are marketed but not often employed in commercial installations. Others, such as switchable windows, have been commercialized but have only very few applications. Yet other promising techniques, including holographic glazings, are only under development.

This section could not cover all interesting new ideas; it is merely intended to exemplify the wide front of innovation in glazings.

KRYPTON GAS GLAZINGS

Several years ago argon gas fill was an interesting development with questionable application. Now argon gas is available for practically any glazing type. A similar path could well be taken by the krypton gas fill. Glazings using krypton achieve U-values that are 25 to 50% lower than those filled with argon. Krypton is costlier than argon, but if very low U-values are needed, the alternative is to select glazings with one or two interpane films—also a fairly expensive option.

The other argument in favor of krypton gas is brought by the integrative design technique. As noted elsewhere, a low U-value window can result in elimination of the perimeter heating system. This approach greatly improves the cost effectiveness of high-performance windows, including those filled with krypton gas.

Krypton gas is also being tested for use in metal wall panels that fit above and below a window. Such panels would eliminate framing short circuits common in steel stud walls.

LASER FRIT GLASS

This glass is cut with a laser to create tiny louvers on the exterior surface of the glass, allowing light to be transmitted from some angles and deflected from others. The size of the panels cannot exceed 24 in in any direction.

The technological considerations of pane size and cost impede the commercialization of this product in the near future.

HOLOGRAPHIC GLAZINGS AND FILMS

Holographic diffractive glazings and films are being developed by the research community. These materials use the same holographic technology that produces the flickering images on many credit cards.

Thin lines are etched into glass or film such that, when light strikes, it is deflected at a different angle. If the top part of a window is treated in this manner (either by processing the glass itself or by applying a holographic film) the light can be reflected along the ceiling, deep into the adjoining space. The lower glass remains clear.

In effect the glass itself becomes a light shelf, throwing light deep into the space, beyond the 7-to-15-ft band which is typical of most daylighting systems. Holographic glazings may illuminate up to 30 ft away from the window. The technique can also be used to increase light uniformity within the cone of light admitted by a window.

Early holographic glazings used to produce a rainbow effect, because they diffracted differently the components of the visible spectrum. This problem has been overcome by researchers at Lawrence Berkeley Laboratory through the use of Bands of Holographic Diffractive Structures (BHDS). However, the holographic area has only up to 20% diffraction efficiency for natural light. Until this efficiency increases, the holographic glazings will not be competitive in terms of energy efficiency.

These materials are still several years from the marketplace. Once available, however, they will provide designers with a sophisticated new technology for utilizing daylight.

THERMOCHROMICS

An interesting concept that is not ready yet for the market is acrylic glazing which can automatically adjust from clear to translucent white in response to heat. As the temperature increases, the glazing, usually installed in skylights, becomes white, reducing the passage of light (and additional heat energy) into the space. As the surrounding air cools, the glazing once again becomes clear.

VACUUM GLAZINGS

The interpane space between two panes of glass can be evacuated, completely eliminating heat transfer through convection. This type of glass can achieve, at center, a U-value as low as 0.16 when using double low-e coatings. Heat is lost through radiation (about 60% according to Lawrence Berkeley Laboratory research) and conduction. Conduction occurs at the glass-sealed edges *and* at the glass pins that keep the two glass surfaces from collapsing under the atmospheric pres-

Figure 2.24 ► Electrochromic glass at the Princeville Hotel, Princeville Resort, Kauai, Hawaii (*courtesy Princeville Resort*).

sure. The cost of vacuum glazing is currently estimated to be about 15% higher than that of other glazings with similar U-value. No commercial applications are envisioned in the near future, but this could change if sealing and reinforcing technology with lower cost can be found.

SWITCHABLE PHOTOCHROMIC AND ELECTROCHROMIC WINDOWS

One manufacturer produces a switchable glass which can change a clear surface to a frosted one. Light transmission is reduced by only a small percent when the glass is frosted. A crystal material is sandwiched between two panes of clear glass. When a weak elec-

tric current is applied, the crystals align and the window becomes transparent. If the current is switched off, the crystals disperse randomly, diffusing the light; as a result, the surface cannot transmit images. To date, most applications have been for building interiors, such as conference rooms with glazed walls. The cost of the material is currently about $50/ft².

In two instances, the switchable glass has been installed as the inner pane in an exterior insulating glass unit: the Princeville Hotel of Kauai, Hawaii (Fig. 2.24), and the church of Scientology in Clearwater, Florida.

The technology is very young yet. As the number of applications increase, cost is likely to be reduced and technical processes to be improved. At this time no new exterior applications are planned.

Case Study: Resort Hotel

In the 9000-acre planned resort community of Princeville, the Princeville Hotel in Kauai, Hawaii, a resort hotel operated by ITT Sheraton Corporation, employs electrochromic glass in each of its 252 guest rooms. The glass is featured as a "magic window" that electronically changes to allow for views or privacy. The vision panels offer privacy without darkness, creating a space that combine natural light and openness with privacy and security. Vision panels are made by laminating liquid crystal film between two sheets of glass. Architectural polybutyral is used in the interlayer. When voltage is applied, the liquid crystal molecules align perpendicular to the glass and it appears clear. In the absence of voltage the glass appears translucent.

CHAPTER 3

EFFICIENT LIGHTING

3.1 ► EFFICIENT LIGHTING—A HIGHLY EFFECTIVE ENERGY CONSERVATION STRATEGY

Lighting uses much energy in commercial structures; in typical office buildings, for example, it accounts for 30 to 50% of the electricity consumption. Additionally, the heat generated by lights must be removed by the cooling equipment.

Because lighting systems are major energy users, they can yield high returns through improvements in efficiency.

This chapter presents advances in lighting technology and lighting system design, and examines how these advances can reduce electricity use. Energy efficient lighting equipment and controls are discussed in Sec. 3.2 (principles) and in Secs. 3.3 and 3.4 (applications). The relationship between lighting systems, fenestration, and HVAC systems is presented in Sec. 3.2.3. The interplay of daylighting techniques and lighting design is presented in Sec. 3.5.

Finally, a glimpse into the future of solar optics is included in Sec. 3.6.

3.2 ► PRINCIPLES OF ENERGY-EFFICIENT LIGHTING SYSTEMS

A well-designed lighting system should attain the desired lighting performance (light levels, color quality, etc.) using energy-efficient means. Technological advances, such as electronic ballasts and compact fluorescent lamps, have increased the energy efficiency of lighting *components*. The efficiency of the entire lighting *system* can be further improved through integration with the HVAC and fenestration systems.

The ballasts in an office building, for example, allow dimming to 20% of light output, taking advantage of glazings with high daylight transmittance. The chillers can then be downsized in response to reduced lighting loads. The often specified VAV system receives fan-powered boxes, in expectation of low cooling loads due to low lighting wattage and low solar gains; alternately, a simpler

► 81

The energy savings achievable from *system integration* rival those obtained from improvements in the lighting equipment and in all other individual components of the HVAC, controls, and envelope systems.

This section presents principles for energy efficient luminaires and control systems; then, it discusses the advantages of system integration during the design phase, as well as maintenance of lighting systems.

3.2.1 ► *Principles of Energy-Efficient Luminaires*

In technical terms, the equipment needed to produce and distribute light is designated as a luminaire. The definition cited earlier lists the components of a luminaire: housing, lamps, electric wiring, and ballasts, if required. Over the past decade the most important advances have involved lamps and ballasts.

PRINCIPLES OF HIGH EFFICIENCY LAMPS

Full Size Fluorescent
A fluorescent lamp is a glass tube with cathodes at each end (Fig. 3.1). The tube is filled with a mixture of gases, primarily argon, and with liquid mercury. When turned on, the fluorescent lamp establishes an electric arc between the two cathodes. The mercury vaporizes and radiates in the ultraviolet spectrum, charging a phosphorous coating on the inner surface of the tube. This coating emits visible light.

High efficiency fluorescent lamps use a krypton-argon mixture. This change in gas composition increases the output by 10 to

constant volume system could yield similar energy use with that of the VAV, if the discharge air temperature is reset using a zone reheat optimization scheme implemented with DDC controls.

DEFINITIONS OF LIGHTING TERMS

BALLAST   A device used with an electric discharge lamp (fluorescent, HID) to obtain the necessary circuit conditions (voltage, current, and waveform) for starting and operating the lamp.

COLOR RENDERING INDEX (OF A LIGHT SOURCE)   Measure of the degree to which the perceived color of objects illuminated by a light source conforms to the color of the same objects illuminated by a reference light source under specified standard conditions.

FLUORESCENT LAMP   A low-pressure electric discharge lamp in which a phosphorous coating transforms some of the ultraviolet energy generated by the discharge into light.

FOOTCANDLE   Unit of illumination. One footcandle measures the level of illumination produced by one candle at a distance of 1 ft.

INCANDESCENT LAMP   A lamp in which light is produced by a filament heated to incandescence by an electric current. Incandescent lamps include tungsten filament for general service and for spot-lighting (e.g., R-lamps and PAR lamps); they also include filament lamps with quartz envelopes (tungsten-iodine or quartz-halogen lamps).

LAMP   A generic term for a man-made source of light. In nontechnical language an incandescent lamp is called an incandescent bulb, and a fluorescent lamp is called a fluorescent tube. (See also LUMINAIRE).

LUMEN   Unit of luminous flux. Lumens measure the rate at which a lamp emits light.

LUMINAIRE   A complete lighting unit consisting of (a) one or several light sources (lamps); (b) housing designed to position and protect these lamps and to distribute the light; (c) electric wiring within the housing; and (d) transforming devices (ballasts) if required. In nontechnical language a luminaire is called lamp (e.g., table lamp). See also LAMP.

20%, from 65 to 70 lumens/watt to 70 to 80 lumens/watt. An improved phosphorous coating can further boost the efficiency to 95 to 100 lumens/watt.

Compact Fluorescent Lamps
Compact fluorescent lamps are shorter and have a smaller diameter than their full size counterparts, so they offer less surface area for light emission (Fig. 3.2). However, the power used to generate the electric arc is relatively constant for all lamp types, and as a result compact fluorescent lamps are less efficient than full size fluorescent lamps—they achieve only 35 to 55 lumens/watt, rather than 65 to 95 lumens/watt.

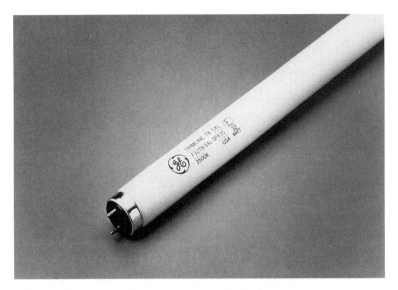

Figure 3.1 ► **Full size fluorescent lamp (*courtesy GE Lighting*).**

Electronic Lamps

Electronic lamps, also referred to as induction lamps, are a variation on the fluorescent lamp principle. Light is emitted by a phosphorus coating on the tube surface, as in all other fluorescent lamps. The phosphorus coating is excited by ultraviolet radiation, also as in other fluorescent lamps. The difference lies in the method used to produce the ultraviolet radiation. Instead of vaporizing mercury, the electronic lamp uses an induction coil which ionizes the gas in the lamp through a magnetic field. Currently, the electronic lamps are similar in size to the compact fluorescents, and at 45 to 50 lumens/watt have comparable efficacy.

Sulphur Lamps

These lamps create light by replacing the mercury of fluorescent lamps with sulphur. The sulphur is excited with microwave radiation. The technology is new but promising. The replacement of mercury with sulphur also presents an environmental advantage, since mercury is toxic.

Infrared Reflective Incandescent Lamps

Incandescent lamps convert only 15% of their energy into visible light. About 75% is emitted as infrared radiation and close to 10% is consumed as the filament burns off. Halogen lamps (Fig. 3.3) offer the opportunity to retrieve some of the infrared radiation. In these lamps a quartz tube contains the filament. The quartz tube itself is encased into an outer glass bulb.

The exterior surface of the quartz tube receives a selective coating which allows visible radiation to pass through, but reflects back onto the filament most of the infrared which cycle the electric arc about 120 times per second. The resulting flicker may be perceptible during normal operation if the lamp is old, and can become annoying if the lamp is dimmed to less than 40 or 50% of capacity.

Electronic ballasts differ from magnetic ballasts in that they use solid-state technology to produce high-frequency alternating current (Fig. 3.5), cycling the electric arc thousands of times per second. This increases energy efficiency in two ways: first, the solid-state circuitry uses less current and has a higher power factor than most magnetic ballasts; and second, because the light is cycling more quickly, the lamps appear brighter.

The power factor (PF) of an electronic ballast is in the 0.90 to 0.98 range. Conventional magnetic ballasts have power factors in the 0.50 to 0.90 range. A power factor of 1.0 indicates that the ballast uses all of the power it draws. A power factor of 0.5 indicates that the ballast uses only half of the power it draws. Consequently, an electronic ballast with PF = 0.95 is more efficient than a conventional magnetic ballast with PF = 0.8. Cooler operation extends the ballast's life.

When used in conjunction with high-efficiency lamps, electronic ballasts may achieve 85 to 95 lumens/watts as opposed to 60 to 70 lumens/watt for conventional magnetic ballasts. However, *efficient* magnetic ballasts can now achieve practically the same lumen/watt ratio as electronic ballasts. Electronic ballasts have a stronger advantage in dimming. Because of their high cycling speed, most electronic ballasts allow a lamp to be dimmed to 20% of capacity, and some go even as low as 5% of capacity, without the annoying flicker characteristic of magnetic ballasts.

Since magnetic ballasts use electric coils, they generate an audible hum which can

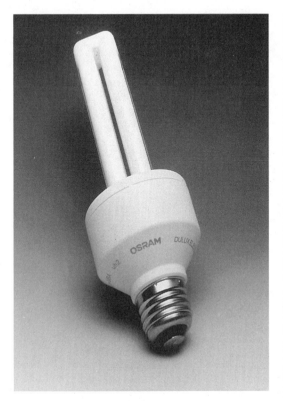

Figure 3.2 ▶ Compact fluorescent lamp (*courtesy Osram Sylvania*).

radiation. This "recycled" infrared radiation maintains operating temperatures for the filament even at 30% lower wattage.

PRINCIPLES OF ELECTRONIC BALLASTS

An important development in luminaire technology has been the electronic ballast for fluorescent lamps. Ballasts are integral to fluorescent luminaires. They provide starting voltage for the tube and regulate the electric arc. Until the early 1980s all ballasts were magnetic or "core and coil" type (Fig. 3.4),

Figure 3.3 ▶ Infrared-reflective halogen lamp (*courtesy GE Lighting*).

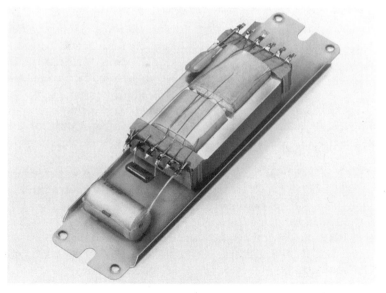

Figure 3.4 ▶ Magnetic ballast (*courtesy Advance Transformer Company*).

Figure 3.5 ▶ **Electronic ballast (*courtesy Advance Transformer Company*).**

accentuate with age. The solid-state components of the electronic ballasts do not create noise.

3.2.2 ▶ *Principles of Energy-Efficient Lighting Controls*

Automatic controls decrease the electricity use of a lighting system by avoiding unnecessary illumination.

With on/off manual switches overillumination is unavoidable. Contributions from sunlight, excess output from new lamps, or simple overdesign can contribute to unnecessarily high light levels. Continuous dimming systems can reduce or eliminate this problem.

Illumination of unoccupied spaces is another cause of unnecessary lighting energy consumption. This problem can be overcome by using scheduled controls and occupancy sensors.

Switching and Dimming Systems
Lighting systems employ three basic switching methods:

- **Manual:** Lights are controlled directly by occupants or maintenance staff.
- **Scheduled:** Lights are programmed to turn on or off at prescheduled times, according to expected occupancy of the space. Manual overrides are provided.
- **Occupancy sensors:** Lights turn on automatically whenever an occupant enters the space. Otherwise, the lights are off.

Similarly, there are three basic methods of dimming control, which can be used along with any of the switching methods:

- **Manual:** Occupants directly control light levels according to their preference.
- **Level of daylight:** Lighting systems adjust their output to compensate for the fluctuating contribution of daylight.
- **Lamp output:** Lighting systems automatically compensate for the changing output of the luminaires themselves.

While manual switching and manual dimming may achieve energy savings, results are unpredictable because they depend entirely upon occupant behavior. Scheduled lighting control is more likely to succeed, but occupancy patterns often change and frequent adjustments could be required.

A typical application for scheduled switching in large buildings is to turn the lights off one or two hours after the regular occupancy period. If the occupants need the lights to remain on in a given area, they call the security service or the Building Automation System technician. The lighting program is reset to "on" for a predetermined period of time, such as two additional hours. To continue beyond the two hours the occupants need to call again. Convenience is ensured by blinking the lights on/off 10 to 15 mins before shutdown, so the occupants are not suddenly left in the dark.

This system is effective in ensuring that lights are not left on overnight. It is not useful in turning off lights as soon as a space becomes unoccupied, be it at the end of the day or during the day. Furthermore, it is not easy to implement in smaller buildings that do not have 24-hour security. The call to keep the lights on must be made to an automated system. Malfunctions of this system can result in significant inconvenience to the occupants.

Automated light switching provides an attractive alternative to scheduled switching, since it responds in real-time to changes in occupancy. In many cases the automated lighting controls complement the scheduled switching, the latter being implemented mainly for areas that must maintain lighting at all times during occupied periods (e.g., corridors). In this case some of the lamps are turned off during unoccupied periods. Automated light switching is achieved with occupancy sensing systems, described below.

PRINCIPLES OF OCCUPANCY SENSING SYSTEMS

During the past decade there has been a proliferation of high quality occupant sensing devices which allow automated control of a lighting system. When a room is unoccupied for more than a specified amount of time, the lights are automatically turned off. The "occupancy sensors," as these devices are commonly called, generally operate on infrared sensing or ultrasound sensing. Newer principles, such as frequency modulation, are being introduced.

Infrared Sensing Principles

An infrared sensor registers infrared (IR) radiation emitted by room surfaces and the human body. The sensor and the controls connected to it are calibrated to ignore any gradual changes in the temperature of, and therefore IR radiation emitted by the room enclosures and furniture. When the controller receives a sustained change in the "thermal signature" of its viewfield (as is the case when an occupant moves), it turns the lights on. The lights are kept on until the space is unoccupied for a preset period of time (e.g., 5 mins).

All bodies radiate in infrared (long-wave radiation) toward one another if in direct line-of-sight. The warmer body radiates more energy than the cooler one, and in effect loses heat. This is one mechanism through which the warmer, interior window pane loses heat to the cooler, exterior pane during winter.

When radiation from a moving human body creates a thermal disturbance, this disturbance is perceived by the sensor. A controller is activated and turns the lights on. For this process to occur successfully, the occupant must be in direct line-of-sight with the sensor. Solid surfaces absorb IR radiation and, if interposed between occupant and sensor, mask the occupant's presence. Even glass is virtually impenetrable for IR radiation. Therefore, IR sensors must be used only in smaller, enclosed spaces with regular shapes and without partitions.

Ultrasound Sensing Principles

Ultrasound occupancy sensing systems operate on a sonar principle, not unlike submarines and airport radars.

A device emits high frequency sound, in the 25 to 40 kilohertz range which is beyond human hearing range. The sound reflects against space enclosures, furniture, and occupants, and is sensed by a receiver.

When people move within the space, the pattern of reflected sound waves changes. The change activates a controller which turns on the lights. The lights remain on until no movement is detected for a preset period of time (e.g., 5 mins).

Unlike thermal radiation, solar or infrared, sound waves are not easily blocked by obstacles. Toilet partitions, for example, absorb IR emissions and mask the occupant's presence from the sensor. Ultrasound permeates the entire space, including partitions, and detects motion even in cubicles and recesses.

Limitations of the system are inherent in its need to receive reflected sound. Large spaces without partitions or with high ceilings tend to produce weak echoes. Perturbations created by movement become hard to detect against this faint background.

PRINCIPLES OF LIGHT DIMMING

Dimming systems operate by adjusting luminaires to keep the amount of light at a particular level (e.g., 40 fc). The sensor is typically placed on the ceiling, where it will not be exposed to direct light from windows or luminaires. An example of such a system is presented in Sec. 3.5.2 on daylight integration.

A smooth and uninterrupted decrease in the light output of a lamp is defined as *continuous dimming*. It is distinguished from *stepped dimming* in which lamp output is decreased in stages by preset amounts. Continuous dimming is usually preferred because there are no sudden fluctuations in light levels and because it saves more energy.

Stepped dimming may see a revival because of the integrative design concept. Software now exists that allows a close analysis of the light intensity and glare in a space. RADIANCE, by Lawrence Berkeley Laboratory, is a high-accuracy program integrated with other tools into a packaged named ADELINE. The ADELINE tool kit helps visualize light patterns in a space. A designer can predict the percentage of time when natural light is sufficient to meet all lighting needs. Glazings with high coolness index (see Chap. 2) can deliver long hours of high light levels free of excessive heat and glare. As a result, conditions are created to keep the lights off through much of the day, during many consecutive days in any season. The dimming system needs only seldomly to change status from on to off or vice versa. The annoying variation in light levels becomes a rare event.

Another reason for the renewed interest in stepped dimming is that, within the integrative design concept, natural light becomes the primary provider of the 30 to 50 fc needed at desk level. The continuous variations in natural light due to time of day and clouds are believed by some medical researchers to be beneficial both psychologically and physiologically.

Dimming systems can also compensate for lamp output degradation, a type of control called *lumen depreciation compensation*. When a lamp is first installed, its lumen output is typically 10 to 20% higher than the rated level. This output decreases over time.

Lumen depreciation compensation systems (LDCS) maintain a constant level of illumination by continuously monitoring the lamps: if output is too high, (e.g., after relamping), it is adjusted downward; as the output slowly declines over months of use, it is adjusted back upward. Such a system saves energy, prolongs the life of the lamps, and maintains the quality of the lighting environment.

Lumen depreciation compensation systems are applied in core spaces. Note that the continuous daylight dimming systems act much like LDCS after hours during cloudy periods, by maintaining light levels no higher than needed and therefore by dimming the excess light output of new lamps.

3.2.3 ► Principles for Design and Maintenance of Energy-Efficient Lighting Systems

Energy-saving lamps, ballasts, and controls are necessary components of an effective lighting system. These parts must be integrated, in turn, into an overall lighting design which fully responds to programmatic requirements and which functions well within the spaces it serves.

The performance of a lighting system can be further improved through integration with the envelope and HVAC systems. In larger buildings, the cost for additional design and planning for integrated lighting/HVAC/envelope is swiftly offset by energy savings. Long-term energy savings are assured through a lamp replacement plan. The following sections briefly address system integration, the design team, and maintenance plans.

SYSTEM INTERACTIONS

The design of lighting systems should be integrated with the design of HVAC, controls, and fenestration systems.

HVAC Equipment

Because of their reduced heat output, high efficiency luminaires allow both the air-conditioning equipment (e.g., chillers, direct expansion packaged units) and the distribution system (fans, pumps, ducts, pipes) to be downsized. Heating equipment retains the same size, since the heat gain from lights is not accounted for in peak heating load calculations. As a result, the additional cost for an energy-efficient lighting system can be offset by the reduced cost of the cooling plant and of the chilled air/chilled water distribution system.

Controls

The same controls can serve both the lighting and HVAC systems, reducing the *combined* cost of building hardware. Occupancy sensors, for instance, can be connected to controllers which turn off lights, close VAV boxes, and reset the space temperature.

Fenestration

With inefficient lighting systems, low U-value fenestration is penalized during the cooling season because, by trapping the heat produced by lights, it increases the cooling load. High efficiency luminaires minimize this problem by producing less heat. Thus low U-value glazing can yield winter-time savings with only a small penalty during cooling periods.

Similarly, buildings with high efficiency luminaires are able to admit more solar radiation without burdening the cooling system. This provides the designer with the opportunity to implement natural daylighting strategies and to expand the color scheme of glazing by using clear glass (usually with low-e coatings), lighter tints, and/or lower reflectance coatings.

DESIGN TEAM AND ENGINEERING TOOLS

HVAC and fenestration systems both influence and are influenced by the performance of lighting systems. The complexity of these interactions requires that professional lighting designers be integrated into the building team from the beginning. The participation of these designers will both encourage energy efficiency and improve the quality of the luminous environment.

For complex buildings such as hospitals, government centers, office towers, or large retail developments, computer simulations should be performed to optimize the configuration of envelope, HVAC, and lighting systems. Such computer models require technical expertise, but offer the only accurate method to evaluate building dynamics.

MAINTENANCE PLANNING

As with all systems in a building, proper operation and maintenance of luminaires and controls increases system life and ensures long-term energy savings.

Planning for maintenance of the lighting system, and particularly for relamping, has additional benefits. As lamps approach the end of their useful lives they produce less and less light. Such depreciation may cause a number of problems:

- First, weak light causes occupant discomfort, which can result in significant, though not easily quantifiable, losses in productivity and revenue.
- Second, the energy use can actually increase as the occupants turn on their own incandescent luminaires (e.g., table lamps) when ambient light levels fall too low. Heat generated by task lights may in turn increase the cooling load of the building.
- Finally, in certain retail situations, lumen depreciation may adversely affect how products appear to customers, giving the impression of dimly lit spaces or distorting the color of the merchandise.

Occupant comfort and optimal energy performance can be maintained, and these problems avoided, by regularly scheduled maintenance and relamping. In most large installations, the periodic replacement of *all* lamps is more cost effective than replacing individual lamps as they burn out, particularly when labor costs are taken into account.

3.3 ► LIGHTING EQUIPMENT APPLICATIONS

Over the past decade, lamps and ballasts became increasingly efficient. This section focuses on energy savings achievable with the new technologies, discusses their applicability, and presents case studies. Specifically, the discussion addresses the following:

- high efficiency fluorescent lamps
- compact fluorescent lamps
- electronic lamps
- infrared-reflective halogen lamps
- electronic ballasts

The principles underlying the functioning of lamps and ballasts were presented in Sec. 3.2.1.

3.3.1 ► *High Efficiency Lamps*

The development and widespread availability of high efficiency fluorescent lamps had a major role in reducing the energy use in buildings. Compact fluorescent lamps further advanced the opportunities for electricity savings, by displacing incandescent lamps in many spot-lighting applications. The electronic lamp, a new arrival in the fluorescent family, extends the trend for higher efficiency and longer life in spot lighting.

Fluorescent lamps are by no means the solution for all lighting situations. In some applications incandescent or high intensity discharge lamps are more appropriate. The energy efficiency of both these lamp types has also improved significantly in the recent past. Most notable is the infrared-reflective technology for incandescent lamps.

HIGH EFFICIENCY FLUORESCENT LAMPS

High efficiency fluorescent lamps provide one of the most cost-effective opportunities to increase lighting efficiency. Compared to conventional fluorescent models, these lamps produce 10 to 20% more light for the same electricity use—70 to 95 lumens/watt versus 65 to 70 lumens/watt. (Typical incandescent lamps, by contrast, only provide 8 to 17 lumens/watt.) Like all fluorescent lamps, the high efficiency types can be dimmed, further saving electricity.

This energy conservation measure requires no modifications to housing, wiring, or overall design of the luminaire. The savings accrue over the 20,000 to 30,000 hours of operation.

All major lighting manufacturers now produce and supply high efficiency fluorescent lamps. Those designated as T-8 are highly efficient, requiring only 32 watts to emit about the same light level as 40-watt lamps. Note that T-8 lamps and T-12 lamps require different ballasts.

Potential Drawbacks

High efficiency fluorescent lamps cost slightly more than less efficient models. Some could also give less accurate color rendition, although "triphosphor" fluorescent lamps have solved this problem and may be appropriate for situations in which color is a consideration.

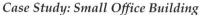

Case Study: Small Office Building

A three-story office building has two 40 ft by 60 ft open office areas per floor. Each of these office areas has been designed with 24, 2 ft by 4 ft fluorescent luminaires, and each luminaire contains four standard 40 watt, rapid-start fluorescent lamps.

High efficiency fluorescent lamps, capable of providing the same number of lumens as the 40 watt lamps but using only 32 watts, are readily available. Assuming that the lights are on 12 hours per day, 260 days per year, and that the cost of electricity is $.10 per kwh, the building could save $1400 per year for six to nine years. Additional savings are achieved because of the reduced demand charges and reduced cooling load.

Case Study: School

A middle school located in Connecticut, has 119,000 ft² of conditioned space. The classrooms are served by rooftop units with VAV distribution and perimeter hot water radiation. All systems have outdoor air economizer cycle with dry-bulb temperature control. The perimeter radiation is sized to meet heat loss up to 60°F (night setback temperature). The supply temperature of the water varies with outdoor temperature. Warm air systems operate during occupied hours only with individual room control. Gymnasium, cafeteria, shops, auditorium, band, and other areas have constant volume units. The electricity costs about $.08/kwh and the natural gas $.50/ccf.

Steven Winter Associates, Inc., performed DOE-2.1 simulations for Northeast Utilities as part of the Energy Conscious Construction program to determine the cost effectiveness of lighting and other energy conservation measures. Based on the computer analyses, the lighting system was designed for 1.6 w/ft² rather than 1.9 w/ft² as originally envisioned.

About 87,000 kwh were estimated to be saved every year in lighting consumption, 1600 kwh in cooling consumption, and 1000 kwh in fans and pumps (8% savings of total electricity usage of the building). The estimated heating energy use increased slightly by 2500 ccf natural gas. The overall effect was savings of $4700/year.

Case Study: Religious Building

In 1985 the Interchurch Center in New York City replaced its conventional 40 watt fluorescent lamps with 34 watt energy-saving lamps in 13,000 of its luminaires. The building also received electronic ballasts to replace its old magnetic ballasts. The payback was below 3 years.

As this example demonstrates, the technology is mature. It has been implemented for a long time in all types of buildings. Note that the most efficient full-size lamps now use only 32 watts instead of 34.

COMPACT FLUORESCENT LAMPS

Compact fluorescent technology is by now well accepted throughout the United States. As the name implies, a compact fluorescent lamp (CFL) is substantially shorter than a full-size fluorescent tube. CFLs have been specifically developed as substitutes for incandescent lamps. They either are self-ballasted, *integral* with a screw base, or require an adapter which contains both the ballast and the screw base (*modular system*). Both CFL systems can be inserted directly into the socket of an incandescent lamp. No additional wiring is needed. For integral systems, when the lamp burns out the ballast also must be replaced. Modular systems permit replacement of the lamps only.

Compact fluorescent lamps are manufactured in a limited range of sizes. They typically use from 5 to 26 watts, and are configured in shapes similar to incandescent bulbs ("light capsule"), or as single- and double-bend tubes (also referred to as "twin tubes" and "quad-tubes"). The lamp depicted in Fig. 3.6 is an example of a twin-tube lamp with an integral ballast. Fig. 3.7 shows a light capsule and quadtube configuration. Triple-tube CFLs use 40 to 42 watts and emit about as much light as 150 watt incandescent lamps.

Several Major Advantages

Although compact fluorescent lamps are not as energy efficient as their full-size counterparts, at 35 to 55 lumens/watt they use much less electricity than typical incandescent lamps, which produce only 8 to 17 lumens/ watt. They also reduce electricity demand

charges, especially since as of 1996 some of these lamps are also dimmable. The service lives of compact fluorescents approach in certain instances 10,000 hours as opposed to 1000 or 2000 hours for incandescents. Finally, because they are more efficient, compact fluorescent lamps produce less heat per lumen than the incandescent lamps, and thus provide additional savings through reduced cooling load.

Drawbacks

Not all compact fluorescent lamps render color as well as incandescent lamps. This may make them inappropriate for some applications such as retail store lighting. Also, compact fluorescent lamps are significantly more expensive than incandescent lamps, although their use can usually be justified on a life cycle cost basis.

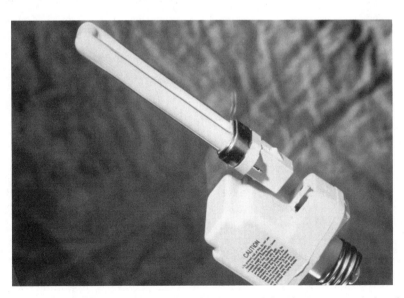

Figure 3.6 ▶ Modular CFL system: Twin-tube lamp with adapter containing ballast and screw base (courtesy Electric Power Research Institute).

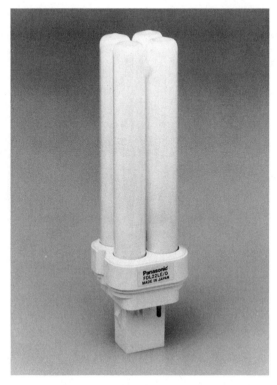

Figure 3.7 ► **Two types of compact fluorescent lamps: light capsule and quadtubes** (*courtesy Panasonic*).

Case Study: Hospital

Energy-efficiency considerations were critical in a decision to relamp the gynecology unit of the Brigham and Women's Hospital in Boston. All incandescent downlights were replaced with 9-watt, screw-in compact fluorescent lamps. The $3500 project paid for itself within a month and a half, and the annual electric bill was reduced by $29,000 in the first year.

Assume that it costs roughly $2 to replace an incandescent lamp and $9 to replace a compact fluorescent lamp. The incandescent lamps, with a life of 2000 hours, were replaced five times per year at a cost of $10 per fixture. The new lamps, which have a life of 10,000 hours, are replaced only once a year, during a group relamping, at the cost of $9 per fixture. Thus an additional $1 is being saved per fixture per year. These substantial savings do not include labor reductions or the reduction in cooling energy use resulting from the lower heat output of the compact fluorescent lamps.

ELECTRONIC LAMPS

These lamps, also called induction lamps, have been recently introduced to the market

Figure 3.8 ▶ Electronic lamp (*courtesy GE Lighting*).

(Fig. 3.8). They are intended as replacement for incandescent lamps in applications that require reflector/spot-lighting. An electronic lamp looks much like an incandescent bulb. On the inner surface of the glass there is a phosphorous coating which emits visible light when excited by ultraviolet light, just as in typical fluorescent lamps. However, this ultraviolet light is generated differently. In the electronic lamp an induction coil creates a magnetic field. The field ionizes the gas in the lamp and produces the UV light.

Currently available electronic lamps are rated at 23 watts and produce about 48 lumens/watt, using about 30% of the electricity of an equivalent incandescent lamp. In this respect they are about as efficient as the compact fluorescent lamps which produce 35 to 55 lumen/watt. Since electronic lamps do not have electrodes, as typical compact fluorescent lamps do, they are unaffected by frequent switching and can have much longer operating lives up to 60,000 hrs. However, at this time electronic lamps cannot be dimmed and cannot be controlled by electronic switches.

SULPHUR LAMPS

The newest development in general lighting technology is the sulphur lamp. Small in size, powerful and efficient, this lamp is well suited for spot-lighting from high levels, such as the top of atriums. Another proposed application is to use the sulphur lamp in conjunction with light tubes. The first installations of sulphur lamps are at the USDOE Forrestal Building and at the National Air and Space Museum of the Smithsonian Institution, both in Washington, D.C.

EFFICIENT INCANDESCENT LAMPS

High efficiency incandescent lamps cannot compete on a lumen/watt basis with full-size fluorescent or even with compact fluorescent lamps. However, they should be specified in situations where fluorescent lamps cannot provide the desired color rendering index or are otherwise inappropriate.

Applications may include showcases, displays, accent lighting, or merchandise lighting.

Specifically, halogen incandescent lamps can now output 20 lumens/watt by using a selective optical coating on the quartz tube which encases the filament (Fig. 3.3). By comparison, typical halogen lamps reach 10 to 17 lumens/watt.

Although the new technology is about 30% more energy efficient than the old, it still rates lower than the 35 to 55 lumens/watt for compact fluorescents, or 60 to 95 lumens/watt for full-size fluorescents. The newer electronic lamps are also more efficient, with 45 to 50 lumens/watt.

Case Study: Strip Shopping Center Store

A store with a strip shopping center has 30 conventional, 100-watt incandescent halogen lamps. By replacing these with infrared reflective lamps, the store can save almost $150 per year. The calculation assumes that the lamps are on 12 hours per day, 260 days per year, and that the cost of electricity is $.10/kwh.

Case Study: Department Store

The Macy's Department Store located in Herald Square, New York City (Fig. 3.9) has in-

Figure 3.9 ▶ Macy's Department Store, New York, New York (*courtesy Macy's*).

stalled infrared halogen lamps for both general and display illumination. The 60 watt lamps provide the same light level yet use about 20% less energy than the standard 150-watt lamps.

3.3.2 ► Electronic Ballasts

Ballasts are devices which regulate the arc current in, and provide starting voltage for fluorescent lamps. Magnetic or "core and coil" ballasts have been in use for about 40 years, are manufactured to uniform industry standards, and can be used with any fluorescent lamp. Electronic ballasts are relatively new. Introduced during the early 1980s, they are now widely specified because of their substantial energy savings.

Advantages

As explained earlier, an electronic ballast with two high-efficiency lamps can yield 85 to 95 lumens/watt, as opposed to 60 to 70 lumens/watt achievable if the lamps are connected to a generic magnetic ballast. However, while electronic ballasts consume 25 to 40% less electricity than conventional magnetic ballasts, they do not use significantly less electricity than newer, *efficient* magnetic ballasts.

Most electronic ballasts allow lamps to be dimmed to 20% of capacity and some can go as low as 5%. In contrast, most lamps connected to magnetic ballasts flicker at less than 40% capacity. Thus, electronic ballasts are more effective for dimming strategies.

Electronic ballasts allow more effective lamp connections. Since magnetic ballasts are wired in series, if one lamp fails the other produces a distracting flicker, which also reduces lamp life. With parallel-wired electronic ballasts this problem does not occur.

Furthermore, an electronic ballast powers up to 4 lamps, versus typical 1 to 2 lamps per magnetic core ballast. This could offset the increased cost for electronic ballasts.

Availability and Cost

Initially, high demand occasionally resulted in low stocks and longer delivery lead times, but this problem has been solved.

The cost for electronic ballasts is less than twice that for magnetic ballasts. Most dimmable electronic ballasts are in turn about 50% more expensive than nondimmable ones—and almost twice as expensive as dimmable magnetic ballasts. These cost differentials will most likely decrease in the near future.

Case Study: Low-Rise Office Building

The 600,000 ft² office building for Apollo Computer in Chelmsford, MA, retrofitted its lighting system in 1988. Core and coil ballasts were replaced with electronic ballasts, yielding over 40% savings for three- and four-lamp luminaires. The lighting savings of $270,000 per year combine with an estimated reduction of $15,000 per year in cooling costs.

Case Study: High-Rise Office Building

The new World Headquarters of the American Express Company, (Fig. 3.10) located in New York City, uses 22,000 electronic ballasts, drawing less than 60 watts of power for each pair of lamps. The system provides the same amount of light as 36,000 core-and-coil type ballasts drawing roughly 86 watts per pair of lamps.

Because fewer ballasts are used and because these ballasts generate less heat than the magnetic versions, air-conditioning costs are reduced. American Express estimates its savings in lighting and air-conditioning costs

Figure 3.10 ▶ World Headquarters, American Express Company, New York, New York (*courtesy American Express*).

to be about $400,000 per year. This does not include savings from lower maintenance and repair costs.

PRACTICAL CONSIDERATIONS FOR LIGHTING EQUIPMENT

Design
- Create performance specifications for the lighting environment and then design an energy-efficient lighting system to meet these specifications.
- In retrofit situations do not delamp without calculating what happens to light quality if there are fewer and brighter sources. Sometimes it is not advisable to simply replace inefficient lamps with half the number of efficient ones, because light levels become uneven. Reflectors help, but a more modest

reduction in light wattage (e.g., by 30% rather than 50%) may be needed to preserve a good lighting environment.

- Efficient lighting hardware is only part of the solution for an efficient lighting system. Consider energy efficiency from the beginning of the design process by providing appropriate footcandle levels for each task, rather than uniform, wall-to-wall, high-intensity lighting. In an open office layout, for instance, circulation areas need only a fraction of the light provided to the work areas. Always consider combining task lighting with general lighting to further reduce energy use and to increase productivity.
- Coordinate the fenestration and lighting design, especially if daylighting strategies are considered. A high-glare, high-contrast fenestration system may make the lighting level appear to be insufficient during daytime. Instead of turning lights off, the occupants will request supplemental light.
- Coordinate lighting and HVAC systems. Specifically, account for the decrease in cooling load due to efficient fluorescent lamps and electronic ballasts. This decrease can result in lower sizes for fans and ducts, pumps and pipes, and primary cooling equipment such as chillers and DX packaged units.
- When selecting energy efficient lighting equipment, consider lamps and ballasts together with housing type. Luminaires with direct-indirect lighting, for instance, are often used to reduce the footcandle level on the work plane by comparison with luminaires that only give direct lighting. The pattern of lamps is different for the two lighting schemes.

- Consider triphosphor fluorescent lamps for applications requiring good color rendition.
- Consider compact fluorescent lamps for new construction where directed light is required but color rendition is not essential.
- Always use electronic ballasts for applications requiring low noise, such as auditoriums.
- Always use electronic ballasts for rooms containing video equipment to eliminate flicker on screens and monitors.
- When specifying electronic ballasts, provide lists of compatible lamps.
- When specifying electronic ballasts check whether they are capable of stepped light output, dimming, and parallel lamp operation.

Operation/Maintenance
- Keep list of compatible lamps for electronic ballasts.
- Develop an appropriate relamping program for the type of luminaires installed.

3.4 ► LIGHTING CONTROL APPLICATIONS

Lighting control systems are composed of switches, dimmers, sensors, microprocessors, and wiring. This section discusses three particularly effective techniques to increase energy efficiency through lighting control systems: occupancy sensors, lumen depreciation compensation, and alternate ballast switching. A fourth technique, daylighting integration, is discussed in Sec. 3.5.2.

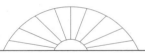

HIGH-EFFICIENCY LIGHTING EQUIPMENT ARE WIDELY SPECIFIED

High-Efficiency Fluorescent Lamps
- Dreyfus Investments, New York, NY
- Mt. St. Michaels Academy, New York, NY
- Nigel French Showroom, New York, NY
- Hue Showroom, New York, NY
- Marriott Travel Plazas, New York, NY
- Caesar's Hotel & Casino, Atlantic City, NJ

Compact Fluorescent Lamps
- Brigham & Women's Hospital, Boston, MA
- Kentucky Fried Chicken, Nationwide Franchises
- Sheraton Tacoma Hotel, Tacoma, WA

High-Efficiency Halogen Lamps
- Bloomingdale's Department Store, New York, NY
- Macy's Department Store, New York, NY
- J.C. Penney Department Store, New York, NY

Electronic Ballasts
- Apollo Computer Offices, Chelmsford, MA
- Four Times Square Tower, New York, NY
- Columbia University, New York, NY
- University of Massachusetts, Amherst, MA, and Lowell, MA
- University of California Resource Library, Los Angeles, CA
- American Express Building, New York, NY

3.4.1 ▶ *Occupancy Sensors*

As discussed earlier, occupancy sensors save energy by turning off the lamps when a space is unoccupied for more than a specified amount of time (e.g., 5 mins). The sensors accomplish this task by detecting movement. Passive infrared sensors (PIR) monitor changes in the low-temperature radiation (infrared radiation) emitted by all surfaces of a room, including its occupants. Ultrasonic sensors send continuous pulses of inaudible sound, and monitor changes in the echos from all surfaces of a room, including its occupants. In some applications both sensor types are combined to increase the reliability of detection.

Cycling of Lamps

An often-voiced concern about occupancy sensors is that cycling lights on and off actually wastes energy and reduces lamp life. This contention is apparently unfounded.

Over a decade ago, the Navy's Civil Engineering Laboratory demonstrated that the energy needed to relight a fluorescent lamp is insignificant relative to that saved by keeping the lamp off. In fact, turning a lamp off for one second saves more energy than is needed for relighting. Although on/off cycling does reduce lamp life, this loss must be weighed against the *overall* amount of time that a lamp is in use before it is replaced.

If a lamp with a rated life of 25,000 hours is operated 24 hours per day it will burn out in 3.9 years (34,000 hours). If the same lamp is cycled on and off, its actual life may be reduced by about 20%, to as little as 28,000 hours; but if as a result it is on only 18 hours per day, its useful life will actually be extended by 10% to 4.3 years. Of course, even longer "off" time will result in further extension of lamp life.

Dimming Applications

In some applications, occupancy sensors save energy by dimming the lamps to a preset level. Warehouses are sometimes illuminated with high-intensity discharge lamps that have a high/low configuration. If an isle is unoccupied, the lamps are dimmed to the low setting. A similar strategy is sometimes applied to halogen lamps located, for example, in file storage areas.

PASSIVE INFRARED SENSORS

Passive infrared sensing systems can differentiate the heat emitted by a moving human body from that emitted by the room enclosure (Fig. 3.11). The PIR system is composed of an infrared sensor, a controller, and wiring. The sensor sends a low voltage signal. The controller compares this signal to the benchmark for background radiation, and decides whether to turn the lights on, off, or whether to maintain the current status.

PIR sensors work best where the lines of sight from sensors to occupants are unobstructed, such as in enclosed offices and high-ceiling open areas. These sensors do not give satisfactory results in bathrooms, because they cannot "see" into cubicles. High desk dividers, high filing cabinets, and even glass partitions can block a sensor's "view." The PIR controller might not recognize small movements (such as the movement of typing fingers) as valid triggers for the "on" status.

ULTRASONIC SENSORS

Ultrasonic sensing systems detect occupants in a room by analyzing the reflections of high-

Figure 3.11 ► **Passive infrared sensor** *(courtesy Visonic, Inc.).*

frequency sound (see Sec. 3.2.2). The system is composed of an ultrasound source, a sensor, a controller, and wiring. The ultrasound source emits sound waves above the range of human hearing. The sensor perceives the echoes of these waves and transmits modulated electrical signals to the controller. As long as the wave pattern changes the controller keeps the lights on. If the pattern remains unchanged for a preset time period (e.g., 5 mins), the controller turns off the lights, under the assumption that the space is vacant.

Because sound waves are not easily blocked by obstacles, ultrasonic sensing systems are particularly useful in those zones where PIR sensors may fail: partitioned areas or spaces with low ceilings. Furthermore, ultrasonic sensors are more sensitive to small movements (e.g., typing fingers). They are not effective in large spaces, unenclosed areas, or rooms with high ceilings, because the sound waves do not bounce back to the receiver with sufficient strength to establish a background pattern against which motion may be detected.

Case Study: Offices and Laboratories
TRW, Inc., installed ultrasonic occupancy sensors in more than 8000 offices, laboratories, and conference rooms in its 27-building Space Park facility in Redondo Beach, CA

(Fig. 3.12). The result has been a 50% reduction in the total number of kilowatt hours used to light the areas where the sensors have been installed, adding up to annual energy savings of $1.3 million. The sensors paid for themselves in just over 1 year of operation.

Case Study: Bathrooms and Corridors
The United States Government is experiencing similar success with an installation of ultrasonic sensors in bathrooms and corridors at six federal office buildings in Washington. Combined yearly savings in all six buildings total $175,000, and the sensors have paid for themselves in an average of 1.5 years.

Figure 3.12 ▶ TRW Space Park Office with ultrasonic occupancy sensors (*courtesy TRW*).

Case Study: Offices and Manufacturing

Abbott Laboratories installed a mix of 500 ultrasonic and infrared sensors in a four-building complex in Dallas, Texas. The ultrasonic units were used in low-ceiling, open office spaces and the infrared units were used in high-bay manufacturing areas. The total cost for all of the sensors was about $100,000. The energy savings covered this cost in just over 1.5 years.

Case Study: Courthouse

A new State Courthouse, located in Connecticut, will be built with 260,000 ft^2 of conditioned space. Infrared and ultrasonic occupancy sensors are considered for installation in offices, conference rooms, and restrooms, covering approximately 30% of the useable space, i.e., 68,000 ft^2. The conservative assumption is that the occupancy sensing system will save only 30% of the lighting electricity use in the areas it covers.

Based on DOE-2.1 simulations performed by Steven Winter Associates, Inc. for Northeast Utilities, the anticipated savings are 49,000 kwh/year in lighting, 4000 kwh/year in cooling, and 300 kwh/year in fans and pumps. This amounts to an approximate reduction of 5% in lighting electricity use for the entire facility. A 550 ccf of gas increase in consumption will also be incurred.

Overall, the building could save almost $6000/year in operating costs.

3.4.2 ► Continuous Dimming Systems

A continuous dimming system is typically installed to increase the responsiveness to ambient conditions and to avoid over-illumination. Continuous dimming of fluorescent lighting systems is a mature technology that has long ago overcome its early problems. Many systems are now available for use with both magnetic and electronic ballasts.

The system is composed of a light sensor, a controller (which performs continuous dimming), switching devices, and wiring. The lighting level is modulated in response to signals from the sensors. These signals can be overridden by switches. Some systems also have a connection into a central control system, which may superimpose on/off status based on occupancy schedules.

Continuous dimming systems can control *both* magnetic and electronic ballasts (see Sec. 3.3.4). As noted in Sec. 3.2.2, most lamps with electronic ballasts can be dimmed to 20% and for some systems down to 5% of light output and electricity use without problems. Magnetic ballasts can be dimmed to as low as 20% of capacity, but problems with flicker usually restrict the reductions to the 40 to 50% range.

Two Types of Dimming Systems

Automatic dimming systems adjust for the contribution of natural light, as will be discussed later in Sec. 3.5.3. Other types are designed to monitor and adjust the light coming from the luminaires themselves. These latter types are called *lumen depreciation compensation* or *lumen maintenance* systems and are presented below.

LUMEN DEPRECIATION COMPENSATION SYSTEMS

In lumen depreciation compensation systems the output of a luminaire is increased or decreased to maintain a preset level of lighting.

Typically, the initial lumen output of a lamp is 10 to 20% greater than the design level. Over time the light output decreases. Sensors placed in the luminaire or on the ceiling detect when this output is too high (which is especially true immediately after relamping) and adjust it *downward* to save energy and to prolong the life of the lamp. Conversely, when the light levels become too low, the control system *increases* the lumen output and maintains good work conditions.

The lumen depreciation compensation systems are usually specified in core spaces. Perimeter spaces generally receive daylight dimming systems. In daylight dimming systems the control system still reduces the light output at night, but has the additional advantage of dimming the lamps much more often and to a greater extent during the day. However, a typical daylight dimming system does not increase the lumen output at night to compensate for the insufficient light levels emitted by aging lamps.

For spaces of some size and with the same number of lamps, the daylight dimming system is more cost effective than the lumen depreciation compensation system. Often though, perimeter spaces are fragmented while core spaces are open. Although the reduction in electricity use per lamp is much greater in perimeter spaces (assuming a glazing with a daylight transmittance above 20 to 30%), the investment per lamp can also be higher. If the light sensor and controller dim the lamps of a core area that is several times larger than the perimeter area, the payback of the two systems is similar.

From the preceding discussion it can be seen that the lumen depreciation compensation (LDC) system is like a daylight dimming system, with the *technological difference* that it increases the light output of the lamps to design levels. The *name difference* is due to historical and marketing reasons.

An LDC system can be placed on the perimeter and will perform all functions of a daylight dimming system, plus the "compensation" duty when needed. A daylight dimming system can be placed in a core area and will reduce the output of new lamps to design levels, but will not increase this output when the lamps age. (Of course, the term *daylight dimming* would be a misnomer unless the core area is also lit with skylights, roof monitors, or clerestories.) Both control systems save more energy when the lighting system is overdesigned and provides unnecessarily high light levels even when the lamps are old.

Case Study: School
A lumen depreciation compensation system was installed in two classes at the Bethel High School in Bethel, Connecticut. Measurements have shown that the electricity use is reduced by 30% in the interior classroom and by 48% in the exterior classroom, while maintaining comfortable light levels.

These high savings are due to some extent to an overdesigned lighting system. The increased savings in the exterior classroom as compared to the interior classroom is due to the combined contribution of excess light from *both* lamps and natural light.

Case Study: Hospital
A hospital located in Connecticut, planned to renovate 17,000 ft² on its ground level floor. A combined lumen maintenance and daylighting system was analyzed by Steven Winter Associates, Inc., as part of the Energy Conscious Construction program of Northeast Utilities.

By applying the two dimming strategies, the lighting electricity use was projected to decrease by 32%, or by 48,500 kwh. Cooling electricity reductions are 8%, or 4100 kwh. Fans and pumps operation also decreases by 2%, or 1500 kwh. After accounting for a 350 ccf increase in gas heating, the total energy savings is estimated at amount $4000/year, or 11% of total energy use cost.

3.4.3 ▶ Alternate Ballast Switching

Alternate ballast switching uses minor wiring modifications, rather than more complex controls, to reduce energy consumption.

Luminaires in which two ballasts power three or four lamps can be wired to allow the lamps to be switched on and off independently. In luminaires with three lamps, one, two, or all three can be turned on; in those with four lamps, the lamps can be turned on in groups of two.

This form of alternate switching allows the lighting of a space to be reduced more evenly than in a system where each luminaire must be entirely on or off. Applications are usually of three types:

- Reduced light levels during unoccupied periods, to allow cleaning of office buildings, schools, and similar spaces at an adequate but not unnecessarily high footcandle level.
- Reduced light levels in circulation areas during unoccupied periods, to maintain an adequate but not unnecessarily high footcandle level for security reasons.
- Reduced light levels during occupied periods in restaurants. Here the electricity savings are achieved during normal occupancy, while the higher light levels are provided for cleaning.

Case Study: University

Columbia University in New York City (Fig. 3.13) uses alternate ballast switching for after-hours maintenance work. In the Center for Engineering and Physical Science Research, for example, the luminaires can be operated with one, two, or three lamps, according to need.

Assuming that for two hours each day and for 260 days per year the lights consume 300,000 watts instead of 600,000, about $8500 is saved per year.

PRACTICAL CONSIDERATIONS FOR OCCUPANCY SENSORS, LUMEN DEPRECIATION COMPENSATION, AND ALTERNATE BALLAST SWITCHING

Design

- Provide clear lines of sight for passive infrared sensors. If occupied areas are obscured from view, lights may be turned off while people are still in the space.
- Divide large spaces into several zones, each controlled by its own occupancy sensor. Overlap the zones so that occupants in border areas do not suffer from inadequate illumination when lighting in an adjacent zone is turned off.
- Design the wiring for lumen depreciation systems to allow effective grouping of luminaires with every sensor. Expect an increased cost over regular wiring schemes, since fewer luminaires are likely to be served by one circuit.
- If the occupancy sensor is mounted on the light switch, ensure that the light switch controls only the room served by the sensor. Otherwise, if the room

Figure 3.13 ► Morris A. Shapiro Center for Engineering and Physical Science Research, Columbia University, New York (*photo courtesy Joseph Pineiro, Columbia University*).

with the light switch/sensor is unoccupied, the light is also turned off in the other space. Although the problem and solution seem obvious, it is not uncommon to find such misapplications in older spaces that have been remodeled many times.

- Some control systems that allow continuous dimming do not work well with energy efficient lamps. Match the control system with the lamp type.

Construction

- Provide additional wiring and space for the control panel.
- Protect occupancy and light sensors from damage.

Operation/Maintenance

- Fine-tune occupancy sensing system after installation; occupant satisfaction with the system is critical. Give special consideration to shutoff timing. If a sensor is set to turn the lights off too quickly after it no longer detects a person in a space, an occupant may be left in the dark. This has been a problem in partitioned office areas and in restrooms.

- Train maintenance personnel to understand the operation of the lighting control system. If, for example, a lighting installation in an office building has alternate ballast switching, the maintenance personnel must be instructed to take advantage of it by using only half of the lights during clean-up periods.
- Do not block the viewing angles of occupancy sensors.

3.5 ▶ DAYLIGHTING APPLICATIONS

When properly utilized, windows, vision panels, clerestories, roof monitors, and skylights provide a significant portion of the lighting needs without overheating and glare.

Computer tools can predict the reduction in energy consumption and electricity demand achieved by daylighting. These tools, discussed in more detail in Chap. 8, are often complex. Their use, however, can result in lower energy use, lower life-cycle costs, and enhanced comfort.

This is especially true where the lighting and fenestration systems are optimized. The glazing should have a high coolness index (CI), i.e., a high ratio between daylight transmittance and shading coefficient. This does not pose a difficulty, since many glazings with CI between 1.2 and 1.5 are available.

For large, unshaded surfaces neither the daylight transmittance nor the shading coef-

EXAMPLES OF BUILDINGS WITH ADVANCED LIGHTING CONTROLS

Infrared Sensors
- World Financial Center, Battery Park City, NY
- World Trade Center, New York, NY
- Grand Central Tower, New York, NY
- C.W. Post Center, Greenvale, NY
- Long Island University, Long Island City, NY
- Point Pleasant School District, Morristown, NJ

Ultrasonic Sensors
- Anchor Savings Bank, Brooklyn, NY
- Francis Perkins, Department of Labor/IRS Headquarters/Herbert C. Hover Building/Dept. of Commerce Headquarters/Dept. of Education's Murray Switzer Building/Federal Suitland Center/Census Bureau Headquarters, Washington, DC
- TRW Space and Defense, Redondo Beach, CA

Lumen Depreciation Compensation Systems
- St. Johns University, Jamaica, NY
- I.R.S., Hempstead, NY
- U.S. District Court, Hauppage, NY
- NYU Medical Center, New York, NY
- World Wide Plaza, New York, NY

Alternate Ballast Switching
- Columbia University, New York, NY
- University of Massachusetts, Lowell, MA
- Alabama Power Co. Headquarters, Birmingham, AL

ficient should be high, to avoid glare as well as discomfort from direct solar radiation. This rule applies to most sunny locations, but even cloudy skies can be a source of glare, especially during winter when the brighter portion of the skyvault is low, toward the horizon. Consequently, the selection of a specific glazing needs to be made according to climate, cardinal orientation of the facade, and type of lamp control.

Computer simulations show that there is almost always a "flat" zone in the optimum range within which the daylight transmittance or shading coefficient can vary without significant effect on lighting energy use. Within a flat zone the designer can select glazings with characteristics that enhance visual comfort. Such analysis is only possible using specialized design software, such as RADIANCE for light intensity and light distribution, and DOE-2 for energy savings. Physical models can also enhance or even substitute the use of lighting design software.

3.5.1 ▶ Core Daylighting Strategies

All commercial buildings can reduce their energy use through daylighting, particularly if they are equipped with light sensors and dimming controls. Most applications involve the first 10 to 15 ft of the building perimeter. To distribute natural light deeper, toward the building core, four strategies have been traditionally used: light shelves, central light courts, atriums, and overhead lighting (skylights, roof monitors, and clerestories).

LIGHT SHELVES

Light shelves are horizontal projections on the outer face of a building. When placed in front of (or projecting through) the upper portion of a window, they reflect daylight deep into a room along the ceiling. In properly designed applications they provide more useful daylight, distributed over a greater area, than do windows alone. Light shelves serve as shading devices for the window area underneath and reduce glare by obstructing the view of a portion of the skyvault. In addition to saving energy, light shelves often serve aesthetic purposes.

Figure 3.14 ▶ Central light court at Lockheed Building 157, Sunnyvale, CA (*courtesy Lockheed Martin Missiles & Space*).

CENTRAL LIGHT COURTS

Central light courts (also called *literiums*) are becoming increasingly common in commercial facilities throughout the United States. Such a court (Fig. 3.14) enhances the value of the building by providing daylight to interior offices. Energy savings do not justify the construction of a light court. If one is to be built for other reasons, however, it should be designed to maximize the daylighting benefits.

ATRIUMS

Atriums are always provided as an amenity, but they can be instrumental in bringing natural light into the surrounding work areas. The conflicting need for daylight and visibility on one side and reduced cooling load on the other side is all too often resolved through massive intervention of the mechanical cooling equipment. Natural ventilation and localized cooling can greatly reduce the energy expenditure for atriums. A passive solar/natural ventilation design will likely require computer analysis of airflows using a three-dimensional computational fluid dynamics model, such as EXACT-3 or CFD-2000.

Case Studies: Office Buildings with Central Light Court

The Lockheed Building 157 on the Sunnyvale, California campus is a five-story, 600,000 ft² construction that uses interior/exterior light shelves on its perimeter and two central literiums to provide daylight to virtually every work station in the facility.

A post occupancy evaluation of the structure conducted in 1989 revealed that both these daylight strategies were functioning properly and that occupant satisfaction with the facility was high.

Annual energy consumption for the building is measured at less than 20,000 Btu/gross ft² per year, about half of the average for the geographic area.

Case Study: Office Building with Light Shelves and Atrium

A 210,000 ft² office building for Blue Cross and Blue Shield in New Haven, CT, also combines light shelves and an atrium (Fig. 3.15). In this case the architects—Ellenzweig Associates, Inc.—used interior light shelves and sloped ceilings to reflect daylight from the atrium into the northern side interior offices. As in the Lockheed building, the combination of increased daylight and an interior atrium space (Fig. 3.16) is highly popular with the occupants.

Both buildings utilize sensors to control and dim the lighting system in response to varying levels of daylight.

OVERHEAD LIGHTING

Overhead glazing is effective in illuminating core spaces. Roof monitors and clerestories (Figs. 3.17 and 3.18) are high performers, since vertical glass admits more sun during winter than summer. Many architectural designs incorporate skylights instead. Because skylights (Fig. 3.19) are either flat or low-slope, they admit more solar radiation in summer. This shortback can be addressed with shading.

A common misperception is that (1) the cost for overhead glazing must be entirely offset by energy savings and that (2) the cost of overhead glazing is high. Overhead glazing creates a better working environment by permitting a psychological connection to the exterior. Placing natural lighting in a core area is akin to placing a window in a perimeter space. The window serves its functional

Figure 3.15 ▶ The Blue Cross/Blue Shield Building in New Haven, CT, employs daylighting strategies (*photo courtesy Ellenzweig Associates, Inc., Cambridge, MA*).

Figure 3.16 ▶ Atrium in Blue Cross/Blue Shield Building (*photo courtesy Ellenzweig Associates, Inc., Cambridge, MA*).

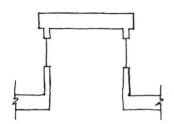

Figure 3.17 ▶ **Typical roof monitor.**

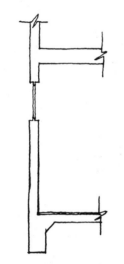

Figure 3.18 ▶ **Typical clerestory.**

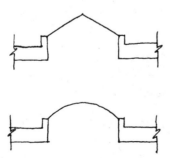

Figure 3.19 ▶ **Typical skylights.**

purpose beyond any energy savings and so do all types of core fenestrations. Thus, overhead lighting does not simply save energy, as might be the case with additional roof insulation.

The cost of bringing natural light to core areas need not be a major issue for a second and important reason: The overhead glazing area can be easily offset by a decrease in the surface area of windows. The window height can be slightly decreased, the window width can be reduced, and if the aesthetics permit, windows on the west and north facades can be reduced in number.

Case Study: Roof Monitors for Office Buildings

Passive Solar Industries Council provided support to the Federal Energy Management Program in introducing passive solar techniques to low-rise office buildings. Energy analyses on a three-story, 70,000 ft² office building were performed for 7 locations.

The building has 14,000 ft² double-pane windows with U = 0.54 and SC = 0.39. The lighting load is 1.57 watts/ft², controlled by a continuous daylight dimming system. Winter temperature setpoint is 72°F with 68°F setback, maintained by 80% AFUE boilers. Summer temperature setpoint is 75°F and off at night, maintained by air-cooled reciprocating chillers.

DOE-2.1 analyses investigated roof monitors that serve 10, 15, 20 and 25% of the core zone. The glass area of facades is reduced by the amount provided for the roof monitors. Consequently, the total fenestration area of the building does not change. Fig. 3.20 shows energy cost savings in 3 cities, for south-facing and north-facing monitors, based on the electricity rate structure of each city.

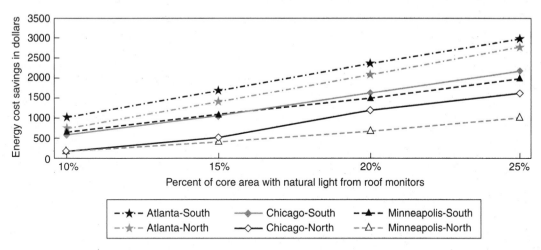

Figure 3.20 ▶ Core lighting with roof monitors.

3.5.2 ▶ *Daylighting Dimming Systems*

Most perimeter zones have excessive illumination during daylight hours. Dimming systems can adjust down the light output, saving electricity and reducing cooling loads in the process.

The simplest form of daylight dimming is accomplished through scheduling programmed into the Energy Monitoring and Control System (EMCS). Light levels are measured during cloudy days in summer and winter. The lamps are dimmed to eliminate excess illumination during these periods. The Energy Monitoring and Control System activates the dimming typically for 5 to 6 hours in winter and for longer periods in summer.

Such systems are inexpensive and can achieve fast payback. The 45,000 ft^2 Hechinger Store, for example, has instituted EMCS-controlled dimming at their Fairfax, Virginia, location, with 25% savings in electricity and 2 years payback. Because of this success

Hechinger installed similar systems at 25 additional stores.

However, scheduled dimming cannot save as much energy, or offer the same quality of lighting as photocell-controlled dimming. This energy conservation measure has been perfected during the last decade and is now one of the most important methods for reducing electricity use and demand.

PHOTOCELL-CONTROLLED DIMMING

Lighting systems can be controlled to effectively compensate for fluctuations in daylight. Because the changes in artificial light levels are so gradual as to be imperceptible, this technique has gained widespread acceptance. Daylight dimming systems increase the quality of the work environment by maintaining a constant level of illumination, and at the same time reduce lighting and space conditioning costs. Daylight dimming is highly effective because it reduces electricity use at precisely the time of highest demand: during hot, clear summer days.

To operate effectively such systems employ the following components:

- Sensors, which measure light levels
- Controllers, which ensure that light output from luminaires slowly compensates for changes in natural light levels, without responding to brief disturbances
- Continuous dimming systems with magnetic or electronic ballasts

The principles of operation for these technologies are discussed in Sec. 3.2.2. For other applications of dimming refer to Sec. 3.4.2.

Case Studies: Offices, Airport, Hospitals

In a retrofit of the lighting system at a research facility in Oakdale, Pennsylvania, Koppers Company installed 210 daylight dimmers while replacing 500 ballasts that were 20 years old. Because of the retrofit, which cost a total of $19,000, the company expected to reduce lighting electricity costs by 45% per year. The project was expected to pay for itself in two to three years.

In 1987, Marriott Corporation installed almost 1800 daylight dimmers in its corporate headquarters in Washington, D.C. The light sensors, dimmers and low-voltage wiring cost $90,000. Although Marriott's lighting system was already efficient, the daylight dimming system reduced lighting electricity costs by 50%, paying for itself in roughly 2.5 years.

At the Allentown-Bethlehem-Easton Airport in Lehigh Valley, Pennsylvania, four daylight dimming systems were installed in the main terminal building at a cost of $4800.

The terminal used 45% less energy for lighting, and the project paid for itself in just over 16 months.

Finally, the Veterans Administration installed 1530 daylight dimmers at its Medical Center in Butler, Pennsylvania. The $110,000 installation saves an average of $6000 *per month*, an annual savings of over $74,000. The project paid for itself in less than two years.

PRACTICAL CONSIDERATIONS FOR DAYLIGHTING

Design

- Examine the effects of daylighting and efficient lighting strategies on the size and type of HVAC systems.
- Use accurate tools (e.g., DOE-2.1, RADIANCE) to perform daylighting simulations. Because of the complexity of the systems, manual analyses are unreliable. Physical models can also be useful, especially to study the aesthetic effects of light. However, computer simulations are needed to optimize the glazing type with the daylight control strategies.
- When evaluating daylighting options, always consider the potential for glare and direct sunlight on occupants. If such unwanted side effects are not reduced or eliminated, the occupants will block the sunlight, preventing any daylighting savings.
- When specifying light shelves, coordinate their dimensions and position with the height and reflectance of the ceiling, and with the shape of the space.
- Examine the effect of light shelves on both direct and diffuse solar radiation. In New York City, for instance, diffuse radiation accounts for about 70 to 80%

of solar radiation that passes *through* south-facing, double-pane clear glass during summer months.

- Use stepped dimming strategies only if the fenestration is designed to provide sufficient natural light for most of the day. The fluctuation in light levels when the lamps step up or down is noticeable. This can be annoying if it happens often. Many occupants feel dissatisfied because of the lack of control over their environment. Continuous dimming, when properly applied, eliminates this problem. However, continuous dimming is more expensive. Ideally, the fenestration system allows the use of stepped dimming or on/off control instead. One possible application is to use stepped dimming only for the row of luminaires closest to the windows.
- Position light sensors out of direct light.
- When installing a daylight dimming system, consider using it as a lumen depreciation compensation system at night. This ensures design light levels even when the lamps age. Additional light level readings need to be made during hours without natural light to properly calibrate the controllers.

Construction

- Protect light sensors from damage.
- Calibrate controllers based on the position of those desks or work surfaces that receive the least amount of light. Typically, this is the area that can be used for work and that is the most distant from windows.
- Refer to Practical Considerations in Sec. 3.4.

THE FOLLOWING ARE EXAMPLES OF BUILDINGS WHICH UTILIZE DAYLIGHTING STRATEGIES

Light Shelves
- Norstar Bancorp Building, Buffalo, NY
- Blue Cross/Blue Shield, New Haven, CT
- National Gallery of Canada, Ottawa, Ontario
- Monticello High School, Albemarle County, VA

Light Court or Atrium
- Blue Cross/Blue Shield, New Haven, CT
- Thresher Building, Minneapolis, MN
- Pacific Museum of Flight, Seattle, WA
- Galleria at Erieview, Cleveland, OH

Photocell-controlled Dimming
- National Westminster Bank, New York, NY
- Point Pleasant Bureau Schools, Morristown, NJ
- Monticello High School, Albemarle County, VA
- Ottis Elevator Offices, Farmington, CT
- St. Raphael Hospital, New Haven, CT
- Walmart Ecomart Store, Lawrence, KA
- Hardware City Associates Office, Farmington, CT
- Marriott Headquarters, Rockville, MD
- Allentown Airport, Lehigh Valley, PA
- The Kopper Co. Offices, Pittsburgh, PA
- Veterans Administration Medical Center, Butler, PA

Operation/Maintenance
- When several years have passed from installation, check whether correct levels of illumination are maintained on work surfaces. Adjustments can be made based on readings from a hand-held light meter.
- Do not obstruct light sensors.

3.6 ► DEVELOPMENTS ON THE HORIZON

Although advances continue to be made in lamp, ballast, control, and sensor technology, some of the most interesting developments involve daylighting the core of the buildings. As noted in Sec. 3.5.1, building cores can receive natural light via light shelves, central light courts, atriums, and overhead lighting. In many situations none of these techniques are feasible.

Light shelves do increase the depth of daylight penetration into the building, but are generally restricted to spaces that do not have walls parallel to the windows within a 20 to 30-ft perimeter band. Central light courts and atriums require distinct architectural solutions which are not always appropriate. Finally some overhead lighting techniques (roof monitors and skylights) are rarely used for more than one or two top floors, while others (clerestories) share the same perimeter-related characteristic of the light shelves.

As a result, core areas in most multilevel buildings are not even considered as candidates for natural lighting. As the examples below show, solutions do exist. Cost and complexity is still a major drawback. Fiber optics may provide a more economical solution to current concepts, in the not-too-distant future.

3.6.1 ► *Light Pipes and Solar Optics*

LIGHT PIPES
Light pipe, or "prism light guide" refers to a hollow conduit lined with prismatic film which can evenly distribute light along its length from an appropriate source. A solar collection system consisting of a computerized tracking mirror and a focusing mirror can be used as input to a light pipe distribution system. A backup electric lamp is used to supplement the light when daylight conditions are inadequate. Although solar configurations have worked well in a few demonstration projects, associated costs currently make the application economically impractical.

Light pipe systems are typically used with electric lamps (e.g., metal halide) in situations where other linear fixtures would be difficult to maintain. An example is accent lighting on the exterior of a tall building. A new development for light pipes is the use of the sulphur lamp, which presents advantages because of its small size yet high lumen output.

Another use for light pipe systems is in areas where it is important to isolate the lamp from the lit environment, such as hazardous areas.

SOLAR OPTICS
Concentrating solar mirrors can be used in standard light wells or in atria to enhance and channel the available daylight. Victoria Park Place, Toronto, Ontario (Fig. 3.21), employs a solar collecting system comprised of tracking mirrors, focusing mirrors, and a light pipe distribution system to deliver daylight to the center core of the top floor area of the complex.

Figure 3.21 ▶ Focusing mirrors deliver daylight to offices at Victoria Park Place, Toronto, Ontario, via light pipes (*courtesy Victoria Park Place*).

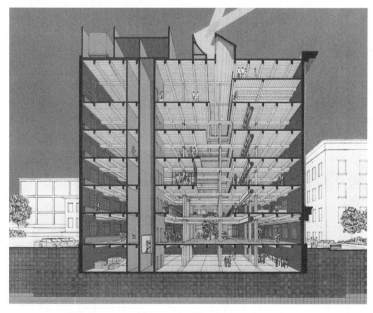

Figure 3.22 ▶ Section through Thresher Square, Minneapolis, MN (*courtesy Hoyt Properties, Minneapolis, MN*).

Figure 3.23 ▶ Thresher Square, Minneapolis, MN (*courtesy Hoyt Properties, Minneapolis, MN*).

Another good example for solar optics is the Thresher Square Office Building. The construction used to be a turn-of-the-century warehouse building. Later it was converted into an office building (Figs. 3.22 and 3.23). The challenge for the remodeling was to maximize useable/leasable space while allowing ample amounts of daylight to penetrate the core of the building. To achieve this, an area of 1386 ft^2 of concentrating lenses, made from reflectorized acrylic film, was employed to project daylight into the various atrium spaces.

A skylight would not have been capable of delivering sunlight to all the atrium spaces. By using the suntracking collector system, all interior spaces are provided with natural light.

CHAPTER 4

HVAC Equipment

4.1 ▶ BROAD ADVANCES IN HVAC EQUIPMENT

During the past decade, the efficiency of heating, ventilating, and air-conditioning equipment for commercial buildings improved substantially. Most technical advances involve refinements of existing technology, such as variable speed compressors for electric chillers and pulse-combustion condensing boilers.

Another significant trend has been the permeation of energy technology from one building sector to another, such as the adaptation of pulse-combustion boilers in particular and of condensing boilers in general from residential/small commercial applications to mid-size commercial buildings.

This chapter reviews the effect of load variations on the efficiency of boilers and chillers. Next, it discusses a particular set of advances in boilers: pulse combustion and modular installations.

A discussion on energy efficiency of electric chillers includes variable speed, scroll, and multiple compressor installations. The discussion on gas chillers refers to double-effect and engine-driven units. Desiccant dehumidification applications are reviewed for their value in reducing the operating costs of chillers.

Emerging applications for desiccants are also noted.

4.2 ▶ PRINCIPLES OF ENERGY EFFICIENCY FOR HVAC EQUIPMENT

Energy efficiency improvements during the past decade have affected virtually every HVAC component, from chiller compressors to boiler burners to fan motors. Equally important, increases in peak efficiencies were paralleled by increases in efficiencies under part-load conditions. Better controls allow closer matching of cooling and heating loads, enhancing the *operating efficiency* of the entire system.

PEAK-LOAD EFFICIENCY
All heating and much of the cooling equipment is most efficient when operating at full capacity. New boiler and chiller technologies have been introduced to boost this peak performance.

BROAD ADVANCES IN HVAC EQUIPMENT

- Condensing boilers in general and pulse-combustion boilers in particular operate at over 95% steady-state combustion efficiencies, and are now used in small to medium-size commercial installations.

   These high efficiency boilers can serve virtually any mid-size building if connected in a modular installation.
- Multiple compressors and variable-speed compressors significantly improve the efficiency of some electric chillers during part-load operation.
- Gas-fired, absorption chiller/heater combination units provide simultaneous heating and cooling. They are particularly effective in applications with year-round hot water needs (e.g., hospitals) and in buildings with significant reheat during the cooling season (e.g., laboratories). The structure of electric and gas rates, as well as utility incentives, are also important factors.

   The double-effect chillers have fully replaced the single-effect types, but now an even more efficient, triple-effect system is being developed.
- Gas-fired, engine-driven chillers approach COPs of 2.
- Desiccants continue to reduce cooling loads in supermarkets and hospitals. Desiccants are also being used more frequently in other building types, such as offices and schools.

For example, some condensing boilers in general and all condensing pulse-combustion boilers in particular can operate at 95% combustion efficiency, much higher than the typical 80 to 85%. Similarly, double-effect (also called double-stage) absorption chillers use 30 to 40% less energy than the older single-effect absorption chillers, by now obsolete. Triple-effect absorption chillers, even more effective, are under development.

Improvements in peak-load efficiency result in lower energy use, but the relationship is not proportional. Actually, when comparing two boilers or chillers, the one with lower peak-load efficiency may use less fuel and less electricity if it has better part-load performance.

PART-LOAD EFFICIENCY

Peak loads occur rarely. First, the design weather conditions are encountered only 1 to 2.5% of the time. A boiler, for instance, may be sized to meet the heating requirements for 10°F, but will operate most of the time at milder temperatures.

Second, the HVAC equipment is routinely oversized by 10 to 30% to account for recovery from night temperature setback, uncertainties in design, problems with construction, and changes in space usage. Therefore even at design outside temperature the boiler is not loaded to capacity.

Finally, a boiler sized for space heating could also be used to generate service hot water. In summer, this boiler will operate at a small fraction of its capacity.

A similar situation is encountered with chillers. As a result, heating and cooling HVAC equipment uses less than half of its capacity for most of the time (Fig. 4.1). Part-load performance is, therefore, essential in determining the annual energy use.

The most inefficient mode of operation is to cycle a boiler or chiller on and off. For instance, when a hot water boiler cycles off it loses heat through the flue. It also loses heat to the boiler room. The water in distribution pipes cools down. All these losses have to be made up when the boiler restarts. If the boiler capacity is much higher than the heating load (e.g., in spring or fall), the cycling is frequent and losses mount, severely decreasing the operational efficiency of the heating system. Although the system does not use much fuel every given hour (since the heating load is low), the amount of fuel used per unit of heat delivered is very high. Much fuel used for little heat delivered means low efficiency.

Should such a condition occur rarely, it would not matter much. In reality, while extremely low heating loads are not frequent, lower-than-capacity heating loads are the norm.

Equipment and controls are widely available to substantially reduce part-load energy consumption. For example, instead of operating in an on/off mode, boilers can use step-firing

Boiler Part Load

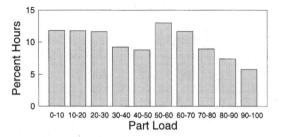

Figure 4.1 ▶ **Boiler part-load for 16-story office building in New York City.**

(high/low/off) or modulating firing (from 100% down to about 20 to 15%). These controls are now common for large capacity equipment, and relatively easy to specify for small units.

Another effective measure is to assemble groups of smaller boilers into modular plants. As the heating load increases, a new boiler enters on-line, augmenting the capacity of the heating system in a gradual manner. As the heating load decreases, the boilers are taken off-line one by one.

Yet another strategy is used for a type of condensing boiler that has *higher* efficiency at lower part-load ratio. Here an automated system fires all boilers simultaneously when such operation results in the part-load range with highest efficiency; otherwise, the boilers are placed on-line as needed.

Many chillers share the same characteristic with the boilers, i.e., they are more efficient at high part-load ratios. This category includes chillers with screw, scroll, and reciprocating compressors. Many centrifugal chillers are more efficient at part-load ratios in the 50 to 80% range. In general, the efficiency of these chillers decreases at full load and also at very low part-load ratios. However, even in these less efficient modes of operation, when the chiller matches the load, the *combined* operation of chiller and cooling tower tends to be more efficient. Furthermore, at 20 to 25% of capacity most centrifugal chillers shut off. Frequent start/stop shortens the life of the equipment. For these reasons, some chillers have been designed to match part-loads by using variable-speed motor compressors, multiple compressors, or multiple-unit installations.

INTEGRATION THROUGH DESIGN

Part-load conditions dominate the operation of boilers and chillers. Typically, higher part-load ratios result in higher efficiencies. Even when the reverse is true, it is rarely if ever cost effective to purchase significantly over-sized equipment. As noted before, not only the first cost is higher, but frequently on/off cycling results in premature aging of the hardware. An economical mode of operation can be obtained through design which selects the boilers, chillers, and their controls based on interactions with the HVAC, lighting, and envelope systems.

Peak-Load Conditions

Cooling equipment needs less oversizing if the design acknowledges *dynamic* interactions with the envelope:

- Solar gains through windows can be closely calculated using hourly computer programs that account for the properties of glazings. Glazings with high daylight transmittance and low shading coefficients can yield significant reductions in peak cooling loads. Shading devices (be they independent or created by the geometry of the building) also help. The effect of thermal mass on peak cooling loads is also taken into account. The cost of detailed simulations is quickly recouped by first-cost savings in the central plant.
- For low-rise buildings, cooling equipment size can also be reduced by calculating the *dynamic* heat loss to the ground during summer.
- The lighting design progresses from a rough estimate in schematic design to a close estimate of watts/ft^2 in design development. If assumptions on lamps, ballasts, and luminaires have changed, it

is worth the additional time to revise the size of chillers.

- The estimate of equipment electric loads should be based on the actual "draw," not on ratings. A computer, for instance, could actually use half or less of the rated electricity.

Heating equipment can have a smaller over-sizing factor by simulating the night thermostat setback and the temperature recovery period. Since the uncertainty in prediction is lower, the oversizing factor can be lower too.

For all equipment, an analysis of peaks can reveal any sharp spikes. These spikes can be reduced through control strategies (e.g., warm-up cycle with outside air dampers closed, optimum fan start) or with hardware (e.g., two boilers at 60% of the load which, when combined, give a 20% margin of safety but which individually operate at high part-load).

Part-Load Conditions

Thoughtful integrated design can also increase the operating efficiency of HVAC systems. For example, occupancy sensing systems can be programmed to turn the lights off and also shut off the VAV box in an unoccupied space. The chilled water temperature can then be increased in accord with the lower cooling load.

Similarly, if the need for service hot water varies considerably in a facility (e.g., hotel), modular boilers or a variable flame boiler will provide improved part-load performance by matching more closely the boiler output with the loads.

Versatility

Finally, heating, cooling, and service water heating systems have been integrated to increase total system performance. As an example, chiller/heaters can provide simultaneous heating and cooling by recovering waste heat. This reduces the total energy use for space conditioning, by comparison to a separate boiler-chiller plant.

4.3 ▶ BOILERS

A boiler is a device which transfers combustion heat to a working fluid (steam or hot water). The working fluid, in turn, heats the building or produces service hot water (Fig. 4.2).

BOILER TYPES

Most commercial boilers are manufactured of steel; some smaller-size boilers use cast iron. Steel boilers transfer combustion heat to the fluid using an assembly of tubes. Based on whether these tubes contain hot gases or fluid, the boilers are designated as firetube or watertube. This classification is important because it is related to the size of boilers. The size, in turn, determines the applicability of high-efficiency condensing boilers (which may or may not use pulse-combustion), and the feasibility of modular installations.

Firetube steel boilers are constructed so that hot gases from the combustion chamber pass through tubes which are surrounded by water. Typically, firetube boilers do not exceed 25 million Btu/hr (MMBtu/hr), but capacities up to 2000 boiler horse power (67 MMBtu/hr) are available.

Figure 4.2 ▶ Typical boiler configuration (*courtesy Cleaver Brooks*).

Watertube steel boilers pass hot combustion gases over water-filled tubes. Sizes for packaged watertube boilers range from small, low pressure units (e.g., around 10 MMBtu/hr) to very large, high-pressure units with steam outputs of 300 MMBtu/hr.

Cast iron boilers are used in small installations (0.35 to 10 MMBtu/hr) where long service life is important. Since these boilers are composed of precast sections, they can be more readily field-assembled than watertube or firetube boilers. At similar capacities, cast-iron boilers are usually more expensive than firetube or watertube boilers.

Both steel and cast iron boilers can operate at low pressure. Low-pressure steam boilers operate below 15 pounds per in^2 gauge pressure (psig). Low-pressure water boilers operate below 30 psig water for cast-iron boilers, and below 150 psig water for steel boilers. Steel boilers also operate at medium and high pressure: above 15 psig steam and above 150 psig water. Medium and high-pressure installations are generally used for larger capacities.

BOILER COMPONENTS

Most commercial boilers are delivered as packaged units. Typically, they contain an insulated jacket, a burner, a mechanical draft system, tubes and chambers for combustion gas, tubes and chambers for water or for steam circulation, and controls.

The actual design of a boiler varies according to the requirements of the application including output, fuel, ease of installation, first cost, maintenance cost, dimensions, etc. While all boiler components have been gradually improved over the years, the burner and control systems account for the most significant increases in energy efficiency.

The following sections discuss energy-efficiency advances for boilers in general, and then focus on condensing boilers and on modular boiler installations.

4.3.1 ▶ *Principles for High Efficiency Boilers*

In this manual, the "overall efficiency" of boilers is defined as the ratio of total Btu output, as measured in the steam or the hot water leaving the boiler, divided by the total Btu of fuel input. The overall efficiency accounts for combustion processes, for stack (chimney) heat loss, and for the loss from the outside surfaces of the boiler. "Combustion efficiency" typically refers just to the effectiveness of the burner.

Other terms are also used. For example, some use the term "boiler efficiency" interchangeably with the term "fuel-to-steam efficiency," and "thermal efficiency" to designate just the efficiency of heat transfer within the unit.

The overall efficiency and the combustion efficiency of boilers are determined according to industry-promulgated standards.

The Annual Fuel Utilization Efficiency (AFUE) is a DOE-mandated efficiency rating for boilers with an output lower than 300,000 Btu/hr. AFUE accounts for both on-cycle and off-cycle losses by combining laboratory measurements with computer simulations. Although similar to the combustion efficiency definition, AFUE provides a lower figure, more representative of actual on/off combustion processes in the field.

Boiler input and output is usually measured in thousands or millions Btu. The industry uses the M symbol for a thousand and the MM symbol for a million. Although elsewhere in the book thousand is usually designated by K, this chapter will use the M designation to maintain consistency with the manufacturers' catalogs. However, it is to be expected that at some point the industry will switch to the international notation.

Manufacturers continue to improve both the overall and the combustion efficiencies of boilers and furnaces. Commercially sized equipment can achieve over 95% combustion efficiency, though anything over 85% is traditionally considered efficient. These highly efficient units, which use condensing combustion, heat small to mid-sized buildings.

In addition to space heating, boilers often provide service hot water (SHW) by means of a dedicated boiler water line to a heat exchanger inside of or external to the boiler. Dedicated high efficiency commercial water heaters are available in the 40 to over 1000 MBtu/hr range (Fig. 4.3). When replacing older equipment, high efficiency boilers could achieve fuel savings of up to 40%.

4.3.2 ▶ *Pulse-Combustion and Modular Boiler Installations*

Manufacturers offer a variety of improved heat exchangers, firing controls, and air/ fuel supply systems. Of these, two technical advances are responsible for the largest increase in the efficiency of boiler plants: condensing combustion (including pulse combustion) and modular design. This section highlights the pulse-combustion process because of its innovation; however, condensing boilers exist that yield similar energy performance without using pulse combustion. The selection of the equipment should be made according to both peak- and part-load performance, in response to the

Figure 4.3 ▶ One type of high efficiency boiler (*courtesy Weil-McLain*).

load variations determined by the building envelope, lighting, plug-load and distribution systems.

PULSE-COMBUSTION BOILERS
This innovative combustion technology was first introduced in the early 1980s for residential water heaters, and is now available in many commercial-size boilers for both space heating and SHW.

Pulse-Combustion Cycle
Essentially, pulse-combustion boilers function like automotive internal combustion engines (Fig. 4.4). First, air and gas are introduced into a sealed combustion chamber in carefully

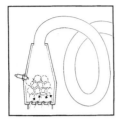

1. The heating process begins as air and gas are introduced into the combustion chamber to mix near the igniter.

2. A spark creates the initial combustion, which in turn causes a positive pressure buildup that closes off the air and gas inlets.

3. This pressure then relieves itself by forcing the products of combustion down a tailpipe. These combustion products are then vented outdoors by means of 2″ PVC pipe (run either vertically or horizontally through a wall).

4. As the combustion chamber empties, its pressure becomes negative, drawing in air and gas for the next ignition.

   At the same instant, part of the pressure pulse is reflected back from the end of the tailpipe.

Fail-Safe Operation

The Pulse design makes it even safer than conventional furnaces. Lockout controls shut down operation long before combustion products could ever escape.

5. It re-enters the combustion chamber, causing the new gas/air mixture in the chamber to ignite and continue to cycle.

   Once combustion is started, it feeds upon itself, allowing the purge blower and spark igniter to be turned off.

AIR CONDITIONING ● HEATING

Made In The U.S.A.

Figure 4.4 ▶ Typical pulse-combustion cycle (*courtesy Lennox*).

measured amounts. This mixture is then ignited by a spark plug, and when completely burned is expelled through an exhaust pipe. Almost all of the energy is used to heat the boiler water, so the exhaust gases have only a relatively low temperature of 120°F.

Once the combustion chamber is fully heated, successive air/fuel "pulses" ignite spontaneously, without the need for an electrical spark (similar to a diesel engine). Thus, no fuel-consuming burner or standing pilot light is required.

When pulse boilers operate, they extract latent heat from the products of combustion by condensing the flue-gas. Thus, they increase overall boiler efficiency. The resulting liquid is drained away; the flue-gas is left with low water vapor content.

The process is similar to that which occurs in an overheated, humid greenhouse. In winter, visitors entering the greenhouse will get water drops on their cold hands and faces. The humid air has condensed on these cold surfaces, converting vapor into liquid. The conversion, also called a phase change, is accompanied by a release of heat. The droplets feel warm. The heat released when water changes phase (vapor to liquid) is latent heat. The reverse process, when water changes from liquid to vapor, is called evaporation. Evaporation extracts heat, making wet hands feel cold.

Prior to this development, heating boilers had to operate with flue-gas temperatures sufficiently high to prevent condensation on cast-iron or steel parts, which can corrode. Lower flue-gas temperatures permit lower water return temperatures in hydronic heating systems.

Under part-load conditions such reduced temperatures further increase the system effi-

ciency. *Reminder:* All pulse-combustion boilers are also condensing boilers over some or all of their part-load range, but not all condensing boilers use pulse-combustion.

Very High Combustion Efficiency
Pulse-combustion boilers can attain *combustion* efficiencies of 95 to 99%. When combined with other high-performance elements for heat transfer, insulation, and control, rated boiler efficiencies higher than 90% are common.

Quick Response and Lower Pollution
In addition to saving energy, pulse-combustion boilers can reach operating temperatures in as

Figure 4.5 ▶ A large commercial pulse-combustion boiler (*courtesy Fulton Thermatic Corporation*).

little as one-half the time of conventional boilers. Pulse-combustion burners also produce lower emissions than conventional gas burners (and considerably lower than coal and oil installations).

Applications

Until recently, only residential and small commercial buildings used high efficiency pulse-combustion boilers. However, commercial boilers of this type now serve the 300,000 to 1,000,000 Btu range, large enough to satisfy mid-sized commercial loads (Fig. 4.5). Condensing boilers that do not use the pulse-combustion technology, yet have 95% combustion efficiencies, also exist in the 1,000,000 Btu range. When several units are connected, the modular plant can meet virtually any heating load encountered in commercial applications.

MODULAR BOILERS

All boilers, regardless of their peak-load efficiency, can be installed in modular configurations to enhance operating performance. This strategy connects multiple boilers to form a modular boiler plant (Fig. 4.6). Theoretically, any number of individual boilers can be used; in one case 36 units have been placed in a single space-heating installation.

Some manufacturers offer preassembled modular boiler packages of various sizes,

Figure 4.6 ▶ Modular boiler installation at Maple Avenue Middle School (*courtesy Aerco International, Inc.*). **The boilers are condensing but not pulse-combustion.**

ranging from approximately 200,000 to several million Btu/hr. Alternately, individual modules can be piped and wired together in the field to form an efficient system.

Energy Savings

Modular boiler installations offer a good way to achieve high operating efficiencies. They are particularly effective in applications with widely varying heating and hot water loads, such as hotels, schools, or high-rise residences.

The design heating load is reached for just a few hours during winter, and domestic hot water loads peak for only short periods each day. Usually the boiler load is lower than the design load by a considerable amount. Additionally, boilers are sized to quickly recover the space temperature from night thermostat setback and to provide a safety margin. Thus, single-boiler installations are rarely if ever fully loaded. The operating efficiency of on-off single boilers, or even of high-low-off single boilers, is significantly reduced. (Modulating flame single boilers, however, are almost as efficient at low part-load as they are at peak-load.) Even in traditional two- and three-boiler installations the boilers are seldom fully loaded, and sometimes operators keep boilers "floating" on-line when they are not needed.

In contrast, modular installations activate just the number of boilers required by a specific load at a given time, using multiple-boiler control panels which sequence the boilers according to loads. Thus, boilers operate for longer periods of time at high part-load ratios, and provide a significant increase in boiler plant operating efficiency (typically 15 to 30%). Additionally, the control panels rotate the order in which boilers fire, to achieve uniform wear on all equipment.

Flexibility in Space Usage

Modular boilers can be transported through doors that cannot accommodate a large boiler. Their smaller size permits positioning of the HVAC equipment in confined spaces.

Case Study: Car Wash

The following case study demonstrates that modular, pulse-combustion boiler technology is mature. A six-bay car wash in Bethalto, Illinois, was fitted as early as 1981 with then-new modular pulse-combustion boilers to replace its conventional gas boiler system.

According to the owner, the boilers had to supply each wash bay with 22 gallons per minute. Peak consumption was 420 gallons of hot water per hour.

This facility was refitted with eight 100,000 Btu modular pulse boilers, while an identical nearby car wash retained its original 1.4 million Btu conventional boiler. During the first year of operation the new system required $1800 for gas use, much less than the $2700 used by the identical, unmodified car wash.

Case Study: Shopping Mall

The 50,000 ft^2 Pioneer Mall in Sergeant Bluff, Iowa, is heated with twelve 150,000 Btu modular pulse-combustion boilers. The mall contains 16 individual stores, including a grocery store, ice cream shop, medical office, and a food service area for up to 150 customers.

Water in boilers is replaced by an antifreeze solution containing 40% propylene glycol, to protect the coils from freezing. The antifreeze solution is pumped from the boilers to air-handling units above each store. There it passes through the heating coils to warm air for the shops.

According to the mall's management, thermal performance has been excellent and the system manufacturer estimates heating cost savings of at least 33% over a conventional gas fueled boiler.

Case Study: School

The 180,000 ft² Maple Avenue Middle School (Fig. 4.7) was built in 1992 in Saratoga Springs, New York. The school has 66 classrooms, a kitchen, two cafeterias, two gymnasiums, and office spaces, accommodating 1200 students.

Eight condensing, modulating-flame, modular boilers are controlled by a staging system to ensure that the heating system responds gradually and efficiently to changes in loads. These boilers are more efficient at *low* part-load ratios, so under such conditions the control module usually operates them simultaneously, rather than sequentially, to minimize fuel use. Service hot water is produced by two separate units. WPS Consulting Engi-

neers, P.C. in collaboration with the school management made the selection based on life-cycle cost rather than first cost. The latter criterion would have resulted in an all-electric installation.

Case Study: Church

The Holy Trinity Greek Orthodox Church in Bridgeport, Connecticut installed in 1989 a modular pulse-combustion system with four 300,000 Btu boilers (Fig. 4.8). The areas heated include the sanctuary with a dome and vaults, ten kindergarten rooms, kitchen, a gymnasium and administrative offices. The boilers step-fire only as needed, according to a controller which maintains the required temperature for supply hot water. A reset algorithm adjusts this water temperature between 200°F and 105°F, corresponding to 20°F and 65°F outside air temperatures. The controller also changes

Figure 4.7 ► **The Maple Avenue Middle School in Saratoga Springs, NY (*courtesy Aerco International, Inc.*).**

Figure 4.8 ▶ The Holy Trinity Greek Orthodox Church, Bridgeport, Connecticut.

the firing sequence of the individual boilers, to even out the on-time for each module.

The manufacturer states that 35% energy cost savings were obtained during the first year, by comparison to the previous, all-electric heating system.

PRACTICAL CONSIDERATIONS FOR BOILERS

Design

- Size the boilers according to ASHRAE/IES Standard 90.1, Section 9, "Heating, Ventilating, and Air-Conditioning (HVAC) Systems." Specifically, do not use a safety factor higher than 10%.
- Consider using computer simulations to calculate the pick-up loads generated by recovery from night thermostat setback. The 30% oversizing allowed by the ASHRAE Standard can be unnecessarily high. Consider specifying controls which implement a gradual increase of temperature from night thermostat set-back, in order to reduce boiler size. Typically, any additional engineering cost is quickly recouped through reduced first cost and lower fuel use.
- Investigate the payback of condensing, or condensing pulse-combustion boilers, even for large installations, by using modular designs. Fuel savings of 10 to 20% over on-off or high-low-off single-boilers can be achieved. Computer simulations should be used for a more accurate estimate.
- When estimating the payback for modular installations also consider drawbacks: increased maintenance costs for multiple units.

- When modular plants are considered, also investigate using boilers with stepped firing or modulating firing.
- Provide boiler condensate drainage for pulse-combustion boilers.
- In small installations, consider through-the-wall venting.

Construction
- Modular boilers may be easier to position in tight spaces than single boilers.
- Maintain proper fresh air intake for boilers.
- Provide commissioning at the end of construction.

Operation/Maintenance
- Maintain hot water temperature as low as possible using hot water reset based on outdoor temperature, return water temperature, monitored load, load anticipators, or other control strategies.
- Regularly clean burner and combustion chambers.
- Perform periodic combustion tests and measure flue-gas temperature.
- In larger installations, periodically analyze flue-gas composition.

4.4 ► CHILLERS

Chillers are devices which chill water to provide space cooling. Typically, commercial chillers extract heat by utilizing vapor compression in a mechanical refrigeration cycle, or by utilizing vapor absorption in a heat-operated refrigeration cycle.

Chiller capacity is rated in tons. One ton of refrigeration is equivalent to 12,000 Btu extracted. Small commercial buildings in tem-

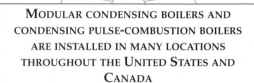

MODULAR CONDENSING BOILERS AND CONDENSING PULSE-COMBUSTION BOILERS ARE INSTALLED IN MANY LOCATIONS THROUGHOUT THE UNITED STATES AND CANADA

- Office of Public Safety, Westchester, NY
- Farm Bureau, W. Des Moines, IA
- Kirtland AFB, Albuquerque, NM
- Stonybrook Museum, Stonybrook, NY
- Maple Avenue Middle School, Saratoga Springs, NY
- Sutherland Middle School, Albemarle County, VA
- U.S. Naval Academy, Annapolis, MD
- Willamette University, Salem, OR
- University of Dayton, Dayton, OH
- Gannon University, Erie, PA
- Red Jacket Inn, Niagara Falls, NY
- Holy Trinity Greek Orthodox Church, Bridgeport, CT
- Allstate Insurance, Roanoke, VA
- Hit & Run Car Wash, Bethalto, IL
- Randolph Street Commuter Rail Station, Chicago, IL
- The Works Hotel, South Bend, IN
- Rochester Airport, Rochester, NY
- Dufferin County Courthouse, Orangeville, Ontario
- St. Francis Xavier Church, Renfrew, Ontario

perate climates (e.g., New York, Pennsylvania, Washington State) have peak cooling needs in the range of 10 to 200 tons. Buildings up to 500 to 600 tons could be considered medium size. Large buildings can require over 1000 tons cooling during design-day conditions. Hot climates, such as Texas or Arizona, can result in loads twice as large. Of course, these figures cannot cover all situations. Very large buildings could require over 50,000 tons cooling.

MECHANICAL REFRIGERATION CHILLERS: ELECTRIC AND ENGINE-DRIVEN

Some chillers use mechanical refrigeration. Electric chillers can be powered by electric motors, fossil fuel engines, or turbines. Basic components include one or several compressors (driven by electric motor, internal combustion engine, or turbines), evaporator, condenser, means to control the flow of refrigerant, and a control panel (Fig. 4.9).

ABSORPTION CHILLERS

Absorption chillers are heat-operated devices which produce chilled water by utilizing an absorption cycle. Absorption chillers can be direct fired, with gas or oil fuel, or indirect fired. Indirect fired units may use as heat source hot water or steam from a boiler, steam from district heating or from industrial processes, or waste heat (air or gas).

Absorption chillers can be single-effect, where only one generator of vapor is used, double-effect or triple-effect, where two or three such generators are employed sequentially to increase unit efficiency. Single-effect chillers can still be found in older installations, but because of their relatively low efficiency are no longer specified for new applications.

Several manufacturers offer absorption chiller/heater units, which use the heat produced by firing to provide space heating and service hot water. (See Sec. 4.4.3.)

Although absorption chillers do not use electricity as their primary source of power, they still consume electricity by operating several pumps, which typically draw from 1 to 10 kw, depending on chiller size.

4.4.1 ▶ Principles for High Efficiency Chillers

Chiller performance depends on both full-load rated efficiency and part-load curves.

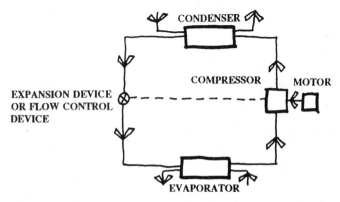

Figure 4.9 ▶ Components of mechanical refrigeration chillers (*courtesy ASHRAE*).

Full-load Efficiency

The efficiency of both mechanical refrigeration and absorption chillers is typically measured by the *Coefficient of Performance* (COP). COP is the heat extracted in Btu divided by the Btu energy input under a predetermined set of conditions (full loading).

The *Energy Efficiency Ratio* (EER) is similar to the COP. It is obtained by dividing the heat extracted in Btu to the energy input in watts. Roughly, EER = COP × 3.413, since there are 3.413 Btu per watt.

Another measure for electric chiller efficiency is the kw required to provide one ton of cooling under full-load conditions (kw/ton). Divide 3.516 by the kw/ton value to obtain an approximate value of the chiller COP.

- Small *air-cooled* electric chillers have 1.6 to 1.1 kw/ton (COP of 2.2 to 3.2).
- Large and medium-sized *air-cooled* electric chillers have 1.4 to 0.95 kw/ton (COP of 3.7 to 4.1).
- Similar *water-cooled* electric chillers have 0.8 to 0.7 kw/ton (COP of 4.4 to 5.0). Lower values such as 0.6 to 0.5 kw/ton chillers (COP of 5.9 to 7.0) may indicate energy-efficient equipment, but part-load performance should also be examined.
- The COP of absorption units is in the range of 0.4 to 0.6 for single-stage chillers, and 0.8 to 1.05 for double-effect, energy-efficient chillers.
- Engine-driven chillers attain COPs of 1.2 to 2.0, where the higher COPs include heat recovery.

The COP is useful only when comparing equipment of the same type and with similar part-load performance. For example, the COP of electric chillers cannot be compared in a meaningful way with the COP of gas-engine chillers, since the cost of one Btu of gas can be very different from the cost of one Btu of electricity.

Also, the comparison between the COP of a screw chiller and a centrifugal chiller has limited value, since part-load performance is different.

Part-load Efficiency Measures

To provide information on part-load energy use a new concept was introduced in recent years: the *Integrated Part Load Value* (IPLV). Many chillers now have both COP and IPLV ratings.

Some chillers also provide heating and/or hot water; the only method to accurately assess the efficiency of such "chillers/heaters" is based on yearly energy use.

Advances in Chiller Efficiency

The energy efficiency of electric chillers improved in recent years with the introduction of two-compressor reciprocating and centrifugal chillers, variable-speed centrifugal chillers, and scroll-type rotary compressors.

Gas chillers also achieve lower energy use in chiller/heater double- and triple-effect absorption configurations, and through high COPs for gas-fired, engine-driven, or turbine-driven chillers.

Another change refers to CFC refrigerants. These refrigerants are replaced in new chillers, sometimes slightly decreasing the energy efficiency. The legislated tradeoff is worthwhile, given the CFC adverse effect on the environment.

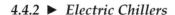

4.4.2 ► *Electric Chillers*

Most electric chillers for commercial buildings use rotary, reciprocating, or centrifugal compressors.

Rotary compressors are specified in chillers with typical capacities of 5 through 500 tons. These compressors raise gas pressure using revolving motions (Fig. 4.10). The innovative scroll compressor (Fig. 4.11) is manufactured in the 1 to 15 ton range. Screw compressors, in several configurations, extend from 40 to 500 tons.

Reciprocating compressors are used in chillers with typical capacities of 10 through 200 tons. These compressors raise gas pressure by operating pistons (Fig. 4.12). Multiple-compressor units match the part-load conditions better and achieve higher operating efficiencies.

Centrifugal compressors are used in chillers with typical capacities of 100 to 7000 tons. These compressors raise gas pressure by rotating an impeller (Fig. 4.13). Above 1300 tons, centrifugal compressors are usually field-erected. As with most HVAC equipment, centrifugal compressor chillers have been experiencing gradual improvement of both steady-state and operating efficiencies.

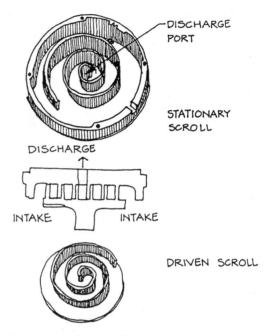

Figure 4.11 ► Scroll compressor (*courtesy Dunham–Bush*).

Variable-speed drives for chillers stand out because of the large energy savings they can achieve (up to 30%) in installations with a wide range of cooling loads.

SCROLL COMPRESSOR CHILLERS

The scroll compressor is an ingenious rotary compression device. The mechanism is elegantly simple; just two primary components, a fixed scroll and an orbiting scroll, are required to compress the gas (Fig. 4.14). These scrolls replace about twice as many parts which are required to do the same work in one piston compressor.

Energy Savings

The good thermal performance of scroll compressors is due, in part, to the physical sepa-

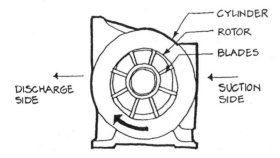

Figure 4.10 ► Rotary compressor (*courtesy ASHRAE*).

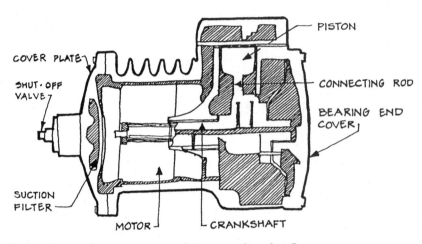

Figure 4.12 ▶ **Reciprocating compressor (*courtesy Copeland*).**

ration they provide between the suction and discharge processes. This separation reduces heat transfer (loss) between the discharge and suction gases.

Five percent energy savings are possible compared with an equivalent reciprocating compressor. Several manufacturers claim EER exceeding 11 (COP above 3.2).

Low Maintenance Costs

In addition to relatively high energy efficiency, field testing and destructive testing of

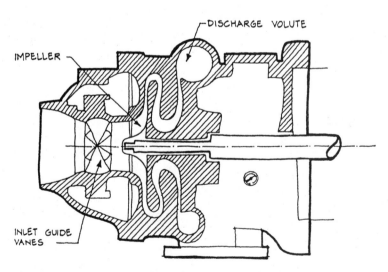

Figure 4.13 ▶ **Centrifugal compressor (*courtesy ASHRAE*).**

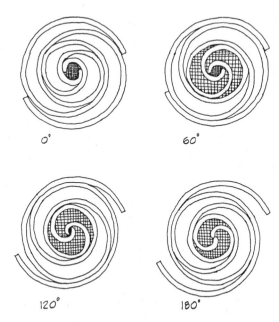

0°   60°   120°   180°

Figure 4.14 ▶ **Operation of scroll processor**
(*courtesy ASHRAE*).

scroll compressors has shown their reliability to be excellent, mainly because of the simplicity of scroll design. Scroll compressors have less rotating mass and internal friction, no valve losses, and a smoother compression cycle.

Unlike piston compressors, many scroll units tolerate liquid slugging and debris within the system, by separating the two scrolls from each other in the presence of contaminants. These "compliant" scrolls are also self-compensating for wear: They lose efficiency very slowly over time because they "wear in."

Quiet Operation

Finally, scroll compressors are quiet. The motion required to compress gas is limited. Also, because suction and discharge flow is continuous, scrolls have very low gas pulses, and since no dynamic valves are required, valve noise (a common problem in piston compressors) is not a factor.

Availability

Scroll compressors are manufactured on 1 to 15 ton sizes. Four-compressor chillers attain 60 ton capacities.

Case Study: Hospital

A small hospital in Connecticut, remodeled 17,000 ft^2 on its first floor that is bermed in the sloping site.

The floor has 3 watts/ft^2 lighting and equipment load and uses a VAV system without reheat. Peak cooling load is 36 tons and is met with a 40-ton chiller. The chiller operates below 50% capacity for most of the time.

The designers considered the merits of a single-piston reciprocal-compressor (EER = 10.2) versus a chiller with four rotary scroll compressors (EER = 11.2). According to DOE-2.1 simulations performed by Steven Winter Associates, Inc. for Northeast Utilities Service Co., the scroll compressor chiller is projected to reduce the electricity cost by 5% per year. More important, lower maintenance costs are also expected.

MULTIPLE COMPRESSOR AND VARIABLE-SPEED COMPRESSOR CHILLERS

Both multiple compressors and variable-speed compressors improve the performance of chillers which operate under partial loading much of the time.

Multiple-compressor chillers are reciprocating, rotary, or centrifugal. Typical capacities range from 30 to 2000 tons. Variable-speed compressor chillers are in general centrifugal.

They operate with variable head pressure and achieve their load-matching capabilities using variable-speed motors, which take advantage of the lower head pressure required at part-load. Typical capacities are in the 150 to 700 ton range.

Selecting between these two energy conserving features requires consideration of both peak cooling load and cooling load profile.

Variable-speed chillers can reduce heat extraction rates to 10% of capacity, but work best when partial loads average over 50% of total capacity. Generally, a reduction in cooling output is matched by a reduction in electricity consumption by the unit. However, when cooling demand falls much below 50%, energy input requirements do not continue to decrease as much, and performance drops off.

However, chilled water temperature reset strategies may improve the efficiency of variable-speed chillers in the 50 to 25% range of capacity.

Buildings may also benefit from the installation of two-compressor chillers. The two compressors operate in concert when the cooling system is fully on, but under partial load one compressor is shut down, so the remaining unit runs close to capacity.

Four-compressor chillers are also used, most notably with scroll technologies. These chillers attain 60-ton capacities. The advantages are similar to those of two-compressor chillers.

Case Study: Hospital

The following analysis compares the relative merits of single-compressor, two-compressor, and variable-speed compressor chillers for a 550 ton chilled water plant serving a 190,000 ft² hospital in Connecticut. The *two chillers* are rated at 0.62 kw/ton (COP = 5.67). For this particular application the chillers are loaded as follows:

▶ Two-Chiller Plant

Part-load Ratio of Individual Chillers	% Time at Part-load
Below 30%	54
31–50%	15
51–70%	18
71–100%	13

The yearly electricity use of the single-compressor chillers is 574,600 kwh. Variable-speed chillers save 21% in cooling electricity use. Two-compressor chillers (equal size compressors) save 19%.

A sensitivity study shows how results could change according to load distribution. If *three chillers* are used instead of two, these chillers operate at higher part-load ratios. As a result, the yearly electricity use of the single-compressor chillers decreases by 11%, to 511,700 kwh.

The savings from two-compressor and variable-speed compressor chillers changes too, since their load-matching advantage is now reduced. Further, there is less difference in the performance of the two energy saving options. In this case both the variable-speed chillers and the two-compressor chillers save about 15% in electricity use for cooling.

▶ Three-Chiller Plant

Part-load Ratio of Individual Chillers	% Time at Part-load
Below 30%	45
31–50%	11
51–70%	22
71–100%	22

Finally, the study compares the cooling energy use of *three* single-compressor chillers versus *two* variable-speed chillers or *two*

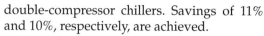

double-compressor chillers. Savings of 11% and 10%, respectively, are achieved.

The summary of the study is captured below:

Two-chiller plant
　　Variable speed saves 21%
　　Two-compressor saves 19%

Three-chiller plant
　　Variable speed saves 15%
　　Two-compressor saves 15%

Three-chiller, single-compressor plant
　　Two-chiller variable speed plant
　　　　saves 11%
　　Two-chiller two-compressor plant
　　　　saves 10%

Other combinations are possible. For instance, it is sometimes economical to use a variable-speed chiller for baseline load and to "top" the load with a single-piston, single-speed chiller.

PRACTICAL CONSIDERATIONS FOR ELECTRIC CHILLERS

Design
- Size the chillers according to ASHRAE/IES Standard 90.1, Section 9, "Heating, Ventilating, and Air-conditioning (HVAC) Systems." Do not use a safety factor higher than 10% and a temperature setup recovery factor higher than 5% unless justified by calculations.
- Consider using hourly computer simulations to calculate the peak cooling load, especially for buildings with large glazed surfaces on several orientations. In low-rise buildings account for the cooling effect of ground coupling.

- Study the annual distribution of part-load ratios before specifying chiller type and size.

　　If the chilled water plant is projected to operate for substantial periods of time over the entire spectrum of part-loads, two chillers, double-compressor chillers, or variable-speed chillers may be more advantageous than one chiller.

　　If the peak load occurs in spike shape over a relatively brief time interval, two chillers of unequal size (a larger one and a "topping" one) should also be considered.
- Use hourly simulations for the actual building or campus served by the chiller water plant to compare the energy use of chillers with different part-load curves.
- Consider using the soft-start motor starters to avoid surges when the chiller is started. This is more important when demand rates are high.

Construction
- Commission the chilled water plant at the end of construction.

Operation/Maintenance
- Provide training, maintenance, and operations manuals for building engineering personnel.
- Use automatic controls to supply chilled water at the highest temperature that meets the cooling load and the specific dehumidification requirements.
- Use automatic controls for centrifugal variable-speed chillers to decrease the condenser water supply temperature when the outside air wet bulb temperature drops.
- Regularly inspect chillers and maintain design operation characteristics.
- Store a supply of important spare parts.

ENERGY-EFFICIENT ELECTRIC CHILLERS ARE INSTALLED THROUGHOUT THE UNITED STATES

Scroll Compressor Chillers
- Two World Trade Center, New York, NY
- City University Graduate Center, New York, NY
- Turner School, New York, NY
- Baby Togs, New York, NY
- Livingston Plaza, Brooklyn, NY
- Carnegie Hall Tower Apartments, New York, NY
- The Mental Health Center, New Haven, CT
- Yale School of Sacred Music, New Haven, CT

Multiple-compressor Chillers
- Rockefeller Center, New York, NY
- Lord & Taylor, New York, NY
- Merrill Lynch, Battery Park City, New York, NY
- Lennox Hill Hospital, New York, NY
- IBM Headquarters, Armonk, NY
- New York Telephone Co., New York, NY

Variable-speed Chillers
- Grumman Aerospace, Bethpage, NY and Calverton, NY
- New York Times, New York, NY
- Citibank, New York, NY
- Southwestern Bell, Little Rock, AR
- Northeast Utilities Headquarters, Berlin, CT
- Ethicon, Albuquerque, NM
- AT&T, Houston, TX
- Trinity Hospital, Cudahy, WI
- Floyd Memorial Hospital, New Albany, IN
- Sears, Roseville, MI
- NE States Power, Minneapolis, MN
- Fresno Hospital, Fresno, CA
- Hershey High School, Arlington Heights, IL
- Household Credit, Salinas, CA

4.4.3 ▶ *Gas-fired Chillers*

Gas-fired cooling systems have been installed in residential, commercial, institutional, and industrial buildings for over half a century, but today high efficiency equipment offers significantly improved thermal performance.

One reason why gas cooling systems are specified is because the price of natural gas has stabilized in recent years and, at least for the foreseeable future, supplies appear ample.

Designers can now consider gas-fired, engine-driven cooling systems, as well as direct-fired and indirect-fired absorption units.

Direct-fired absorption chillers utilize an open flame to generate energy for cooling. Indirect-fired absorption chillers use the heat from steam, hot water, or hot gases produced elsewhere.

Some of the direct-fired chillers can simultaneously provide both chilled and hot water. They are commonly designated as chiller/ heaters.

Direct-fired Absorption Chillers/Heaters

Direct-fired absorption chiller/heaters are especially effective in applications where the combustion heat can be used during the cooling season (e.g., buildings with large service hot water needs). Sizes range from about 30 to 1500 tons. Because direct-firing generates high temperatures, these chillers are well-suited for the efficient double-effect or triple-effect configurations. Advances in energy efficiency are covered later in this chapter.

Indirect-fired Absorption Chillers

These chillers need a readily available heat source, such as low pressure steam (15 psig) or medium temperature hot water (300 to 330°F). Refrigeration capacities from 50 to 1500 tons are available, but typical sizes range from 400 to 1000 tons. Double-effect configurations can be used only with high temperature steam, high-temperature/high-pressure hot water, or with hot industrial waste gases.

For this reason double-effect indirect-fired chillers are used mostly for hospitals, prisons, universities, and other institutional facilities with campus-type layouts. Industrial plants, of course, frequently have high-temperature hot water or high-pressure steam available.

Engine-driven Chillers

Engine-driven chillers use reciprocating, rotary, or centrifugal compressors to provide mechanical refrigeration. The engine can be automotive or gas-fired. Capacities for most chillers of this type range from 30 to 350 tons, but can go as high as 1500 tons.

Gas-fired, turbine-driven chillers are also available up to capacities of 5000 tons, but have a high first cost.

This chapter focuses on advances made by gas-fired engines in providing high COPs and close load matching.

Applicability of Gas-fired Chillers

Although gas-fired chillers can significantly reduce the demand for electricity, they are not necessarily more cost-effective than electric chillers. The first cost of gas-fired chillers is often twice as high as that of electric chillers. Designers must also consider other variables when selecting chillers, including fuel prices, utility demand changes, maintenance requirements, and the cost of pollution controls. Rebates paid by electric and/or gas utilities may also be a significant factor.

DIRECT-FIRED, DOUBLE-EFFECT ABSORPTION CHILLER/HEATERS

Absorption cycle chillers have been in use since the 1950s, but energy-efficient, direct-fired, double-effect chiller/heaters are a relatively new development.

Double-effect units typically require 30 to 40 percent less energy per ton of cooling than do the now-obsolete single-effect chillers. In addition, chiller/heater units provide both cooling and heating at greater combined efficiency. Some of those units have heat exchangers which permit simultaneous cooling, heating, and domestic hot water cycles.

The Double-effect Absorption Cycle

Figures 4.15 and 4.16 illustrate the basic absorption cooling and heating cycles. The primary difference from single-effect units is that double-effect chillers extract usable heat from the hot water vapor that boils in the

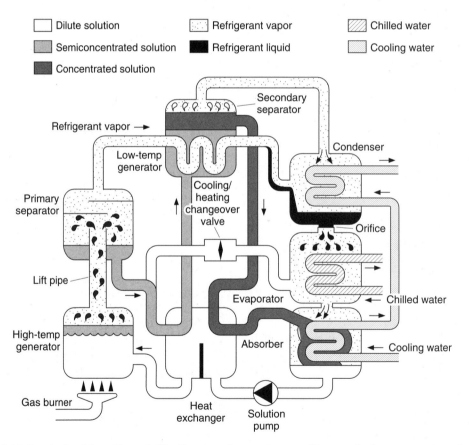

Figure 4.15 ▶ A double-effect chiller/heater absorption cooling cycle (*courtesy American Yazaki Corporation*).

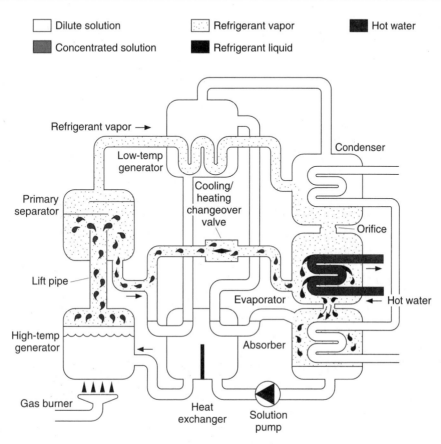

☐ Dilute solution   ▨ Refrigerant vapor   ▮ Hot water

▨ Concentrated solution   ▮ Refrigerant liquid

Refrigerant vapor →

Low-temp generator

Primary separator

Cooling/ heating changeover valve

Condenser

Orifice

Lift pipe

Evaporator

Hot water ←

High-temp generator

Absorber

Gas burner

Heat exchanger

Solution pump

Figure 4.16 ► A double-effect chiller/heater absorption heating cycle (*courtesy American Yazaki Corporation*).

first stage generator—heat which would be expelled as waste through a cooling tower. This hot vapor is then recycled, by means of a second low-temperature generator, to produce a very concentrated lithium-bromide solution for additional cooling.

Despite all the subsystems present in absorption chillers, manufacturers have developed compact packages.

Direct-fired chillers provide the high temperature required by the two-stage absorp-

tion process. Most direct-fired chillers use gas as fuel; some use both gas and oil.

Energy Efficiency

Double-effect chiller/heaters are now available in capacities up to 1500 tons, and with COPs approaching 1.05, the highest achieved with such equipment. While the COPs of compressor-based electric chillers are considerably higher, modern absorption equipment is sometimes less expensive to operate, because the cost of gas on an equivalent Btu basis could be lower than that of electricity.

Other Advantages

These units also have several other advantages:

- operate at relatively high efficiency under partial load
- are quiet
- require less maintenance than typical electric compressors (except for scroll compressors)
- can utilize recovered process heat or heat from cogeneration as input

In the past, gas-fired chillers had the additional advantage of not creating environmental problems with CFCs. This, however, has become less of an issue for electric chillers. Non-CFC electric units are produced, and the replacement refrigerants are more benign (although not problem-free).

Cost

While double-effect chiller/heaters can offer low energy costs, they typically have higher initial costs than electric chillers. This higher first cost must be recovered over time through energy savings, and the cost recovery schedule will vary considerably with local fuel prices and specific building energy demands. Life expectancy of the chiller/heaters could also be lower, because of the double-duty performed.

Selection of Absorption Chillers

To take full advantage of the superior energy performance of a chiller/heater, designers must carefully integrate heating and cooling systems within a building, and find a use for the hot water generated during the cooling season. Many buildings (e.g., hospitals, multifamily housing, and manufacturing plants) have significant hot water requirements year-round, and thus are particularly well suited to use double-effect chiller/heater systems.

Absorption cooling can also be used in combination with electric cooling. Since two chillers are usually provided in a central plant to ensure reliability, one can be electric and one absorption. In this configuration, it is possible to reduce the peak load with the absorption system and to use the electric chiller for the base cooling load. This can be cost effective in areas with high electric demand rates.

A similar strategy involves using a chiller/heater sized to meet the heating load. In many large buildings the cooling requirement exceeds the heating requirement, and an electric chiller can be used to make up the difference.

Case Study: Office Building

The 820 Second Avenue Office Building in Manhattan (Fig. 4.17) had its older single-effect absorption chiller and steam boiler replaced with a new 500-ton double-effect chiller/heater. First year energy savings in the nineteen-story building were $53,000, or more than 50% over the older equipment. The compact design of the new chiller/heater, and its relatively light weight, allowed easy installation in the small machine room on top of the building.

Case Study: Hospital

The consulting engineers for the six-story, 332-bed hospital, St. John's in Queens, New York, (Fig. 4.18, p. 144) selected two 400-ton direct-fired chiller/heaters, after comparing them to a conventional system that uses two

Figure 4.17 ▶ **Installing a new double-effect gas chiller/heater in this Manhattan office tower reduced its annual gas consumption by 54%.**

electric centrifugal chillers and a gas boiler. According to the engineer's calculations, the installation will save over $20,000 every year in energy costs.

Case Study: Hotel

This case study demonstrates that the technology is mature. The 318,000 ft^2 Doral Arrowwood Hotel in Ryebrook, NY, has been using two 430-ton direct-fired chiller/heaters since as far back as 1982. The hotel has a con-

ference center which sometimes requires cooling while guest rooms need heating. The ability of the equipment to perform simultaneous cooling and heating solves this problem in an energy-efficient manner.

GAS-FIRED, ENGINE-DRIVEN PACKAGED CHILLERS

Gas cooling COPs approaching 2.0 can be achieved by coupling modern gas-engine and compressor technologies. In gas-fired, engine-driven cooling, a natural gas motor rather than an electric motor, drives the compressor (Fig. 4.19, p. 145). The compressor itself can be reciprocating, rotary-screw, or centrifugal. The natural gas engine can also indirectly supply hot water or steam to operate an absorption chiller by using the rejected heat from its cooling and exhaust system.

Although gas-driven chillers have been in use for over 20 years, current models have better performance, lower maintenance requirements, and longer operating lifetimes.

Advances in Engine Technology

Many of the older systems were custom-built using industrial gas engines. Systems of this type have been improved and packaged into compact units offering capacities from 30 to 500 tons.

Some of the latest designs are built around automotive engines which have been modified for continuous operation on natural gas. The advantage of this approach is lower cost—an automotive engine is roughly one-fifth the cost of its industrial counterpart.

Flexibility

Gas-engine-driven cooling systems are quite flexible. They can be configured as water chillers, direct-expansion units, or rooftop

Figure 4.18 ▶ Installing an energy-efficient gas chiller/heater should save this hospital about $20,000 a year in energy bills.

packages. (For example, 15-ton and 25-ton rooftop units are now becoming available.) Such new configurations provide designers with additional energy-efficient ways to cool commercial buildings.

Case Study: Restaurant

One restaurant in the Fuddruckers chain (Fig. 4.20, p. 146) installed two 15-ton gas-fired, engine-driven heater/chillers on the roof to provide heating and cooling. The chiller/heater facility is located in Howard Beach, NY. These units were chosen over gas heating and electric air-conditioning due to rebate incentives and estimated lower operating costs. The system proved effective with a 35% savings in energy costs and an estimated savings of $39,000 over 15 years.

Selection of Gas-fired, Engine-driven Chillers

A gas engine (Fig. 4.21, p. 147) can use less energy than a comparable electric motor. However, these savings must overcome the higher first cost of an engine-based system. Two-year payback was achieved in areas with high electricity costs and using utility subsidies. Substantial operating cost reductions over electric units are not always possible, especially when the comparison is made against electric chillers with efficient part-load operation, such as variable-speed chillers. Further, the cooling tower of an engine-driven chiller is likely to use more energy than that of an electric chiller.

Since engine-driven chillers generate much heat, it is sometimes economical to recover this heat instead of rejecting it through the

Figure 4.19 ▶ Typical Gas-fired, engine-driven packaged chiller with reciprocating engine (*courtesy Trico*).

radiator and/or the cooling tower. Buildings with simultaneous need for cooling and hot water present opportunities for this energy-saving strategy. Hospitals, hotels, and apartment buildings are prime candidates, just as they are for chiller/heater applications. However, the cost of heat recovery could be relatively high and needs to be independently evaluated.

Case Study: Hospital
The Ralph M. Johnson Veterans Administration Medical Center in Charleston, South Carolina, required a new cooling system for 24,000 ft^2 of intensive care and operating rooms. In 1994 the hospital installed a 125-ton

gas-fired, engine-driven chiller to provide the required cooling while reducing the summer peak demand charges for electricity. The cost savings potential was estimated to be in the $8,000 to $12,000 per year by comparison with an equivalent electric chiller. In addition the engine-driven chiller gave extra capacity for the emergency power systems. (Courtesy Tecogen)

Case Study: College
The new Gudelsky Institute for Technology Education is located on the Montgomery College Campus in Rockville, Maryland. In 1992 a 150-ton gas-fired, engine-driven chiller was installed in the central plant to meet the additional load in conjunction with the other existing chillers. The chiller uses an automotive-type engine to power a screw compressor. The output can be modulated down to practically zero. The engine-driven chiller charges an ice storage system during the night. During the day the chiller is used to reduce peak electric demand charges. Finally, recovered engine heat can be used to produce service hot water. The multiple use of the chiller has extended its operation from an estimated 1500 hours to about double that amount. (Courtesy Tecogen)

4.4.4 ▶ Gas-fired Desiccant Dehumidification as Adjunct to Chillers

Desiccants are materials, either solid or liquid, which have affinity for moisture. In effect, they extract water vapor out of the air.

Desiccant dehumidifiers have been used for many years, typically for specialized process-drying, swimming pools, dry-storage pharmaceutical, or supermarket applications as an alternative to mechanical cooling.

Figure 4.20 ▶ Fuddruckers Restaurant, Howard Beach, NY (*courtesy Brooklyn Union Gas*).

Energy Savings

A typical HVAC system dehumidifies by cooling the air below *dew-point* temperature. Once the moisture is extracted, the air is reheated to the desired interior temperature. This reheat operation uses additional energy, and lowers the overall efficiency of the system.

Desiccant air drying can save energy and cost by eliminating the need for reheat. In effect, when using desiccants the compressor sees only the sensible heat load. Often, desiccant dehumidification makes it economical to maintain lower relative humidities than would be practical with a chiller alone. In such instances comfort can be maintained with a higher dry-bulb temperature. For example, 72°F at 55% relative humidity yields about the same comfort as the higher temperature of 75°F at a lower

relative humidity of 50%, obtained with desiccant dehumidification. The chiller size could be reduced helping offset the cost of the desiccant dehumidification unit.

During the past decade, mechanical engineers have been actively specifying gas-fired desiccant dehumidification systems for supermarkets, which need to maintain low humidities in order to avoid frosting of, and therefore the expensive defrosting process for, refrigerated display cases.

Desiccant dehumidification can also reduce the volume of air required for cooling in other applications, such as hospitals, restaurants, hotels, and even office buildings. If the sensible load is not great (e.g., office building in Southern California), the cooling system could operate with 100% outside air, where the outside air is close to the minimum required for

Figure 4.21 ▶ Typical gas-fired, engine-driven packaged chiller with screw compressor (*courtesy Tecogen*).

ventilation purposes. First costs for fans and ducts can be reduced, together with operating costs.

HVAC Components for Desiccant Dehumidification

The central component of desiccant cooling systems is a rotating wheel packed with solid desiccant material (Fig. 4.22). It dries the conditioned air stream, while a second, heated air stream removes and exhausts the absorbed moisture. The required heat may be provided by a natural gas burner or may be recovered from a cogeneration engine.

Case Study: Hotel

The Marriott Courtyard Hotel in West Palm Beach, Florida, uses a gas-fired desiccant dehumidifier unit. The desiccant unit passes moisture-laden outside air over a wheel coated with silica gel. The gel dries the air, which is then cooled by the through-the-wall air-conditioning units and distributed to the hotel. The reverse process occurs with the exhaust air stream. This air is heated by a gas burner and absorbs moisture from the silica gel in the wheel.

According to the Gas Research Institute, during the first year of operation this system maintained relative humidities in the mid-40s in the three-story wing it serves. Another wing, which uses conventional air conditioning, experienced relative humidities in the high 50s.

Case Study: Supermarket

Since 1983 the H.E. Butt supermarket chain in Texas has used desiccant systems to control humidity in several dozen stores. One HEB store in San Antonio, Texas (Fig. 4.23), requir-

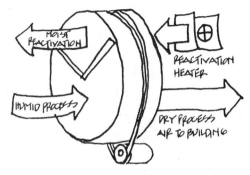

Figure 4.22 ▶ Diagram of desiccant wheel.

ing major remodeling, reduced first costs by installing a new desiccant system to work with the existing HVAC system, rather than replace the entire system. The desiccant system supplies all outside air needed by the stores. The outside air moisture accounts for over 80% of the latent cooling load of the store. This load is removed by the desiccant system before it enters the building. The desiccant system also warms the air as it removes the moisture. This warm air keeps the aisle temperature at comfortable levels, without the need for supplemental heat.

Case Study: Hospital

The Northeast Baptist Hospital in San Antonio, Texas (Fig. 4.24), faced a problem common to many surgical hospitals constructed during the late 1970s and early 1980s. Chang-

ing surgical procedures have forced the original HVAC systems to cool the air more than originally intended. Operating rooms are now maintained at 62 to 65°F instead of 68 to 72°F. At these low temperatures, the original cooling systems cannot control humidity, which rises above the 60% rh maximum required by regulations.

The hospital's designers installed a desiccant system in front of the air handler which supplies outside air to the operating rooms. That ventilation air accounts for over 95% of the moisture load on the operating rooms, so the excess humidity is eliminated before it has a chance to enter the building. Because the desiccant system could be located on the inlet of the make up air unit, nearly all construction was completed while operating rooms remained in use.

Figure 4.23 ▶ **HEB Supermarket in San Antonio, Texas, uses desiccant systems to control humidity (*courtesy Mason-Graut Company, for Munters DryCool*).**

Figure 4.24 ▶ **Northeast Baptist Hospital, San Antonio, Texas (*courtesy Mason-Graut Company, for Munters DryCool*).**

PRACTICAL CONSIDERATIONS FOR GAS-FIRED CHILLERS

Design

- Size the chillers according to ASHRAE/ IES Standard 90.1, Section 9, "Heating, Ventilating, and Air-conditioning (HVAC) Systems." Do not use a safety factor higher than 10% and a thermostat setup recovery factor higher than 5% unless justified by calculations.
- Consider using hourly computer simulations to calculate the peak cooling load, especially for buildings with large glazed surfaces on several surfaces on several orientations. In low-rise buildings account for the cooling effect of ground coupling.

- Study the annual distribution of part-load ratios before specifying chiller type and size. If the chilled water plant is projected to operate for substantial periods of time over the entire spectrum of part loads, two gas-fired chillers, or a combination of electric and gas-fired chillers may be more advantageous than one gas-fired chiller.
- If the peak load occurs in spike shape over a relatively brief time interval, two chillers of unequal size (a larger one and a "topping" one) should also be considered. The topping chiller could be electric or gas-fired.
- Use hourly simulations for the building or campus served by the chiller water plant, to compare the energy use of chillers with different part-load curves.

- Examine heat recovery from engine-driven chillers.
- Plan from the beginning for location of gas exhaust.

Construction
- Commission the chilled water plant at the end of construction.

Operation/Maintenance
- Provide training, maintenance, and operations manuals for building engineering personnel.
- Use automatic controls to supply chilled water at the highest temperature that meets the cooling load.
- Regularly inspect chillers and maintain design operation characteristics.
- Store a supply of important spare parts.

4.5 ► DEVELOPMENTS ON THE HORIZON

The pace of improvement for energy-efficient HVAC equipment continues. Of specific interest is the gas-fired desiccant dehumidification for office buildings.

GAS-FIRED DESICCANT DEHUMIDIFICATION FOR 100% OUTSIDE AIR SYSTEM IN OFFICE BUILDINGS

The concept has been pioneered by Dr. Meckler several years ago, but may find its true application only in the future. Office buildings have relatively low latent loads. These loads are mostly generated by humid outside air. The outside air can be dehumidified by means other than condensation over a chilled water coil, e.g., by a gas-fired desiccant dehu-

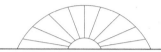

ENERGY-EFFICIENT GAS-FIRED CHILLERS ARE INSTALLED THROUGHOUT THE UNITED STATES

Double-effect Chiller/Heaters
- Caledonia Hospital, Brooklyn, NY
- St. John's Hospital, Queens, New York
- Consolidated Edison Energy Education Center, Long Island City, NY
- Delta Airlines Terminal, LaGuardia Airport, Queens, NY
- SIAC Metro-Tech Center, Brooklyn, NY
- Polytechnic University, Bern Dibner Library and Center for Advanced Technology in Telecommunications, Brooklyn, NY
- Maine College of Art, Portland, ME
- Jewish Museum, New York, NY
- Doral Arrowwood Hotel, Ryebrook, NY
- Campbell Soup Company Headquarters, Camden, NJ
- Four Times Square Tower, New York City, NY
- New York Telephone Building, John F. Kennedy Airport, New York, NY

Engine-driven, Gas-fired Chillers
- The Wyndham-Bristol Hotel, Washington, DC
- Robert Marlin Office Building, Elmsford, NY
- American Airlines Terminal, John F. Kennedy Airport, New York, NY
- Parker Hill Health Care Center, Roxbury, MA
- Crusader Clinic, Rockford, IL
- Brookpark Motor Lodge, Brookpark, OH

midification unit. The dry outside air is then cooled by conventional refrigeration. This air could be sufficient to take care of all sensible loads. The office building would therefore use 100% outside air, with small ducts, low fan energy use, and high efficiency.

The problem in applying such an idea was that sensible loads needed to be small. A decade ago this may have been difficult to achieve. Today, with the integrative design concept, cooling loads can be reduced to a fraction of what they were.

High-performance windows provide sufficient daylight with low shading coefficients. The lighting system achieves densities of 1 w/ft^2 and below. Energy-efficient computers, printers, and faxes further decrease the on-line electricity use from its peak reached in the mid-80s. Together, these measures can

decrease peak cooling by over 50%. Off-peak loads can be even lower through the use of economizer controls that are enthalpy-based.

The system can achieve significant first-cost savings through smaller chillers, ducts, and fans. An additional expense could be the fan-powered boxes needed to ensure at least 1 cfm/ft^2 air movement in occupied areas, since outside air alone may not be delivered at that rate.

Another point in favor of this concept is that current design practice has quadrupled the minimum outside air requirement from 5 cfm/person to 20 cfm/person. In mild climates the amount of outside air needed to remove peak cooling loads will not be very different from that required for ventilation. The 100% outside air system becomes more attractive.

CHAPTER 5

HEAT RECOVERY

5.1 ▶ RENEWED INTEREST IN HEAT RECOVERY

Many heating, cooling, and ventilating processes reject heat, either intentionally or as a side effect.

The idea of recouping at least some of this heat for other useful purposes is not new, but the technology to do so has advanced in recent years. This chapter highlights technical improvements made in air-to-air plate heat exchangers and heat pipes. Improvements in equipment for the recovery of waste heat from electric and from gas-fired, engine-driven chillers are also discussed.

While heat recovery devices are often integrated within other HVAC equipment (chillers, heat pumps, cogeneration engines) the benefits of heat recovery are both distinct and high. For this reason heat recovery is treated separately in this manual.

5.2 ▶ PRINCIPLES OF ENERGY-EFFICIENT HEAT RECOVERY

The concept of heat recovery was formulated in the industrial sector, where for centuries by-product heat from manufacturing processes has been reclaimed to perform other functions. Waste incinerators, for example, often generate process steam or hot water. The recovery of waste heat from buildings is a more recent development.

Principles for Recovery of Building Exhaust Heat

The heat content of air can be classified as *sensible* and *latent*. When sensible heat is added to air, the air temperature increases. When latent heat is added to air, the air becomes more humid but retains the same temperature. This latent heat can eventually result in a change in temperature. If, for instance, the moisture in the air is made to condense on a cool surface, the water vapor releases sensible heat, and increases the air temperature during the transformation from vapor to liquid (also called change of phase).

Evaporation is the reverse of condensation. Water evaporating into the air draws heat from the air (and from the surface on which it is located, if any) to complete the phase change. This lowers the temperature of both air and surface.

Air-to-air plate heat exchangers, heat pipes, and glycol loops reclaim sensible heat

▶ 155

energy from building exhaust and use it to preheat the intake air (see Figs. 5.1, 5.2, and 5.3). Latent heat may be recovered using desiccants, as discussed in Sec. 4.4.4.

The effectiveness with which sensible heat is recovered depends on the temperature differential (ΔT) between the two air streams—intake and exhaust. In winter ΔT varies between 30°F to 50°F for most of the time, and heat recovery is efficient. In summer, however, the ΔT typically ranges only between 10°F and 20°F. Exceptions are hot climates, such as those encountered in Arizona, Nevada, and Southern Texas where ΔT can

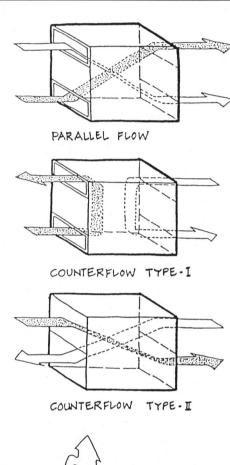

PARALLEL FLOW

COUNTERFLOW TYPE-I

COUNTERFLOW TYPE-II

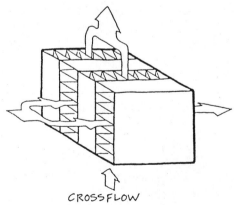

CROSSFLOW

Figure 5.1 ▶ Schematics for air-to-air plate heat exchangers (*courtesy ASHRAE*).

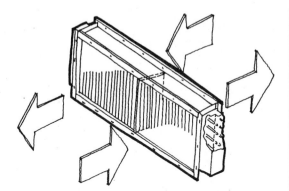

Figure 5.2 ▶ Schematic for heat pipe module (*courtesy ASHRAE*).

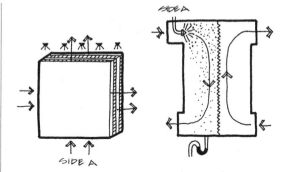

Figure 5.4 ▶ Two types of air-to-air heat exchangers with IDEC (*courtesy Z-Duct*).

remain at 30°F for extended periods. For this reason intake air precooling is rarely effective unless aided by auxiliary measures, such as indirect evaporative cooling (IDEC).

In the IDEC process the exhaust air is directed through side A of the heat exchanger (Fig. 5.4). A water spray deposits moisture on the interior surfaces of the exchanger, and this moisture evaporates into the exhaust air stream until close to saturation. The evaporation lowers the temperature of the metal sheet separating the exhaust and intake air streams, cooling the latter.

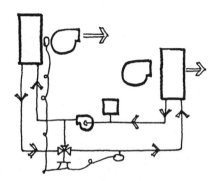

Figure 5.3 ▶ Schematic for glycol loop (*courtesy ASHRAE*).

The IDEC process also can operate by spraying the outside air and cooling the return air. Because it uses evaporation, IDEC is most effective in climates without high humidity in summer. Houston, Texas, for instance, would present challenges to an IDEC application. However, the climate need not be dry in order to use IDEC. Successful applications can be seen in states such as New York, where summer relative humidities are often in the 70 to 80% range.

Another factor influencing the effectiveness of the heat recovery is the magnitude of the contact surface between heat exchanger and air stream. (This surface is always highly conductive.) Most heat exchangers retrieve 45 to 65% of the heat from the exhaust air. Beyond this range the number of plates, fins, or coils of the heat exchangers must substantially increase. The pressure drop across the heat exchanger increases too, and this pressure must be overcome with additional fan power.

Consequently, heat exchangers that have heat transfer efficiencies much beyond 65% could be associated with higher first costs and even with higher operating costs. This issue cannot be resolved by optimizing the heat exchanger only, since the increase in fan energy use caused by the heat exchanger affects the building heating and cooling loads. The best method, for investments that are large enough to justify the engineering, is to perform a whole-building energy simulation based on an hourly computer program such as DOE-2.1.

Applications with high temperature exhaust air and high outside air ratios may justify high heat recovery efficiencies. Hospitals, for example, often maintain winter temperatures of 74 to 78°F and operate entire building wings on 100% outside air. Health clubs, prisons, auditoriums, and even shopping malls offer similar opportunities.

Principles for Recovery of Chiller Waste Heat
Chillers release heat extracted from water. This heat can be recovered and used for space heating or for service hot water.

Electric chillers can recover relatively low-temperature heat from condensers. Service hot water preheat is a typical application.

Figure 5.5 presents a schematic of a chiller. The compressor powers the cycle, heating the refrigerant. Hot refrigerant gas moves to the condenser. The condensation process converts the gas into liquid, releasing heat. This heat is absorbed by the water in the cooling tower loop where it is rejected.

The refrigerant, now liquefied, moves to the evaporator. There it changes phase again, becoming gas. The evaporation process extracts heat from the chilled water circuit, through a heat exchanger. The water, thus chilled, is pumped to cool the building.

A heat recovery electric chiller (Fig. 5.6) can retrieve most of the heat that is otherwise rejected. To this end two condensers are

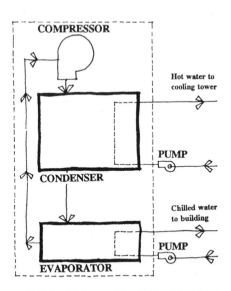

Figure 5.5 ► Schematic of electric chiller.

used, or the condenser circuit is split in two sections. One section recovers heat; the other section still rejects heat through the cooling tower, since a building would rarely need all the heat that can be extracted from the chiller.

Heat in condensers is available from two sources: compressor, which powers the cycle; and evaporator, which extracts heat from the water (chills the water). A chiller with 0.7 kw/ton (COP of 5) extracts 5 Btu in the evaporator for every Btu input into the compressor. Since heat from both compression and evaporation processes are available for recovery, 6 Btu heat could theoretically be retrieved for every 5 Btu of cooling. This would be equivalent to 1.20 Btu recovered heat for every Btu of cooling.

However, the refrigerant-to-water heat recovery in the condenser is only about 95% efficient. As a result, an electric chiller with COP of 5 and with heat recovery delivers

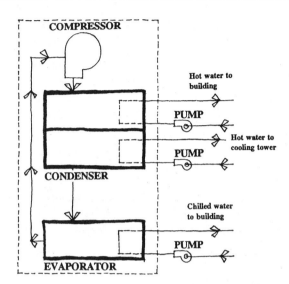

Figure 5.6 ▶ Schematic of electric chiller with heat recovery.

approximately 1.15 Btu of usable heat for every Btu it extracts for cooling purposes.

Less efficient chillers achieve higher ratios of heat recovery, but the improvement is a reflection of higher energy use, not of more effective heat recovery. For example, a chiller with air-cooled condenser may be rated at 0.9 kw/ton (COP of 3.2). The recoverable heat is 4.2 Btu for every 3.2 Btu extracted during cooling. By accounting for a 95% heat recovery efficiency, this chiller can deliver 1.25 Btu of heat for every Btu of cooling.

Direct-fired absorption chillers use heat to power the absorption cycle. This high-temperature heat can be used for both space heating and service hot water. Refer to Chap. 4, HVAC Equipment, for a discussion of this technology.

Specifically, Sec. 4.4.3 contains a description of the absorption cycle and of direct-fired, double-effect chiller/heaters. These units can provide simultaneous cooling and heating, or can reject the heat to a cooling lower when hot water needs are low.

Gas-fired, engine-driven chillers recover heat directly off the engine jacket, engine exhaust, and oil cooler (Fig. 5.7). The high-temperature heat can be used for both space heating and service hot water.

For example, a centrifugal engine may use one or two compressors. The compressors operate at high speed and release heat. The engine is wrapped in a jacket, and water circulates between jacket and compressors. This water cools the compressors by absorbing heat.

The compressors are lubricated with oil. The oil gets heated at high temperatures and this heat is also recovered.

Finally, the exhaust gas has elevated temperature, and a heat exchanger retrieves part of this heat too.

Recent Advances in Heat Recovery

All types of heat recovery equipment used in commercial buildings have been upgraded during the past decade, either through innovation or through assimilation of concepts from the industrial sector. This chapter discusses two areas of change:

- Recovery of building exhaust heat through air-to-air plate heat exchangers and through heat pipes
- Recovery of heat from electric chillers and from gas-fired, engine-driven chillers

As with all HVAC equipment, heat recovery devices function more efficiently not only because of hardware improvements, but also

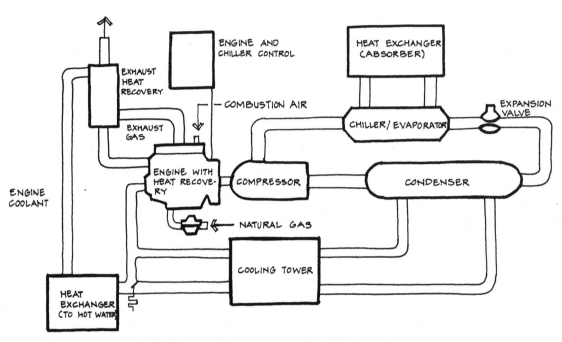

Figure 5.7 ► Gas-fired, engine-driven chiller with heat recovery.

because of better controls. See Chap. 7, HVAC Control Systems.

5.3 ► AIR-TO-AIR HEAT EXCHANGERS

Air-to-air heat exchangers can be defined as devices which transfer heat between air supplied to and air exhausted from a building.

These heat exchangers consist of plates, fins, or coils that extend in both intake and exhaust ducts. In winter, exhaust air is forced through the exchanger and releases some of its heat. The plates, fins, or coils transfer this heat to the intake duct, warming the outside air.

The reverse occurs during summer operation. However, in most U.S. locations, the out-side air temperature is rarely more than 20°F above the exhaust air temperature, and the opportunity for precooling is limited. Indirect evaporative cooling could be used to increase the air-conditioning savings if the outside air is not very humid.

Air-to-air heat exchangers obstruct the air passage through ducts and therefore increase the fan energy use. As a result operation costs during mild and warm weather could actually be higher. Bypass dampers are sometimes installed to circumvent the heat exchangers in spring, summer, and fall. The dampers can be manually adjusted or can be temperature activated. Temperature-activated dampers ensure that the heat exchanger is on-stream only when the temperature differential between incoming and outgoing air is high.

PLATE AIR-TO-AIR HEAT EXCHANGERS

Plate air-to-air heat exchangers are made of several hundred aluminum plates tightly sealed together by a joining method that is usually patented (Fig. 5.8). Intake and exhaust air pass over the plates and exchange heat using several configurations illustrated in Fig. 5.1. The joining method ensures a complete separation of the intake and exhaust air streams, which are virtually free of cross-contamination.

Energy Efficiency

Most plate air-to-air heat exchangers are 45 to 65% efficient, depending on configuration and temperatures of the air stream. Highest heat recovery is obtained in winter, but summer performance can be improved in appropriate climates by using indirect evaporative cooling to the 50 to 70% range. Cold climates and high exhaust air temperatures make these exchangers attractive. High amounts of outside air, typically above 30% of the air delivered to a space, ensure a high level of utilization of the devices, and therefore a shorter payback.

Reliability and Low Cost

Plate heat exchangers are usually selected over fin-tube heat exchangers in most situations where it is important that exhaust air does not mix with intake air. Even for office building applications, plate heat exchangers

Figure 5.8 ▶ A typical plate air-to-air heat exchanger (*courtesy Z-Duct*).

offer greater certainty that the supply of air remains clean.

Installed costs start at about $.75/cfm and are somewhat higher than for glycol loops. However, plate heat exchangers are significantly less expensive than heat pipes, which provide another pollutant-free method to retrieve heat.

Applications

Industrial settings were the original beneficiaries of this technique, but commercial applications now include restaurants and hospitals, as well as specialized functions within any building, such as kitchens, pools, and exercise rooms.

One constraint on the use of plate heat exchangers is the fact that the exhaust and intake air streams must be in proximity so that both can be channeled through the heat exchanger. During design this is not difficult to achieve. Retrofitting existing mechanical rooms is more problematic unless the adjacency between intake and exhaust is already present. Glycol loop heat exchangers are commonly used for remote location of exhaust and intake.

Case-Study: Factory

Sparkomatic, a manufacturer of automotive stereo sound equipment, uses plate air-to-air heat exchangers to recover heat from a waste-burning incinerator at its Milford, PA, headquarters. This supplies enough energy to heat the 60,000 ft² manufacturing and warehousing facilities eliminating the need to operate the existing gas-fired space heaters (2 mm Btu/hr). Payback is calculated at 2 years.

Case Study: Laboratory

The Laboratory of Experimental Medicine and Surgery in Primates of the New York Medical Center (Fig. 5.9) uses plate air-to-air heat exchangers to preheat 2400 cfm outside air supplied to the ape holding and breeding area. According to the manufacturer, the facility reduced its fuel use by 2800 gallons of oil in the first year of operation of the heat exchanger. The estimated payback is 1.5 years.

Case Study: Mid-rise Condo

Camelot, a 21-story condominium in Hackensack Heights, New Jersey (Fig. 5.10), uses plate air-to-air heat exchangers to precondition the supply air to its pool, exercise room, and sauna areas. Air-conditioning requirements are estimated to have decreased by 30% and heating requirements by 75%, yielding energy savings of 39,000 and 139,000 Btu/hr, respectively. Payback is calculated at 2 years.

HEAT PIPES

Heat pipes are simple yet effective devices for thermal energy transfer. The basic concept was developed by General Motors and the Atomic Energy Commission during the 1940s and eventually found its way into commercial buildings during the 1970s as a heat recovery mechanism.

Heat pipes have no moving parts. Physically, a heat pipe is simply a copper tube lined with a wick structure and filled with refrigerant. When one end of the pipe is placed in the exhaust air stream and the other end in the intake air stream, refrigerant vapor circulates within the pipe. In winter the refrigerant transfers heat from the warm exhaust air to the cool intake air. In summer, the cool exhaust air is used to lower the temperature of the intake.

The heat pipe itself has a heat transfer efficiency of 99%, or about 1000 times higher than copper. The entire heat exchanger has a recovery rate of 50 to 70%.

Figure 5.9 ▶ The Primate Lab at the New York Medical Center uses plate air-to-air heat exchangers (*courtesy Des Champs Laboratories, Inc.*).

A typical heat pipe system uses factory-assembled modules (Fig. 5.11) which can be readily installed in ventilation ducts or built into an air handler. Each module consists of an integrated finned heat pipe, and a supporting frame. The frame incorporates a center partition to prevent mixing of exhaust and supply air.

While heat pipes are typically used for intake air preheat, the indirect evaporating cooling (IDEC) system has been introduced to extend their usefulness during the cooling season.

In IDEC/heat pipe installations, a water spraying system wets the pipes on the exhaust side, lowering the temperature of the rejected air through evaporation. The ΔT between intake and exhaust is therefore increased, and cooling-mode operation of the heat exchanger becomes more attractive.

This method, however, requires a relatively plentiful supply of water—which may be a problem in some areas such as Long Island in New York State. Additional costs are associated with water treatment.

Energy Savings
While fairly expensive to install ($.90–$3.25/cfm), heat pipes can significantly reduce HVAC energy requirements of buildings in both winter and summer cycles, recovering 50 to 70% of the exhaust energy. With the addition of IDEC, it is possible to achieve up to 20% cooling energy savings, in comparison with conventional chillers alone.

Other Advantages
Since heat pipes have no moving parts, their maintenance requirements are negligible and operation is silent. Useful life expectancy is over 25 years.

Figure 5.10 ▶ **Camelot Condos in Hackensack, NJ, use plate air-to-air heat exchangers for its health club** (*courtesy Des Champs Laboratories, Inc.*).

Case Study: School Building

A heat pipe heat recovery system was incorporated into the HVAC system of a secondary school in Douglas, NY (Fig. 5.12). The system, which includes indirect evaporative cooling, delivers 210 tons of cooling capacity to the school for about 1/8 the electric power costs of conventional mechanical cooling. During the cooling season, the peak day energy savings are roughly 1.5 million Btu per hour.

PRACTICAL CONSIDERATIONS FOR AIR-TO-AIR HEAT EXCHANGERS

Design

- When selecting air-to-air heat exchanger types, consider that both plate exchangers and heat pipes require proximity of intake and exhaust air streams. For distant locations of the two air streams, glycol loops provide a better solution.
- Optimize the pressure drop across the heat exchanger by considering both heat recovery potential and fan energy use increase.
- Consider providing bypass dampers for heat exchangers that are not specifically designed to precool the intake air. Provide a sensor to signal the position of damper.
- Provide easy access for cleaning heat exchanger surfaces.
- If heat is recovered off heavily polluted exhaust (e.g., industrial, garages) consider providing a gas analyzer and an alarm in intake stream.

Figure 5.11 ▶ A typical heat pipe module.

THE DOUGLAS MIDDLE SCHOOL

Figure 5.12 ▶ A heat pipe IDEC system saves this school about 1.5 million Btu/hr during peak cooling days (*courtesy Quinn/Richardson, P.C.*).

- When considering an IDEC/heat pipe system analyze the potential for evaporative cooling during periods of high demand for the application. Schools are particularly well-suited because they have small cooling requirements in summer, when humidity is high and IDEC is less efficient.
- Consider cost and availability of water for IDEC systems. High water usage may be problematic for some New York areas such as Long Island in New York State.

Construction
- Commission heat exchanger operation.

Operation/Maintenance
- Include maintenance of heat exchangers in the training of personnel and in the operation manual.
- Clean the heat exchanger on a rigorous schedule to avoid infestation with microorganisms.
- If the heat exchanger is designed for preheating only, bypass it at the end of the heating season.

5.4 ▶ HEAT RECOVERY FROM CHILLERS

This section discusses heat recovery from electric and engine-driven chillers. Absorption chillers, which use heat generation as the driving mechanism, are discussed in Chap. 4, HVAC Equipment.

Heat recovery chillers are practical in large commercial buildings, where different zones require simultaneous heating and cooling and where there is high service hot water consumption.

AIR-TO-AIR HEAT EXCHANGERS ARE USED IN MANY BUILDINGS THROUGHOUT THE UNITED STATES

Plate Air-to-Air Heat Exchangers
- IBM Office Building, New York, NY
- Hamilton Park Conference Center, Florham, NJ
- Painesville YMCA, Willoughby, OK
- Children's Hospital, Little Rock, AK
- Federal Courthouse, Greensboro, NC
- Bascom Elementary, Woodstock, GA
- Hammocks Middle School, Miami, FL
- Pleasant Grove Elem., Texarkana, TX
- Rhode Island DOA, Providence, RI

Heat Pipes
- Disney World, Orlando, FL
- U.S. Navy, Norfolk, VA
- Sony Corporation, Dothan, AL
- Sam's Wholesale Club, Nationwide
- Finast Supermarkets, Canton, OH
- Marsh Supermarkets, Indianapolis, IN
- Kentucky Fried Chicken, Biloxi, MI
- University of Miami, Miami, FL
- Giant Supermarkets, throughout Pennsylvania

Prime candidates include offices, hospitals, laboratories, educational complexes, large mixed-use urban centers (retail, hotel, convention), and airport terminals.

HEAT RECOVERY FROM ELECTRIC CHILLERS
As shown in Sec. 5.2 on principles of heat recovery, electric chillers may be equipped

with a double set of condensers; one to reject heat to the environment through a cooling tower, and a second *heating condenser* to recover heat for other purposes. These two-condenser heat recovery chillers are sometimes called *double-bundle* chillers, since some models have two separate condensers (shell and tube bundle) as shown in Fig. 5.13. Manufacturers also offer two separate condenser circuits housed in a common shell.

Energy Efficiency

Refrigerant flows as needed through the second condenser to preheat domestic hot water or to warm portions of the building. Heat recovery chillers deliver roughly 1.15 to 1.25 Btu of heating energy for each Btu of cooling.

However, because of the need to provide relatively high condenser temperatures, the compressor performs more work. For this reason the COP of electric chillers tends to be lowered to some extent by heat recovery.

While heat recovery chillers may use centrifugal, reciprocating, or rotary compressors (see Chap. 4), there are functional differences.

Centrifugal compressors provide the greatest efficiency, but their heat output temperatures are limited to about 110°F to 125°F, mostly appropriate for service hot water preheat. Reciprocating and rotary screw compressors have slightly lower performance, but they can produce hotter output water temperatures, usable for some types of space heating.

Double-bundle chillers may cost about 10% more than standard chillers, but this extra first cost can be amortized in a few years through energy savings if the heat recovered can be used during most of the cooling season.

Case Study: Office Building

The operation of a 3-story, 50,000 ft² office building located in New York City was simulated with the DOE-2.1 program. A double-bundle chiller produced estimated energy savings of 4720 therms over a standard electric chiller.

Case Study: Office Building

The Seafirst Building in Bellevue, Washington, is a 21-story, 390,000 ft² office block (Fig.

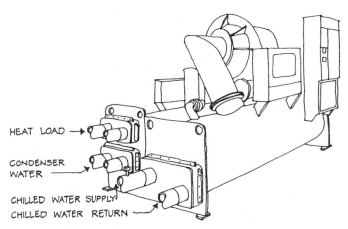

HEAT LOAD →

CONDENSER WATER →

CHILLED WATER SUPPLY

CHILLED WATER RETURN →

Figure 5.13 ▶ A double-bundle heat recovery chiller (*courtesy York International Corp.*).

5.14). The complex is conditioned with a 200-ton reciprocating heat recovery chiller and a 320-ton, high-efficiency centrifugal chiller with ice storage. The heat recovery chiller operates at a heating COP of 3.5 while simultaneously making ice and heating water. According to the Electric Power Research Institute, this facility consumes 31% less energy than a typical building meeting the state energy code, for a total estimated savings of $56,400 per year. Bellevue Place was awarded the Energy Edge Award in 1986.

HEAT RECOVERY FROM GAS-FIRED, ENGINE-DRIVEN CHILLERS

The compressor, powered by a gas engine, sends hot refrigerant gas into the condenser.

There the gas releases heat to the cooling tower circuit and liquefies. The refrigerant then flows into the evaporator. The evaporation process extracts heat from the chilled water circuit through a heat exchanger.

During this cycle the condenser gets heated. In turn, it heats the lubrication fluid. This heat is recovered off the engine jacket, oil cooler, exhaust manifold, and exhaust heat exchanger, yielding about 1 Btu for every 2 Btu of gas input. If all heat recovered were used (a theoretical assumption), the chiller COP could be as high as 2.2.

Multiple Uses for High-Grade Heat

Engine-driven chillers with heat recovery (Fig. 5.15) can deliver hot water at 240°F, sufficient for practically all commercial heating

Figure 5.14 ▶ The Seafirst Office in Bellevue, WA, uses a heat recovery chiller to help save $56,400 a year (*courtesy Bellevue Place, Bellevue, WA*).

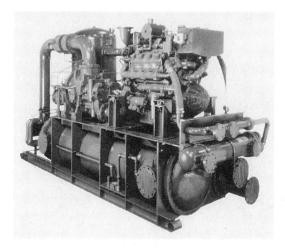

Figure 5.15 ▶ Gas-fired, engine-driven chiller with heat recovery.

applications: space heating, hot water for personnel needs, kitchen, and laundry. Furthermore, hot water at such elevated temperatures can activate existing single-effect absorption chillers or can be effective as preheat in modern double-effect absorption chillers.

For these reasons gas-fired, engine-driven chillers can be effective in hospitals, nursing homes, laboratories, prisons, multifunctional buildings with restaurants and pools, etc.

Advantages and Disadvantages

While these chillers reduce both electric demand and energy use, they cost more than heat recovery electric chillers and are more expensive to maintain.

Air pollution at site may be another consideration. However, total pollution resulting from cooling with electric chillers (e.g., where electricity is generated with oil or coal) is similar to that of gas-fired, engine-driven chillers.

Case Study: Hotel

The 8-story Wyndham-Bristol Hotel in Washington, D.C., was built in 1949 and renovated in 1984 (Fig. 5.16). In 1987 one 150-ton gas-fired, engine-driven chiller was installed to replace an aging 180-ton electric chiller. The waste heat from the unit is used for service hot water.

According to the manufacturer, this recovered heat meets all service hot water needs from May through September.

PRACTICAL CONSIDERATIONS FOR HEAT RECOVERY IN CHILLERS

Design

- Consider heat recovery for chillers in all applications with substantial service hot water needs, or with simultaneous heating and cooling.

  Consider selecting SHW equipment that can use the heat from chillers. For example, in a hospital coordinate the purchase of laundry equipment (steam versus hot water) with the selection of chillers.
- When selecting the type of chiller, consider its potential for heat recovery. This includes electric (lower temperature heat) versus engine-driven (higher temperature heat). Within electric chillers, consider the potential for heat recovery of the centrifugal types (again lower temperature heat) versus rotary and reciprocating types.
- Maximize the effectiveness of heat recovery in electric chillers by optimizing the size of the two condensers, or of the two sections of a split condenser.

Construction

- Commission the heat recovery function of chillers.

**HEAT RECOVERY IN CHILLERS IS USED IN MANY
INSTALLATIONS THROUGHOUT THE UNITED STATES**

Electric Chillers with Heat Recovery
- IBM, Poughkeepsie, NY
- Chemung Canal Bank, Main Office, Elmira, NY
- Southside High School, Elmira, NY
- Rochester Telephone, Rochester, NY
- YMCA, Rochester, NY
- Jewish Home, Rochester, NY
- AETNA, Middletown, CT
- Ralph H. Johnson Veterans Administration Medical Center, Charleston, SC
- ITT, Shelton, CT
- Union Carbide, Bethel, CT
- Bell Laboratories, Piscataway, NJ

Gas-Fired, Engine-Driven Chillers with Heat Recovery
- The Wyndham-Bristol Hotel, Washington, D.C.
- 18-Story Condominium, New York, NY
- The Masonic Home of Florida, a long-term health care center, St. Petersburg, FL
- Green Briar Nursing Center, Miami, FL
- The Armed Services YMCA of Boston, Boston, MA
- Wilma and Harold Good Library at Goshen College, Goshen, IN

Operation/Maintenance
- Provide training and operation manual to building maintenance personnel.
- Periodically clean condensers of electric chillers.
- Check for corrosion of heat exchangers at exhaust of gas-engine chillers.

5.5 ▶ DEVELOPMENTS ON THE HORIZON

While heat recovery concepts and hardware continue to be perfected, the most profound changes are taking place in *system integration*. Chillers have control packages that comprise

Figure 5.16 ▶ The Wyndham-Bristol Hotel, Washington, D.C.

monitoring, fault and safety diagnostics, as well as interfaces into Building Automation Systems. The Building Automation Systems, in turn, often include Energy Management and Control Systems (EMCS).

Since the operation of heat recovery devices consumes energy, it is advantageous to imple- ment this feature at the time when needed, and to the extent to which it is needed. The dissemination of EMCS increases the role of monitoring and control functions within chillers (and heat recovery chillers), and provides impetus for the extension of the functions to air-to-air plate heat exchangers and heat pipes.

CHAPTER 6

COGENERATION

6.1 ► COGENERATION— MORE INTEGRATED, MORE EFFICIENT

Cogeneration—the process of generating both electricity and heat on site—is not new, but until the 1980s was primarily applied to industrial facilities and campuses with demands of 1000 kw or higher.

Now cogeneration is practical for a wide range of commercial buildings. The equipment can be sized more precisely, since computer simulations give a better understanding of the dynamics of heating, hot water, and electrical loads. Cogen packages are easily produced in sizes of 30 kw or even lower. In addition, cogen control systems closely track the electricity and heat output, and help schedule preventative maintenance.

Closer sizing, factory engineering, and field monitoring not only extend the applicability of cogeneration, but also increase its efficiency.

This chapter briefly discusses underlying principles for cogeneration, presents advantages of monitoring and control, and outlines emerging techniques for increased efficiency.

6.2 ► PRINCIPLES FOR ENERGY-EFFICIENT COGENERATION

Cogeneration systems are devices typically powered by gas or diesel oil engines, or by gas turbines. Dual fuel cogeneration units are also available. The equipment produces electricity using a generator, and releases heat in the process. The heat is reused for space heating, service hot water, or absorption cooling, via heat exchangers which are located at the engine jacket and at the manifold of flue and exhaust gas. High temperature cogenerators may produce steam, which can be used directly on site (e.g., laundry, absorption cooling, or process) or can be converted to hot water through a heat exchanger.

For most applications involving one building the cogeneration system is "packaged," that is, preengineered and preassembled in a factory. Most manufacturers offer natural gas-powered packaged cogeneration systems in the 30 to 600 kw size range (Fig. 6.1). In addition, there are smaller "microsystems" ranging from 4 to 25 kw (Fig. 6.2). Designed to minimize engineering and field installa-

COGENERATION—MORE INTEGRATED, MORE EFFICIENT

- Packaged cogeneration reduces engineering and field installation costs. Typical systems range from 30 to 1000 kw, with most experience obtained in the 60 to 600 kw range.
- Systems with as little as 4 kw generating capacity have also been produced.
- Multiple cogeneration modules achieve high part-load utilization and are proven to save energy.
- Applications for cogeneration now include offices and restaurants, in addition to the more traditional installations for hospitals, nursing homes, and multifamily buildings, and, of course, campuses and industrial complexes.
- The appeal of cogeneration has been increased by using the heat output in summer for absorption and desiccant cooling.
- Microprocessor control and remote monitoring increase the reliability and efficiency of cogeneration units.

tion costs, many of these smaller modules can be put on line in just a few days with little or no interruption of service. All packaged cogen systems now benefit from advanced controls that improve reliability and save energy.

Operation of Cogeneration Systems

The cogen system may be designed to track (match) either the thermal or the electric load of the building. In thermal tracking the cogenerator is usually sized to carry baseload heating and/or hot water, with a supplemental boiler to meet peak demand. As heat and hot water requirements decrease, some of the cogenerated heat is rejected through radiators or cooling towers. If the need for heat becomes low the cogenerator may be shut off.

Thermal tracking is typically used in small and medium-size applications, up to 1000 kw. Cogen systems below 100 kw are increasingly attractive, since small buildings tend to pay higher utility rates than large industrial or commercial users.

Electricity tracking is a strategy where the cogenerator supplies baseload power needs. Peak demand is met with the help of grid electricity. Again, low heating/hot water needs may trigger a shutoff sequence. Electricity tracking is typically used in large installations, common for industrial users or campuses.

Peak-shaving cogeneration is not employed often because the engines and turbines operate most cost effectively when they run for long periods of time.

Energy-Efficient Cogeneration Systems

The key to energy-efficient cogeneration lies in finding a use for most of the recovered heat.

Gas and diesel engines usually generate electricity with a 30 to 35% efficiency. Gas turbine generating efficiency is generally lower than that of an engine, ranging from 20 to 35%. However, the percentage of recoverable heat in a turbine installation is greater, and the heat is also of a higher quality (hotter)

Figure 6.1 ▶ Factory-assembled (packaged) cogeneration system (*courtesy Tecogen, Inc.*).

than that from an engine—800°F or more, compared with about 250°F heat from an engine jacket. Gas turbines are generally used in large applications, above 1000 kw.

While cogeneration produces electricity at only about 30% efficiency, heat recovery can boost the overall system efficiency up to 70%. In contrast, purchased electricity is also produced at about 30% efficiency, but there is rarely an opportunity to use the heat from a central power plant.

Since heat recovery is essential to the effectiveness of a cogeneration system, applications are restricted to facilities characterized by year-round, simultaneous need for both electric power and heat. Buildings need heat for a variety of purposes, including space heating, service hot water (SHW), absorption cooling, or process. Hospitals, prisons, colleges with dormitories, hotels, multifamily residences and, increasingly, restaurants are typical candidates.

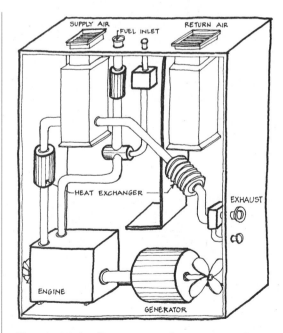

Figure 6.2 ▶ Prototype microcogen unit (*courtesy Tecogen, Inc.*).

Small installations may be designed solely to meet SHW needs—especially when laundries and kitchens are present—since SHW is usually produced in constant amounts year-round. If space heating is also covered, summer operation may be less efficient unless some of the heat can help reduce cooling needs. This may be achieved by combining cogeneration with absorption cooling or desiccant dehumidification. However, absorption cooling requires high temperature hot water or steam.

Economic Feasibility

Cogeneration systems are relatively expensive to procure and maintain—about $1000 to $1500 per kw installed and $.01 to $.015 per kwh maintenance. For this reason, it is important that the thermal load be closely matched with the needs of the facility and that maintenance be minimized. Better control systems, presented on the following pages, have helped the efficiency and reliability for cogeneration units.

Obstacles to Cogeneration

The increased use of cogeneration is hampered by three obstacles: concern over local pollution, concern over maintenance costs, and difficulty in providing cost-effective engineering for small installations. The first two issues are technical in nature and can be addressed by today's technology. The design issue is institutional.

When a building needs a boiler or chiller, the design path is predictable, the cost foreseeable, and the engineering time relatively short. A cogeneration system, in contrast, requires first a feasibility study which examines the matching of electricity and heat loads, and which selects a size range for the cogeneration unit. This study can be expen-sive and the results are not guaranteed, unless the firm has significant experience in cogeneration, allowing it to predict in advance the probable results.

Given the cost of the study, it is rarely cost effective to specify one 20 kw or even one 60 kw unit. As a result, small cogeneration applications are infrequent. However, the case can be made that a small unit in a medium building will run more hours at peak capacity and therefore will be more cost effective. Small units can also open numerous opportunities in small buildings. There is a need for a simple guide on cogeneration for small buildings, to eliminate the feasibility study. Such a guide could be based on a synthesis of numerical studies and could be sponsored by professional societies or by manufacturers.

6.3 ► ADVANCED MONITORING AND CONTROL TECHNIQUES

Cogeneration equipment includes three main subsystems: engine or turbine, electricity generator, and heat exchanger. The orchestration for optimum performance requires close monitoring and control.

If system components get damaged, peak- and part-load performance suffer and the maintenance time increases. This, in turn, leads to fewer hours of operation and longer payback time. Cogen manufacturers have addressed these issues during the last decade, and have increased both the efficiency and the reliability of their equipment.

By being more reliable, today's cogen systems are specified more often. When installed they deliver predictable savings.

CONTROLS FOR HIGH RELIABILITY AND EFFICIENCY

Reliability

Microprocessor-based control systems take readings from several sensors within the cogen system to enact an automatic shutdown if damage to the unit appears likely. Monitoring is performed via remote data links.

For example, the temperature in the hot water return line is compared to a predetermined setpoint. The cogeneration unit is shut down if this setpoint is exceeded, avoiding engine and building overheating. A warning message appears on the EMCS monitor of the facility, and, if applicable, on the monitor of the shared energy savings company that has installed the system.

Shutdown occurs when sensors indicate low water level, low oil level, and low oil pressure.

If the system produces steam, shutoff occurs at pressures too high or too low.

Irregular engine operation (too high or too low speed), power failure, and electricity output beyond design parameters (e.g., voltage too high or too low) also causes shutdown.

Because of such safety features and of effective display and alarm functions, modern cogeneration systems have considerably reduced maintenance downtime. Most systems operate 20,000 to 25,000 hours before requiring any major overhaul. The condition of cogen subsystems is also better. As a result, the energy efficiency has improved.

Energy Efficiency

Advanced cogeneration systems modulate the electricity and heat output. For example, a gas engine cogeneration unit could operate an absorption chiller (Fig. 6.3).

At maximum thermal load all heat from the cogen unit is reused. As the load decreases, the jacket hot water is modulated, with some of the heat being redirected to a radiator. Next, the hot water obtained from exhaust gas is reduced. Should the heat output decrease below a setpoint—sometimes chosen at 10%—the cogen unit is turned off.

When most of the heat is rejected, the radiator or cooling tower fans work at full capacity. However, if the need for thermal output is high, two-speed or variable-speed fans reduce the electricity use.

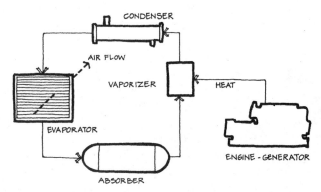

Figure 6.3 ▶ Diagram of cogeneration and absorption cooling (*courtesy Waukesha*).

One manufacturer offers an option for *electricity modulation* in steam cogen. The unit has an additional compressor which can boost steam pressure (e.g., for laundry). When the compressor is operated, it uses some of the electricity which was previously supplied to the building. Consequently, the unit can operate efficiently during periods of decreased electricity demand but increased thermal demand.

Case Study: Hospital

The Resurrection Medical Center (Fig. 6.4) in Chicago, IL, uses two 725 kw cogeneration modules to shave the electric demand beyond 2400 kw. The 10,000 lb/hr steam provides heat during winter and runs a 550-ton absorption chiller during summer. Since its installation in May 1989 the cogeneration system has been providing 80% of the electricity, resulting in over 30% savings in the electric bill and $400,000 in demand costs. The payback period is four years.

Case Study: School

The 200,000 ft^2 Waverly High School, located in Waverly, NY, was built in the 1960s. It has a population of one thousand students, educators, and administrators. Until 1990 the facility was all electric. A packaged, modular, gas-fired cogen system (Fig. 6.5) was then designed by Francis Harper of Hunt Engineers & Architects. The cogen plant consists of 5 modules, 75 kw each. The modules can also use LP gas as fuel, to confer added flexibility in purchasing. The electricity generated from the cogen plant is used for lighting, plug loads, fans, and pumps. The hot water is pro-

Figure 6.4 ► **Resurrection Medical Center in Chicago uses two packaged cogeneration modules (*courtesy Resurrection Health Care Corporation*).**

duced at a rate of 470,000 Btu/hr. This water is piped to new hydronic radiation in winter and to a new 125-ton absorption chiller in summer. Since the chiller is single-effect, it can use the low-temperature water produced by the cogeneration units. The cogeneration plant saved $309,000 during its first 3 years of operation, exceeding the more conservative prediction of the designers. It received the 1993 New York State Governor's Award for Energy Excellence.

PRACTICAL CONSIDERATIONS FOR COGENERATION IN SMALL- AND MEDIUM-SIZE APPLICATIONS

Design
- Clearly determine the goal for the cogeneration system: baseload thermal demand, baseload electric demand, peak thermal demand, peak electric demand, or shortest payback period.

Often, tracking of the thermal base load results in the lowest life-cycle cost. However, depending on economic parameters such as fuel and electricity costs, financing terms, and cost of maintenance contracts, a larger cogeneration system may result in a shorter payback period.

- Strategies that reduce the peak electric demand are sometimes justified by the structure of electricity rates. For example, a hospital which receives low rates in exchange for reducing the demand when requested by the electric utility could use a generator or a peak-shaving cogen unit. The cogen has higher effi-

Figure 6.5 ▶ Packaged, modular, gas-fired cogen system installation at Waverly Junior/Senior High School, Waverly, NY (*courtesy Tecogen*).

ciency through the utilization of thermal load, and can be used more often because it is more economical.

- Size the cogeneration unit to minimize the amount of heat rejected. When possible, provide controls to modulate electric and thermal output.
- Provide the full complement of controls and monitoring options. This cost will be quickly recovered in avoided downtime and repairs.
- Consider modular cogeneration units for facilities with widely varying thermal loads.
- Consider measures to minimize local pollution.

Construction
- Commission the cogeneration unit, including emergency response and operation at low part-load.

Operation/Maintenance
- Perform preventative maintenance.
- Preserve low level of pollution through clean fuel burning.

6.4 ► DEVELOPMENTS ON THE HORIZON

Future cogeneration systems could be integrated with other energy equipment, including heat pumps, desiccant dehumidifiers, thermal storage, and fuel cells.

COGENERATION AND HEAT PUMPS
Cogen can be effectively integrated with electric heat pumps. Heat from the cogeneration unit is fed into the heat pump loop

EXAMPLES OF COGENERATION SYSTEMS FOR SMALL AND MEDIUM APPLICATIONS

Up to 100 kw Total
- Grenadier Housing, New York, NY
- Catholic Field Nursing Home, Westchester, NY
- Drew University, Madison, NJ
- Microfab, Amesbury, MA
- Harvard University, Blodgett Pool, Cambridge, MA
- Arden Wood Bencoolent Association, San Francisco, CA

Up to 300 kw Total
- Taunton High School, Taunton, MA

Up to 500 kw Total
- Yonkers Memorial Hospital, Yonkers, NY
- Eger Nursing Home, Staten Island, NY
- Seco-Warwick, Co., Meadville, PA
- Waverly High School, Waverly, NY

Up to 1000 kw Total
- Dresser Industrial Instruments Division, Stratford, CT
- University of Richmond, Richmond, VA

Up to 1000 kw per Module
- New York University, New York, NY
- New York Telephone, New York, NY
- Resurrection Medical Center, Chicago, IL
- Chicago Art Institute, Chicago, IL

or stored for nighttime use. Cogenerated power is used to reduce building peak demand, which improves overall system cost effectiveness. Such an arrangement would, however, only be cost effective in buildings with significant heating requirements during the hours of peak electrical demand.

COGENERATION AND DESICCANT COOLING

Cogenerated heat can also be used to regenerate the liquid in desiccant dehumidifiers, in systems where the sensible cooling is performed by a chilled water plant, and where the latent cooling is provided by desiccants. Supermarkets are prime candidates for this approach, but the strategy can be effective for other building types as well. For example, one prototypical cogen/desiccant installation in a Long Beach, California, office building reduced its energy costs by 31%.

COGENERATION AND FUEL CELLS

Finally, fuel cell systems may eventually offer excellent performance for combined heat and power generation. Originally developed for use in spacecraft as battery substitutes, fuel cells can produce both electricity and high temperature heat, by converting chemical energy to electrical energy and vice versa. These cells can also store electrical energy longer and more efficiently than batteries, and can be repeatedly charged and discharged without performance degradation.

In operation, fuel cell capsules are charged by a cogeneration system during periods of low electrical demand, and then discharged when demand is high. This allows the cogenerator to operate almost continuously at high efficiency, and minimizes the need to purchase outside power. Both electric and heat energy from the fuel cells, of course, can be put to a variety of uses.

CHAPTER 7

HVAC CONTROL SYSTEMS

7.1 ▶ ADVANCES IN ALL AREAS OF EQUIPMENT CONTROL

Today, almost all commercial buildings rely on some form of electronic control to manage the operation of their mechanical and electrical systems.

Much of the advanced HVAC equipment discussed in this manual simply could not function without modern controls. Modular boiler systems, for example, use electronic controllers for sequencing instructions, and some chillers owe their high efficiency to variable speed control and to "soft" startup.

At a higher level, energy monitoring and control systems allow centralized management of dispersed mechanical equipment, and can govern whole building control strategies such as demand control and limit.

This chapter examines controls which offer significant energy-saving benefits to HVAC equipment such as boilers and chillers, and to distribution systems such as fans and pumps. System integration advan-

tages, at both zone and whole building level, are also examined.

7.2 ▶ CONTROL STRATEGIES FOR ENERGY-EFFICIENT OPERATION OF HVAC SYSTEMS

Because the usefulness of a controller is largely determined by its programming, it is more appropriate to think of the controls discussed in this chapter as strategies, rather than discrete components.

Four basic control methods are typically used to improve the efficiency of HVAC systems: optimization of equipment performance, load tracking, load anticipation, and systems integration.

OPTIMIZATION OF EQUIPMENT PERFORMANCE

As discussed in Chap. 4, HVAC equipment operates over a wide range of part-load conditions, and electronic controls determine to a

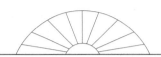

ADVANCES IN ALL AREAS OF HVAC
EQUIPMENT CONTROL

- Oxygen trim controls in boilers optimize the combustion process and reduce fuel use by 2 to 7%.
- Multiple boiler systems achieve fuel savings of 10 to 20% over single boilers by operating at higher part-load ratios.
- Temperature controls for service hot water save between 20 to 30% by tracking use patterns.
- Variable speed drive and multiple-compressor chillers achieve high performance at mid-range part-load ratios, with 10 to 20% savings over many single-speed, single-compressor chillers.
- Fans and pumps with variable speed controls use 10 to 30% less electricity than their constant speed counterparts.
- Occupancy sensors control local cooling, heating, and ventilation.
- Energy monitoring and control systems optimize the interaction between HVAC, lighting, fire, safety, and other systems.

great extent the efficiency with which these part-loads are met. For example, boiler combustion efficiency can be increased by modulating the air/fuel mixture according to demand, and centrifugal chillers may change their speed to match cooling loads.

Increases in equipment operating efficiency, although important, address only one facet of the energy use in buildings. Load tracking and load anticipation are equally important to reduce energy use.

LOAD TRACKING

Load tracking ensures that the equipment responds to real space conditioning needs. For instance, some boilers can modulate their burner output to deliver heat according to demand. Outside temperature sensors could give a satisfactory indication of the demand for heat. However, the load on the boiler is calculated with higher precision if hot water flow, and hot water supply and return temperatures are monitored. The firing rates can thus be adjusted more closely and greater energy savings are obtained.

Load tracking is essential because it provides heating and cooling to the HVAC equipment. However, in large buildings and on campuses even a precise measurement of the load at the central plant may not be sufficient, since this load reflects past conditions in the occupied zones. By the time the HVAC equipment alters its operation, and these changes affect the heat delivered to or extracted from a space, the needs of that space may be already different. Load anticipation techniques are being developed to respond to this problem, and to achieve energy savings at a global level.

LOAD ANTICIPATION

Load anticipation is a more sophisticated form of load tracking, in which the computer records building operating data, examines them for patterns and, based on these patterns, learns to anticipate future events. Sometimes the prediction is fine-tuned by corroborating past energy use with weather readings (e.g., air temperature, solar radiation).

For example, a hot water controller in a hotel might "decide" to increase hot water temperatures every morning only from 7 a.m. to 9 a.m., after having observed repeated heavy demand during those hours—since this is when most of the guests take their showers.

Other mechanical equipment can be similarly controlled. For instance, optimum fan start may be predicted according to occupancy patterns *and* to outside air/inside air temperature recordings over the past 6 hours. System recovery time might also have been "learned" and utilized as an additional prediction tool.

SYSTEMS INTEGRATION

Systems integration is the final and most complex step in decreasing energy use in buildings. Here the HVAC system does not simply comply to demands for space conditioning. Rather, a central Energy Monitoring and Control System (EMCS) assesses the interaction between the HVAC system and other systems, such as lighting and office equipment (Fig. 7.1).

Systems integration through controls introduces a need for hierarchy and optimization of dynamic interrelationships.

For example, in a space with daylighting controls and movable shades there is an optimal relationship between the reduction in

Figure 7.1 ▶ **Components of the Energy Monitoring and Control System** (*courtesy Johnson Controls*).

lighting energy use, because of natural light, and the increase in cooling, because of solar gains. A more common situation is encountered in spaces where the temperature is allowed to float during summer nights. The pre-cool period is best determined through an optimization which accounts for the mass of the building, the maximum space temperature allowable over night, and the air temperature during the past few hours.

To solve such complex problems, much research activity is devoted to inserting Expert System routines into EMCS software. Although the effort expended on systems integration is high, the potential for energy use reduction is equally substantial.

The following sections examine practical applications of HVAC controls from simple burner output modulation to chiller plant optimization, and to the complex integration strategies discussed above.

7.3 ▶ BOILER CONTROLS

Boilers can be equipped with microprocessors which control air-fuel mixtures, firing rates, water temperatures, and various other parameters, in response to changing system loads, to variations in outside air temperature, or to switches in fuel types.

For multiple boiler systems, the controllers also coordinate the operation of individual boilers to improve total system performance under part-load conditions.

7.3.1 ▶ Control Strategies for Efficient Boiler Operation

As discussed in Chap. 4, the energy performance of boilers continues to improve, as measured by their rising Annual Fuel Utilization Efficiency (AFUE). Some equipment for mid-size commercial buildings is now rated at up to 95% AFUE, though anything over 85% is traditionally considered efficient.

Essentially, boilers are heat conversion and transfer devices which operate in an environment where the demand for heat varies continuously. Thus, strategies to improve boiler efficiency include optimizing the combustion process, maximizing the percent of heat transferred to the working fluid, reducing standby and piping system losses, and matching heat output with heat demand.

Maximum combustion efficiency results when virtually all fuel is consumed in the combustion chamber, with little heat wasted up the stack. This requires careful regulation of the air/fuel mixture introduced to the combustion chamber, and exact timing of ignition and exhaust.

Any heat loss reduction from the boiler system saves energy. This is achieved through better insulation and through improved heat exchangers, but also by controlling water temperatures in response to a decrease in heating demand.

Finally, load tracking is of critical importance for fuel economy. Overheating can be prevented by delivering hot water at the minimum temperature required by the load. The boiler plant can respond to such fluctuations in demand by using electronically staged modular boilers, each operating close to full capacity, or variable flame boilers.

Section 7.3.2 discusses applications of these energy-efficient control strategies for boiler systems.

7.3.2 ▶ Control Applications for Boilers

OXYGEN TRIM CONTROL
Modern oxygen trim systems can be installed to improve boiler combustion efficiency.

These systems monitor the oxygen content in boiler flue gases, and then regulate the volume of the incoming combustion air to maintain an optimal air/fuel ratio.

Improved Combustion Efficiency

By automatically adjusting the air/fuel ratio, typical boiler efficiencies can be usually improved by 2 to 7% or more.

To operate at peak efficiency, boilers require the correct blend of air and fuel. If there is too little air, the fuel burns incompletely; with too little fuel, burner temperatures and thermal output decrease.

Traditionally, air/fuel mixtures are preset by technicians during routine maintenance. While this approach ensures reasonable efficiency for average conditions, performance suffers with shifts in operating loads, burner condition, and fuel characteristics. It is not uncommon for a boiler to start the heating season well tuned and to have its performance significantly degraded by spring.

Components of Oxygen Trim Systems

Oxygen "trim control" systems have three primary components: a sensor probe, a trim control analyzer (Fig. 7.2), and a mechanical interface which operates the incoming air damper (Fig. 7.3). Typically, the probe consists of a zirconium-oxide sensor permanently mounted in the boiler flue stack. The sensor produces a low-voltage electric signal which varies with the amount of oxygen detected.

This signal is transmitted to a trim-control analyzer unit. The analyzer compares it with prerecorded, optimal data and orders the necessary air supply adjustments. Some analyzers can be programmed to accommodate either gas or oil fuel.

Precise oxygen trim systems analyze both oxygen and carbon dioxide flue-gas content.

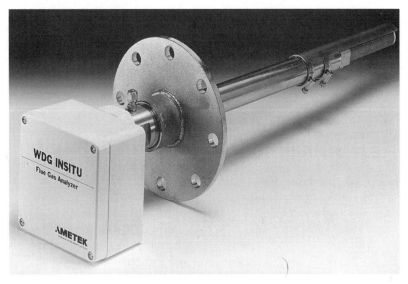

Figure 7.2 ▶ Flue-gas analyzer probe (*courtesy Ametek*).

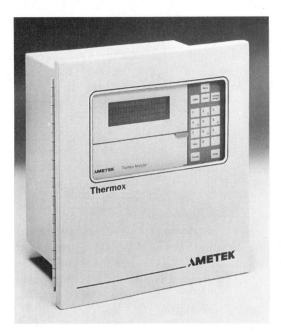

Figure 7.3 ▶ Combustion air trim system (*courtesy Ametek*).

However, these systems are expensive and generally used only for large applications of over 25 million Btu/hour or about 750 hp. Simple oxygen sensor equipment can return most of the potential fuel savings at a fraction of the cost.

The most advanced units use *adaptive control* strategies to anticipate load swings and to preadjust the dampers for performance optimization. These "smart" analyzers record data on building HVAC operation, detect patterns, and "learn" to anticipate certain conditions of occupancy and thermal loading.

Applications

Hospitals, schools, shopping centers, apartment complexes, and hotels with central boilers can all benefit from the installation of an oxygen trim installation. Because these systems cost from $5000 to $15,000 to install, they are generally considered cost-effective for boilers larger than 3.5 million Btu/hr or about 100 hp. In many cases, the initial system costs can be recovered through fuel savings in 1 to 3 years.

Case Study: Hospital

The steam boilers in the Johnston Willis Hospital, in Richmond, Virginia, were equipped in 1987 with oxygen trim controllers. Efficiency of the two, 6900-pound-per-hour, dual-fuel boilers was improved by 7 to 8%, and maintenance time was cut in half. Fuel savings were sufficient to pay back the $19,000 investment in control equipment in just 16 months.

BURNER FLAME CONTROL

Traditionally, boiler water temperatures were maintained by burner cycling, i.e., by turning the flame on and off as needed. A more energy-efficient procedure, made possible by the introduction of microprocessor-based controls (Fig. 7.4), involves starting the burner at low fire, and then increasing its firing rate only according to demand. Operating boiler efficiency is increased by 5 to 15% or more, depending on how oversized the boiler is and how much the load varies. Highest savings are associated with extended service at low part-load.

Cost and Payback

Equipment cost for burner flame control is relatively modest, usually less than $2000, and can often be recovered in the first year of operation.

Figure 7.4 ▶ Typical boiler controller capable of modulating burner flame (*courtesy Honeywell, Inc.*).

Case Study: Medical Center

The Kaiser Permanente Medical Center in Los Angeles, CA, uses a boiler control system that modulates the firing. The control system also monitors the operation of the two 350 hp boilers via a link to a microcomputer. A separate oxygen trim system adjusts the oxygen level and activates an alarm when this level drifts beyond the optimum range.

DEMAND-SENSITIVE WATER TEMPERATURE CONTROL

These microprocessor controllers can be thought of as thermostats with microchips. They operate by lowering the water temperature during off-peak periods, in order to avoid overheating of the building, or of the service hot water.

These controllers monitor water temperature several times per minute at two or three points: on outbound hot water pipes, on hot water return pipes, and sometimes at the storage point (Fig. 7.5). The data are then analyzed to determine the optimum water temperature setpoint.

The most advanced systems use adaptive control strategies. They record energy consumption over time and examine the use patterns to anticipate load changes. While it is ideal to have a full year of data in the microprocessor's memory, two to three months are sufficient to start improving the performance of the heating or hot water system. The data are weighed differently in the decision-making logic, with information from the past few days receiving the highest weight. The goal is to ensure that sufficient thermal energy is always available, without having to produce an excess. Such close "tracking" of energy supply and demand is impossible with purely responsive systems. Savings of 20 to 30% can be achieved.

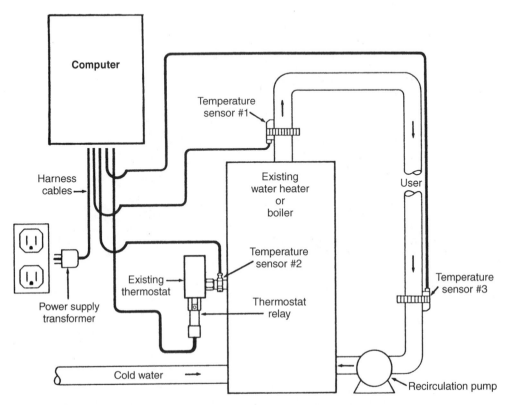

Figure 7.5 ► **Schematic layout for demand-sensitive water temperature control (*courtesy Pro-Temp*).**

Applications

Demand-sensitive water temperature control is particularly effective for hotels, multifamily buildings, hospitals, and other similar occupancies which have widely varying, but predictable demands for hot water. As Fig. 7.6 shows, most hot water recirculating systems with constant water temperature settings are not very efficient, because in an effort to meet the day's heaviest demand for hot water, they keep the water unnecessarily hot at all times.

As a result, hot water systems with controlled temperature adjustment can yield substantial energy savings over their constant temperature counterparts.

Case Studies: Hotels

The Green Tree Marriott Hotel of Pittsburgh, Pennsylvania, installed a water heater controller in 1986. At the end of a six-week test period, energy savings averaged 33% or $1300. The control unit cost about $4000 and paid for itself in less than one year through energy savings.

The 225,000 ft^2 Dulles Airport Marriott in Washington, D.C., as shown in Fig. 7.7, installed in 1992 a water heater controller for its 4 million Btu gas-fired boiler for service hot water (SHW). The boiler has a high/low flame control. It serves an SHW loop with 25 gpm recirculation and 3500 gallons storage.

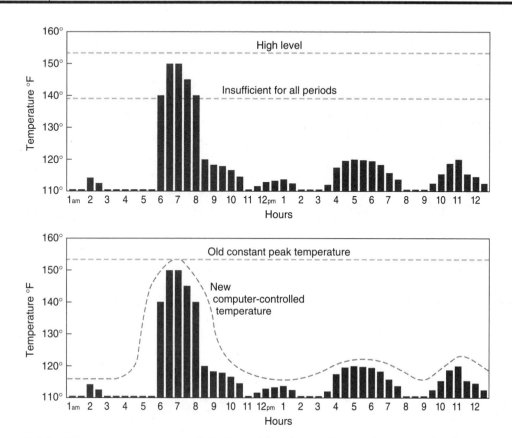

Figure 7.6 ▶ Water temperature modulation with a demand-sensitive controller (*courtesy Pro-Temp*).

The controller adjusts the water temperature from its former 135°F setting to lower temperatures, as indicated by the data received from supply and return water several times per minute. The water temperature setting also depends on historical data recorded by the controller. During the first summer of operation, the controller saved over 25% of the gas formerly needed for SHW (i.e., over $6000 savings). Payback is below one year.

Case Study: College Dormitory
La Grange College, in Georgia, reduced heating bills in four of its dormitories by approxi-mately 20% after installing a reset controller system. Prior to the installation, water temperatures had been maintained at a constant 150°F, to ensure that an adequate supply of hot water was available when needed. Once the controllers were operating, water temperatures were automatically reduced, ranging from 105 to 130°F—always just high enough to meet the demand.

WATER RESET CONTROL BASED ON OUTDOOR TEMPERATURE
Boiler system efficiency can be measurably improved by lowering the supply water tem-

Figure 7.7 ► Marriott International Hotel, Dulles Airport (*courtesy Marriott Corporation*).

perature setpoint as the outside air becomes warmer and less heating is required. An external sensor informs the controller of the outside air temperature. The hot water temperature is monitored by a sensor in the supply header or hot water manifold. The controller changes the hot water supply temperature according to the outside air temperature. While the technology is well established and used, it should be considered more often because of the large energy savings it provides at low first cost.

Energy Savings
Water temperature reset reduces fuel consumption by decreasing heat loss from unnecessarily hot water in boilers and distribution piping. There is also less space overheating. Typical fuel savings of 5 to 15% can be achieved. The method is less efficient than the demand-sensitive hot water temperature control previously discussed for the following reason.

Most modern buildings have relatively high internal heat gains from lighting, office equipment, and elevators. Additionally, as the envelope thermal integrity increases, the fraction of solar heat retained rises too. Windows and vision panels, for example, achieve overall R-values of 3 to 6, compared to R-2 only a decade ago. Air retarders practically eliminate air infiltration in perimeter zones. The heat load is therefore less coupled to the outside air temperature.

Since heating demand cannot be closely predicted based on the outside air temperature readings, a certain amount of overheating still occurs. (This overheating is substantially reduced with the demand-sensitive controls.)

Components
This system is very simple: An outdoor air temperature sensor transmits a low voltage electric signal to a controller, which adjusts the setting for hot water temperature. Many boilers now come with this proven technology built in. Some even incorporate a sensor for return water temperature, to further fine-tune the reset of supply water temperature.

Applications

Because of its limitations, the water temperature reset control is best used in buildings with large envelope-to-floor area ratios, and where solar gain is not high. The return water temperature sensor makes it attractive for a wider range of buildings. Its low cost and simplicity makes the technique worth considering for situations where more advanced controls are either too expensive or too difficult to operate by maintenance personnel.

Case Study: Office

DOE-2.1 simulations on a four-story, 55,800 ft² office building located in Hartford, CT, show that the outdoor water temperature reset can reduce the gas consumption in heating by 16%. At $.80/ccf this is equivalent to $3500 per year.

Case Study: University

Kutztown University in Kutztown, PA, uses a 781 point energy monitoring and control system incorporating, among others, a boiler water reset function. Expected payback for the entire system was calculated at two years.

Case Study: Hotel

Days Inn, a 216-room hotel facility in New Orleans has been saving about 25% on monthly heating and hot water bills by using a water temperature reset controller.

CONTROLS FOR MULTIPLE BOILERS

The general operation and benefits of multiple boiler systems were described in Chap. 4. Essentially, an array of small modular boilers allows more efficient part-load operation than a single large boiler operating in a high-low-off mode. Modular boilers are turned on and off as needed, each operating closer to peak capacity and thus at higher efficiency.

The boiler control algorithms are typically based on hot water temperature. Some use the water temperature reset control based on outside air temperature to improve efficiency.

The more advanced controllers allow reprogramming to optimize the control sequences for particular buildings and to adjust for changing base conditions (e.g., new building uses). Most controllers that serve modular boilers change boiler sequencing from one operating cycle to the next, in order to ensure uniform wear on the equipment.

Many controllers also monitor boiler operating hours and reschedule their sequencing as necessary. This technique is even more effective in equalizing system wear, ensuring consistent operating efficiency, and also facilitates the scheduling of maintenance at regular, predictable intervals.

Example of Operation Strategy

The particular unit shown in Fig. 7.8 allows the simultaneous control of eight boilers and programming of up to 14 variables, depending upon operating requirements. It automatically resets the supply water setpoint as outdoor air temperature changes, and increases or decreases the number of operating boilers as required to maintain the desired supply water temperature.

Systems Components and Cost

Multiple boiler systems are made practical by microcomputer control algorithms that determine which boilers fire, for how long, and in what sequence. In most instances these controllers are locally based with the boiler system, but they can also be part of a building-wide energy monitoring and control system.

Figure 7.8 ► **Programmable controller for multiple boilers** (*courtesy Weil McLain*).

The cost of the controller usually ranges from $2000 to $5000 and has a typical payback of 1 to 3 years.

Applications

In general, the most sophisticated control systems can be cost justified in larger buildings. The complexity of these systems may also increase the need for routine electronic system checks and for sensor calibrations. However, even small applications can benefit from simple, yet efficient, multiple boiler controls.

Case Study: Nursing Home

A 60,000 ft², 95-room wing was recently added onto the Rest Haven West Nursing Home, in Downers Grove, Illinois. The original plans called for the installation of a single 5 million Btu boiler, but these were changed to include four modular boilers of 1.2 million

Btu capacity each. The modular installation cost more than the single boiler, but is expected to yield significant energy savings.

Case Study: Church

In 1989, the Holy Trinity Greek Orthodox Church in Bridgeport, Connecticut, was refitted with a gas-fired multiple boiler system to reduce its energy consumption. The system consisted of four 300,000 Btu boilers, which replaced an electric heating system. The boilers were connected to a central controller with software which permits step-firing according to need.

An indoor-outdoor reset algorithm constantly adjusts the boiler firing and regulates the water temperature according to the outdoor temperature. For every degree drop in the outside temperature, the boiler water is set to rise about 1.5 degrees. The boiler sequencing is automatically rotated to reduce maintenance and wear on the units.

During the first winter the new system saved $6400, or 35% of the heating bill.

PRACTICAL CONSIDERATIONS FOR BOILER CONTROLS

Design

- Select an oxygen trim system that is compatible with the boiler combustion controls, which may be manual, microprocessor-based, analog electronic, or analog pneumatic.
- Select a blower motor which can withstand the voltage fluctuations imposed by the burner flame controls.
- In modular boiler installations, integrate the functions of (1) the boiler sequencing controller and of (2) the controller that resets water supply temperature based

on outdoor air temperature. Specifically, set the control algorithms so that a decrease in supply water temperature ordered by the OA controller is not immediately followed by a call for heat from the sequencing controller.

- Consider providing simple decentralized backup controls so that, for example, the equipment can heat the building even if the EMCS breaks down. Display readouts on local controllers are always desirable, since they provide operating data from which building engineers can quickly evaluate system performance, and if necessary, guide manual operation.

Construction

- Seal any small cracks around oxygen sensor probes, since these could allow room air leakage into the stack, causing improper oxygen content readings and control errors.
- Place outdoor air sensors for water reset control in shade to ensure proper functioning of reset systems.
- Commission the operation of control systems over the range of operating conditions expected.

Operation/Maintenance

- Clean and calibrate the oxygen sensors regularly to ensure accurate readings.
- Calibrate regularly hot water temperature sensors and especially flow meters.

7.4 ▶ CHILLER CONTROLS

Chiller controls improve the performance of the cooling equipment itself, and integrate its

BOILERS WITH ADVANCED CONTROLS ARE IN PLACE IN MANY BUILDINGS

Oxygen Trim Control
- Harlem Hospital, Harlem, NY
- Kings County Hospital, Brooklyn, NY
- Coney Island Hospital, Brooklyn, NY
- North Shore Hospital, Nassau County, NY
- New York University, New York, NY
- Queens College, Queens, NY

Burner Flame Control
- Battery Park City Offices—Bldg. 4, New York, NY
- 30 East 33rd St. Offices, New York, NY
- New York State Dept. of Health, Albany, NY
- Trump Riverside South Highrise Development, Manhattan, New York
- Port Washington Schools, Port Washington, NY
- Correctional Facility, Bridgeport, CT
- Naugatuck High School, Naugatuck, CT
- Trumbull High School, Trumbull, CT

Demand-Sensitive Water Temperature Control
- Green Tree Marriott, Pittsburgh, PA
- Days Inn of North America, Six Locations
- La Grange College, La Grange, GA
- Northrop High School, Fort Wayne, IN
- Hyde Park Hilton Hotel, Chicago, IL
- Best Western Inn, Chicago, IL

operation within the dynamics of the building energy systems. During their history, chillers have been controlled manually, semi-automatically, pneumatically, hydraulically, electrically, electronically—utilizing vacuum tube and then solid-state technology—and finally by microprocessor. This evolution has produced distinct improvements at each stage. Today, the technical impetus is for control simplification and improved communication with higher order energy monitoring and control systems.

During the 1980s, chiller manufacturers began incorporating microprocessor controls into their products. There was a simultaneous trend toward distributed processing—that is, positioning the "intelligence" closer to the controlled devices.

During this same period, chillers themselves became more complex in an attempt to improve their energy efficiency. Such advances as multiple compressors, variable-speed drives, accurate metering devices, and many other internal machine enhancements would not have been possible without microprocessor controls to regulate the complex interactions involved.

7.4.1 ► *Control Strategies for Efficient Chiller Operation*

Commercial chillers are devices which use mechanical power or vapor absorption to extract heat from water. This heat is then rejected into the air, or partly reused for other purposes. The chilled water is pumped into coils in the building, where it meets cooling loads. Consequently, chiller system efficiency is improved by optimizing the heat extraction/rejected process, reducing piping system losses, and matching heat extraction rates with cooling demand.

Energy input to mechanical refrigeration chillers originates from drive motors. These motors are usually electrical, but may also be gas-powered (engine or turbine-driven). Thus, strategies to reduce compressor energy use are largely directed at reducing drive energy use.

Absorption chillers use heat to operate physiochemical cycles. Improvements in efficiency are obtained by increasing the number of these cycles. Single-effect absorption chillers are least efficient and by now obsolete, but can still be found in existing installations. Also, these chillers may sometimes be attractive if used in conjunction with a cogeneration system which supplies heat for the absorption cycle. Double-effect absorption chillers are now typical, while triple-effect chillers are about to be introduced to the market.

As with boilers, water temperature set-points for chillers can be adjusted to minimize energy loss in the piping system and to avoid overcooling, by reducing the temperature differential between the chilled water and the environment. However, a countervailing effect is that pump energy can be saved if circulating water is made cooler (i.e., since less water must be pumped to extract a given number of cooling Btu).

The most effective control strategies must, therefore, adjust chilled water temperatures so the system will function with the least possible combined energy input to compressor, pump motors, and to cooling tower or condenser fans.

Finally, load tracking and load anticipation allow chillers to deliver the required amount of chilled water, at maximum temperature, to meet space cooling loads. These strategies are

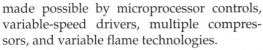

made possible by microprocessor controls, variable-speed drivers, multiple compressors, and variable flame technologies.

The following sections present practical means of accomplishing the energy saving strategies delineated here.

7.4.2 ▶ Control Applications for Chillers

CHILLER SPEED CONTROL

As discussed in Chap. 4, variable-speed chillers can effectively track the cooling demand in a building.

Variable chiller speed is typically achieved with variable frequency controllers (VFD) for standard induction motors. A VFD responds to changes in load by adjusting the frequency and voltage of the power supplied to the motor, which in turn adjusts its speed. (The same principle can also be applied to save energy in the air and hydronic circulating systems, as discussed in the next section.) In effect, VFD adjusts motor output to match the demand.

Fig. 7.9 shows that a VFD uses nearly the theoretical minimum power predicted by the centrifugal fan and pump affinity laws.

Improved Part-Load Performance

Because chillers are sized to meet the maximum cooling load of a building, they operate below full capacity for over 95% of the time; part-load efficiency is therefore essential in determining the energy use for cooling.

Constant speed, single-compressor chillers meet partial loads by unloading the compressor and/or using hot gas bypass down to 15 to 25% of capacity. In both unloading and bypass strategies the compressor uses less gas and therefore performs less mechanical

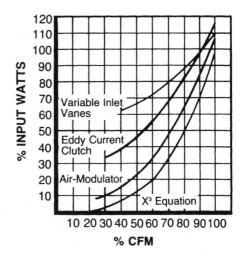

Figure 7.9 ▶ Power requirements of VFD (air-modulator) versus other control strategies (*courtesy York International*).

work, which results in lower electricity consumption. Below the 15 to 25% range these chillers typically cycle on and off.

The cycling is inefficient, but can occur frequently in buildings where high internal loads require chiller operation at low outside temperatures—often in the 50°F to 60°F range.

Variable-speed chillers reduce the cooling costs in two ways:

1. They match better the load/compression profile, and in a more efficient way. Therefore, they require less electricity per ton of cooling delivered than constant speed, single-compressor chillers.
2. They do not need to cycle until they reach 10 to 20% of capacity.

One drawback of VFD-driven motors, including those used in chiller applications, is that they use about 5% more energy than constant speed motors at and around peak capacity. However, variable speed is usually an attractive option, since chillers rarely run for extended periods of time at full capacity.

Because of the higher part-load performance, one manufacturer claims average savings of 30% over its own line of constant speed centrifugal chillers without the variable frequency drive.

However, variable speed chillers are not necessarily the most cost-effective strategy for widely varying loads. Multiple compressor chillers or multiple single-speed, single-compressor chillers could prove better suited in some applications. The selection of chillers is best achieved by performing hourly energy analyses with a computer program such as DOE-2.1.

The variable speed capacity of chillers is enhanced by coordination with other chiller functions. Advanced control systems (Fig. 7.10) monitor the chilled water temperature, refrigerant pressures, prerotation vane (PRV) setting, and current motor speed to derive a motor speed and PRV position close to optimum.

Some local control systems for chillers are designed to interface with energy monitoring and control systems, which also coordinate cooling tower operation, cooling water temperature, demand scheduling, etc.

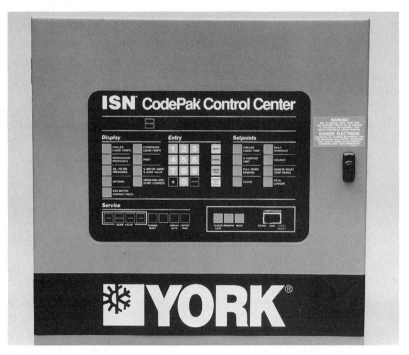

Figure 7.10 ► Control panel for microprocessor chiller controller (*courtesy York International*).

Other VFD Advantages

In addition to using more energy, the cycling of constant speed chillers tends to inflict considerable wear on the equipment. Microprocessor controls for variable speed chillers adjust the chiller speed down to 10% of capacity. At that point, the controller allows the chiller to continue running and to stabilize itself. Only if the stabilization effort fails to accommodate the change within a safe period of time is the chiller cycled off.

Case Study: Medical Center

In January of 1983, centrifugal chillers in the Castle Point, New York Veterans Administration Medical Center, were equipped with variable-speed controllers. Annual cooling load for the facility is about 200 tons. Following the installation, a study was conducted to determine the energy savings. During the first two years of operation savings averaged 32%.

The study also concluded that savings would have been even greater in other regions and for applications where the cooling season was longer. Finally, no compromise on comfort was made, as supply chilled water design temperatures were maintained at all times.

Case Study: Bank

In 1984, the Bank of Chicago (formerly Continental Bank) in Chicago, Illinois (Fig. 7.11), received a new 480-ton variable-speed compressor. Annual operating costs with the new

Figure 7.11 ▶ Bank of Chicago, Chicago, IL (*courtesy Bank of Chicago*).

system were about $31,000, or roughly $27,000 less than with the older system it replaced. Payback time through energy savings was six years.

A Mature Strategy

As the two case studies show, variable-speed controllers for chillers have been in use many years. The technology is proven and mature. New applications continue to be implemented.

CHILLED WATER PLANT OPTIMIZATION PACKAGES

The efficiency of chilled water production can be measurably improved by simultaneously controlling all essential variables in the chilled water plant. Control strategies include chilled water reset, condenser water reset, chiller sequencing, soft-starting of chiller motors, and demand control.

Control packages are also available for smaller capacity systems and single chillers. Optimizers can be used as stand-alone chiller controls, or they can in turn be controlled by higher order energy monitoring and control systems.

Functions

An array of sensors, meters, controllers, and software reduces the electricity consumption by minimizing the sum of the kw power drawn by compressors, pumps, and fans required to produce each ton of air conditioning. Similar controls are applied to gas-fired chillers. Systems of this type provide daily, monthly, and annual reports of energy use and savings. (See Fig. 7.12.)

Water temperature reset controls save energy because they base the temperature of water on continuous measurements, rather than on maximum cooling load estimates. Chiller optimization algorithms match production to need, by simultaneously consider-

ing demand, outside air temperature, humidity, high temperature of the day, history, and other factors. Resets can be made in both the condenser water and chilled water loops.

The data collected are used to minimize the simultaneous energy consumption of all chiller plant components. For example, if the condenser water is reset to a lower temperature, the cooling tower will need to reject more heat. Most cooling towers have multiple single-speed fans, multiple two-speed fans, or variable-speed fans. As the need to reject heat increases the cooling tower will consume more electricity. The controller calculates a setting which establishes a minimum combined electricity use for both chiller and cooling tower fans.

Soft-starting of chillers is also typically provided by plant controllers. This feature begins chiller operation at the lowest practical power level, which significantly reduces the electrical demand peak produced each time a compressor is started. It also prevents the energy waste associated with overcooling the chilled water at startup. Additional capacity is brought on-line at timed intervals, as needed.

Demand control is another way to reduce cooling energy consumption at times of very low cooling demand. Normally, under such conditions the chiller capacity would be reduced to a point where its operation was very inefficient, since only a small amount of cooling would be produced relative to the energy input.

Optimizer programs cycle chillers off for a minimum amount of time, and keep the system off until the demand for cooling returns. The net result is that the compressors operate at more favorable efficiencies, by avoiding unnecessary starts and stops due to transient demand drops.

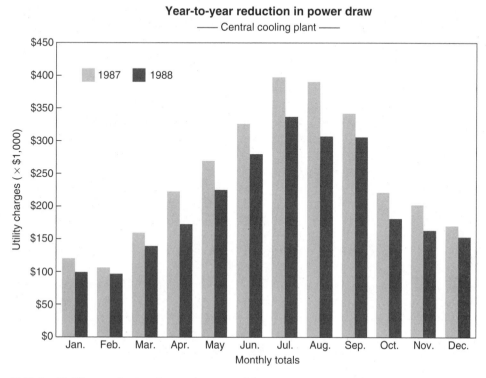

Figure 7.12 ▶ Chiller optimization software with energy savings display *(Courtesy Landis & Gyr).*

The demand control function also operates during higher part-load conditions. Specifically, the controller disallows brusque changes in cooling capacity, smoothing fluctuations in demand. Without such functions the chiller can have periods when it "hunts," undershooting and overshooting the proper chilled-water temperature. Such operation wastes energy and creates discomfort.

The most effective optimization software can document and "learn" the operating characteristics of individual chillers under its control, and can determine how best to use them under various loading conditions. Typically, these packages must be customized for specific installations. Most systems are also equipped with self-test diagnostics—that is, they can check to see if their own internal components are functioning properly.

Energy Savings

Chiller optimization packages save the most energy for facilities which have many operation possibilities with differently sized chillers, multiple or VFD compressor chillers, multiple-fan, or VFD fan cooling towers.

Energy savings are also large for inefficient, existing facilities with older chillers. Actual savings depend on the specific chiller part-load performance, operating requirements, climatic conditions, and utility rates. Typical optimization packages can save up to 20% on energy consumption in large cooling plants of over 500 tons.

The controller units are built with microprocessor technology and designed for unattended operation. They are now offered by several established manufacturers with good reputations. The technology has overcome its inception difficulties of the early 1980s, when it had suffered from some reliability and support problems.

Case Study

Research Laboratories at AT&T Bell Laboratories in Holmdel, New Jersey (Fig. 7.13), fitted its 2 million ft^2 facility with a comprehensive energy monitoring and control system, including advanced software to optimize chiller usage. This system obtains data from 352 sensors, monitoring relative humidity and the temperatures of inside and outside air, return chilled water, refrigerants, and evaporator water. It then controls the cooling functions of the center through output points at air dampers, condenser modulating valves, refrigerant inlet vanes, variable-speed drives, etc. Energy savings are estimated to be about $500,000 annually.

PRACTICAL CONSIDERATIONS FOR CHILLER CONTROLS

Design

- Consider using control systems that optimize the entire chiller plant, rather than controls that enhance the operation of individual pieces of equipment (such

Figure 7.13 ▶ AT&T Bell Laboratories, Holmdel, NJ.

as chillers, cooling towers, and pumps) separately.

- Provide simple decentralized backup controls so that, for example, the equipment can condition the building even if there is EMCS servicing or down time. Display readouts on local controllers are always desirable, since they provide operating data from which building engineers can quickly evaluate system performance and, if necessary, guide manual operation.
- Provide filters against noise feedback into power lines and into microprocessor-based controls when using VFD chillers.
- Provide separate hard-wired safety devices for all central plant equipment, including devices which monitor fail-safe limits. These devices ensure that critical temperatures, pressures, and flows are not breached. For instance, such devices can offer assurance that the optimization package does not reduce the fan speed of cooling towers too much, endangering the chiller.
- Examine the performance of optimization packages for low part-load conditions, which are prevalent in most chiller plants.

Construction

- Place outdoor air sensors for water reset temperature control out of direct sunlight.
- Commission the chilled water system controls over the full range of conditions of operation.

Operation/Maintenance

- Clean and calibrate sensors and flow meters regularly to ensure accurate readings as well as proper and accurate control responses.

ADVANCED CHILLER CONTROLS ARE USED THROUGHOUT THE UNITED STATES

- Gruman Aerospace, Bethpage, NY
- Memorial City Mall, Houston, TX
- Hofstra University, Hempstead, NY
- Conrad Hilton, Chicago, IL
- Owens Corning, Columbus, OH
- Farm Bureau, Indianapolis, IN
- State University of New York, Amherst, NY
- Exxon Corporation, Thousand Oaks, CA
- Sloan Kettering Memorial Hospital, New York, NY
- Equitable Life Building, Los Angeles, CA
- National Institute of Standards and Technology, Gaithersburg, MD
- Miami Valley Hospital, Dayton, OH
- America West Airlines, Las Vegas, NV
- Champion Paper, Hamilton, OH
- AT&T Bell Laboratories, Holmdel, NJ
- Merchants National Bank, Fort Smith, TX
- Northwest Medical Center, Atlanta, GA
- EI Dupont Haskell Labs, Newark, DE

7.5 ▶ FAN AND PUMP CONTROLS

Fans and pumps are part of both central plant and energy delivery system, and account for a large portion of energy demand in commercial facilities. To illustrate just how large, Fig. 7.14 shows the breakdown between different electricity-using systems in a mid-rise office building.

7.5.1 ► *Control Strategies for Efficient Fan and Pump Operation*

The energy use of fans and pumps is reduced through improvements in both hardware effi-

ciency and operating strategies. High efficiency motors, better-shaped fan wheels, better fan blades, and better pump impellers can be specified for maximum savings in installations that employ multiple fans and pumps, or variable-speed drives. While the choice of better equipment is relatively straightforward, the selection of multiple units versus

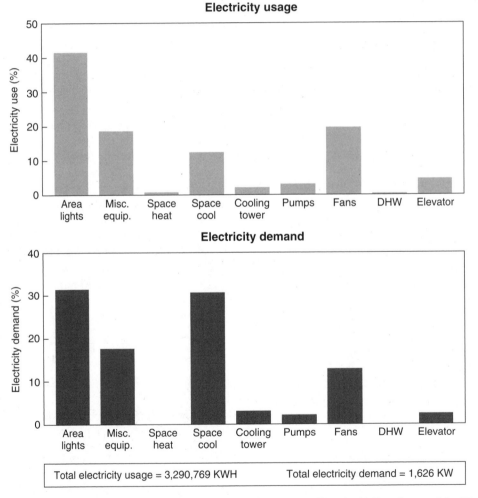

Figure 7.14 ► Distribution of energy demand in 16-story office building located in New York City.

variable-speed units depends on both first cost and part-load profiles.

Multiple fans and pumps operate in stages: one unit meets the demand to capacity, at which point the second unit comes on line, etc. If all units have the same size, stocking of spare parts is simplified and problems in case of failure in one of these units are alleviated; however, two or three equal-size units may not approximate very well the load profile, while many units may be too expensive.

If the units are of different sizes the load profile is better followed, but the maintenance costs increase and the system redundancy is lowered.

Variable-speed fans and pumps can closely track any load variations. They may be more expensive than multiple units, in both first cost and maintenance. If the loads vary widely both on a diurnal and seasonal basis, the additional expenditure may well be justified.

Variable-speed control has two basic operating advantages:

1. It can soft start motors, which reduces the electrical power demand during startup.
2. It can precisely modulate air and water flow rates to match thermal demand, which improves energy efficiency under part-load conditions.

7.5.2 ▶ Control Applications for Fans and Pumps

The benefits of variable-frequency control have already been described with regard to chillers (Sec. 7.4.1). The same advantages can also be extended to fans and pumps throughout the HVAC system, to yield substantial energy savings.

Most variable-speed drives are controlled locally, but they can also be centrally controlled through a building-wide energy monitoring and control system.

Costs for electronic speed control usually range from $300 to $500 per motor hp.

VARIABLE-SPEED FAN APPLICATIONS

Variable Air Volume (VAV) systems have long been accepted as an energy-efficient method of air distribution. A typical VAV system has the following components: a fan which can vary the airflow, ducts, air supply boxes which can modulate closed or open to different degrees; pressure sensors in the duct, near to the fan; proportional controllers, automatic valves, and damper operators; and room thermostats or sensors. The VAV boxes sometimes have coils.

During the cooling season the thermostat or sensor may register a space temperature toward the bottom of the throttling range. In order to reduce the cooling rate, the thermostat or sensor sends a signal to the VAV box. According to the magnitude of this signal, the box closes its dampers to a percentage of delivery area.

When the box closes, the air pressure in the supply ducts increases. A pressure sensor relays a command to the fan to reduce the amount of supply air.

HVAC suppliers have traditionally offered *variable inlet vanes* on their air handler units to reduce airflow rates, but the newer *variable frequency controllers* can save far more energy by reducing fan speed, and therefore airflow, with higher precision.

One problem with VAV systems is that, as the cooling or heating load decreases, the air volume also decreases to rates as low as 30% of design. This can result in very low airflow rates throughout most of the fall, winter, and spring. Low flow rates cannot efficiently disperse local concentrations of pollutants and odors, giving rise to indoor air quality complaints. Fan-powered VAV boxes address this problem by maintaining a constant rate of air movement, which in offices is generally between 0.8 to 1.2 cfm/ft². This solution comes with an increase in first cost and some decrease in operational efficiency (since even the small local fans use electricity). However, if night heating is achieved with the heating coils located in the VAV boxes, the small, local fans can save electricity. This is because fan energy is used only in the zones which require heating, and because the small fans are located close to the space and do not need to use energy to overcome significant duct friction.

Cooling tower fans are also relatively high electricity users. These fans cool water in the condenser loop to a setpoint (sometimes determined by the central energy monitoring and control system). Rather than simply turning the fans off and on as needed, it is often more efficient to modulate fan speed to achieve the required temperature. Another cost-effective option is to specify multiple fans with two speed controllers.

Case Study: Office Building

A variable-speed controller was installed on the cooling tower fan at the corporate headquarters of the Preferred Risk Group, an insurance company based in Des Moines, Iowa, where 750 people are employed. The 15 hp fan uses 20% less electricity as a result of the retrofit.

Case Study: Office Building

The 600,000 ft² headquarters office of the Boston Globe Newspaper (Fig. 7.15) has been fitted with a comprehensive energy monitoring and control system, which includes variable-speed drives on its 35 air handlers. In combination, these measures save an estimated $425,000 per year in energy costs, which could pay for the installation in about four years.

Case Study: New Courthouse

The new GSA Courthouse in New York City (Fig. 8.14) has 26 floors and 715,000 ft² of cham-

Figure 7.15 ▶ The Boston Globe Newspaper building (*courtesy Boston Globe*).

bers, courtrooms, and administrative offices, as well as other functions such as a data processing center, auditorium, cafeteria, and lobby. All office and chamber areas have fan-powered VAV systems. A DOE-2 analysis performed by Steven Winter Associates, Inc. and sponsored by Consolidated Edison projected that, by replacing inlet guide vanes with variable-frequency drives on the AHUs serving the VAV system, the Courthouse could save 407,000 kwh per year, or close to $45,000.

VARIABLE-SPEED PUMP APPLICATIONS

The circulating pumps on the condenser and the chilled water loops can also be speed controlled. In general, greater energy savings are achieved by modulating the flow through the chilled water loop.

The decoupling of the chilled water production and distribution piping is a prerequisite to effective chilled water pump speed control. This scheme allows the chilled water delivery rates to the building to fluctuate based on demand.

In the chilled water loop, optimal flow rates decrease with building load. However, this is not a strictly linear relationship, since chiller efficiency, pump energy demand, and fan power requirements must all be simultaneously considered.

Traditionally, chilled water flow rates are controlled by throttling valves and bypass loops, but this strategy still requires full input energy to the pump motors at all times. Speed controlling of the pumps eliminates the need for bypass circuits, because it slows down the pumps in response to pressure increases caused by the closing of throttling valves. (The throttling valves close in response to reduced cooling demand.) The electricity use of the pump motor is greatly reduced as the pump operates at lower speeds. The same considerations apply to the hot water distribution loops.

The rate of circulation for condenser water depends on the cooling load on the chiller. When the cooling load decreases, the temperature of condenser water also decreases. When the ambient temperature drops, the cooling tower cools more of the water and its temperature also decreases. In either or both cases less condenser water has to be pumped to the cooling tower in order to reject the same amount of heat. Pumps with variable-frequency drives can achieve savings by reducing the flow rate and therefore the electricity used for pumping.

Variable-speed pump strategies are most effective where (1) the chillers operate at low outdoor ambient temperatures, (2) low chiller loads are common, and (3) the chiller operates under the previous conditions for extended, uninterrupted periods of time.

Case Study

Dallas-Fort Worth Airport (Fig. 7.16) uses variable-speed pumps for a chilled water, primary distribution system to cool a 3.4 million ft^2 building complex with four terminals, offices, and hotel spaces. The buildings are connected to the central chiller plant which has three chillers, 8500 tons each. Two chillers use steam turbines (one is standby) and one chiller uses a variable-speed electric motor drive.

The electric chiller is used down to less than 10% of capacity. It operates from late fall to early spring, and then during peak summer months covering the base load. The steam turbine chiller is used down to 40 to 50% of capacity. It operates from early spring to late fall.

Figure 7.16 ▶ **Dallas-Fort Worth Airport uses variable-speed pumps (***courtesy Dallas-Fort Worth Airport***).**

The central plant is located at a distance of 4000 ft from the buildings. Energy savings of 20% are attributed just to the advanced design of the cooling distribution system. The oldest part of the system has been in continuous, reliable operation since 1974 and has produced cumulative savings of over $2 million. The airport saved over $40 million since 1985 on a whole range of energy conservation measures including variable-speed pumping.

PRACTICAL CONSIDERATIONS FOR FAN AND PUMP CONTROLS

Design

- When selecting fans and pumps consider all options: two-speed, multiple units, variable speed. Two-speed or two-unit configurations are often cost effective for pumps and for cooling tower fans, although variable-speed units out-

perform other configurations in energy use reduction.
- In most VAV systems variable-frequency drives for fans are cost effective when compared to inlet vanes. One option that yields energy use between inlet vanes and VFD fans is the plug-in fan with scroll damper.
- Always decouple the chilled water and hot water distribution system from the production system to allow effective utilization of VFD pumps.
- If VFD pumps are used on the condenser circuit, provide safeguards against low flows which could damage the chiller.
- When possible, integrate the operation of VFD pumps within a higher-order system, which optimizes their use with chiller or heater operation. This will ensure that low pumping rates do not

result in unreasonably high costs for operating the primary equipment.

- When the building served by VFD fans and pumps contains sensitive electronic equipment, consider specifying electronic filters to avoid feedback into power lines.

Construction

- Commission the operation of variable speed fans and pumps over their expected operation range.

Operation/Maintenance

- Establish a regular chiller maintenance schedule. This is especially important for variable-speed units, which may need more maintenance then simpler designs.

7.6 ▶ VENTILATION SYSTEM CONTROLS

The amount of outdoor air introduced by HVAC systems has been receiving greater attention in recent years, from both the standpoint of energy use and indoor air quality. In an effort to prevent sick building syndrome, ASHRAE has increased its recommended outside air rates. At the same time, energy-conscious building designers have tried to limit the amount of required fresh air, in order to reduce heating and cooling costs.

Fortunately, it is possible to reconcile these two apparently conflicting goals through a combination of heat recovery and demand-based ventilation controls.

7.6.1 ▶ Control Strategies for Efficient Ventilation

Forced circulation of air within a building consumes electrical power. Outside air intake consumes thermal energy.

VARIABLE-SPEED FANS AND PUMPS ARE USED IN ALL TYPES OF BUILDINGS

Variable-Speed Fans
- Pan Am Building, New York, NY
- 1166 Avenue of the Americas, New York, NY
- Merrill Lynch, New York, NY
- Federal Reserve Building, New York, NY
- Syracuse University, Syracuse, NY
- BMW World Headquarters, Camden, NJ
- Rutgers University, Piscattaway, NJ
- Princeton University, Princeton, NJ
- Trenton Office Building, Trenton, NJ
- Acmat Corp., New Britain, CT
- American Cynamid Co., Stamford, CT
- Yale University School of Medicine, New Haven, CT
- SNETCO, Bridgeport, CT
- Phoenix Mutual Life Ins. Co., Hartford, CT
- Connecticut Natural Gas, Hartford, CT
- IBM, Southbury, CT

Variable-Speed Pumps
- Williamantic Housing Authority, Nathan Hale Terrace, Williamantic, CT
- Acmat Corp., New Britain, CT
- Cheshire Correctional Institute, Cheshire, CT
- Phoenix Mutual Life Ins. Co., Hartford, CT
- Phoenix Mutual, Enfield, CT
- Connecticut Natural Gas, Hartford, CT
- Goodwin Square, Hartford, CT
- IBM, Southbury, CT
- Durst Building, New York City, NY

The simplest and most common way to reduce unnecessarily high outside air rates is to close the outside air intake at night and on weekends, when a building is unoccupied. However, approaches also exist for the occupied periods.

One way of limiting energy use is to closely track the ventilation rate to the actual occupant requirements in each conditioned zone, based on number of occupants, on carbon dioxide level, and/or volatile organic compounds (VOC). (As described in Sec. 5.3, air-to-air heat exchangers also make it possible to bring in more outside air, without a proportional increase in thermal energy loss.)

7.6.2 ► Control Applications for Ventilation Systems

PEOPLE COUNTERS

The control strategy called *people counters* is based on occupancy sensors which count people entering or exiting a space. These data are then fed into an electronic controller which keeps a running tally of the number of occupants, and adjusts the air replacement rate by opening and closing powered dampers in the ductwork.

The counters are usually simple infrared beam devices, like those used in security systems and automatic door openers.

Buildings with greatly fluctuating occupancies can derive significant energy benefits from this ventilation control strategy. These include stores, theaters, restaurants, banks, libraries, and convention centers. Here, ventilation rates have traditionally been based on the expected maximum occupancy, which may occur less than 5% of the time.

Retail store ventilation systems, for example, are often designed to supply about 10 to 15 ft^3 of outside air per minute (cfm) for every occupant. If the building's capacity is 2000 people, the HVAC system must be able to provide 20,000 to 30,000 ft^3 of outside air per minute to comply with the store's maximum requirements. Though most stores are rarely filled to capacity, their HVAC systems are continuously circulating this maximum volume of fresh air. According to ASHRAE/IES Standard 62-1989, theater lobbies must supply 20 cfm/person and the auditoriums for theaters or schools 15 cfm/person. All these high ventilation rates are designed for maximum occupancy, which is sporadic.

By counting the number of people in a space and adjusting the outside air rate, heating and cooling savings of up to 30% are possible in some cases.

Case Study: Stores

One of the first tests of occupancy-based ventilation control was sponsored by the U.S. Energy Research and Development Administration in 1977. Three Lechmere discount department stores in Massachusetts were equipped with occupancy-based ventilation controls, and their performance was monitored for 20 months. The installation reduced heating and cooling energy use by an estimated 26%.

Case Study: Supermarket

DOE-2.1 simulations were undertaken on a large supermarket located in Connecticut. The building has 113,000 ft^2 out of which 45,000 ft^2 is retail, and the rest refrigerated storage and offices. On peak hours 1150 people go through; however, the occupancy varies from 100% between 5 pm and 8 pm to 17% at 7 am or 11 pm. Overnight about 50 people clean and arrange the merchandise.

The retail area is air conditioned with DX rooftop units (EER = 8.2, AFUE = 78%, which supply 15 cfm outside air/person, maintaining a maximum of 55% relative humidity.

Basecase energy use is calculated to be 5,588,000 kwh (including refrigeration) and 94,800 ccf gas. If occupancy sensors modulate the outside air ratio based on the number of people present, the electricity is projected to decrease to 5,027,000 kwh and the gas to 79,700 ccf. This would translate to $11,000 savings per year, or about 10% of the entire energy cost.

CARBON DIOXIDE SENSORS

A relatively new method to control outside air volume is by regulating the carbon dioxide level. Essentially, as more people enter a space they breathe more oxygen and replace it with carbon dioxide; this raises the CO_2 level. When CO_2 content reaches a predetermined limit, an analyzer (Fig. 7.17) sends a signal to the controller which increases the ventilation rate.

This control strategy is similar in function to occupancy counters, but more precise; it can adjust for different rates of occupant demand based on their level of physical activity, age, health, etc.

However, the outside air rate cannot be based solely on CO_2 levels. Sufficient outside air must be supplied to remove emissions by building materials and equipment.

CO_2-based ventilation control has been used in Europe and has proven to be particularly effective for spaces like auditoriums, where major occupancy shifts can occur at irregular intervals, and in gymnasiums, where vigorous physical activity generates large amounts of carbon dioxide.

Figure 7.17 ▶ Wall-mounted CO_2 analyzer (*courtesy CEA Instruments*).

In the United States CO_2-based ventilation control applications have been initially applied to industrial settings (e.g, Anheuser-Busch Breweries) and to motor vehicle garages, but now schools, colleges, and office buildings are also using the technique.

Case Study: Office Building

Tops Markets, Inc. Corporate Headquarters in Williamsville, New York, installed CO_2 sensors as an integral part of the constant evaluation of the building's overall performance. The 200,000 ft^2 building depicted in Fig. 7.18 incorporates these sensors to ensure superior indoor air quality with the high concentration of people that work in the facility. At the same time, these CO_2 sensors save energy by avoiding excess ventilation during periods of low occupancy, such as evenings, weekends, or lunch breaks.

Figure 7.18 ▶ Tops Markets, Inc. Corporate Headquarters, Williamsville, New York (*courtesy Ciminelli Development Company, Inc.*).

SCHEDULED OUTSIDE AIR MODULATION

While people counters and CO_2-based systems provide automatic means to control the rate of outside air supply, simpler methods are sometimes used with a good degree of success. One effective strategy is to schedule the outside air rate for periods of low occupancy on a time clock. During such times the outside air rate as well as the exhaust air rate is reduced. An override is provided to reset the outside air back to design rates, should there be an unexpected increase in occupancy. This strategy works best in spaces with predictable variation in population during occupied hours. The spaces also need to be small enough so that the manager can assess the situation and use the override in a timely manner, should it be needed.

Case Study: Fast Food Restaurants

The McDonald's Restaurant at Guilderland (Fig. 7.19), close to Albany, New York, serves an interstate thruway, so it must be open 24 hours per day. Steven Winter Associates, Inc. (SWA), collaborated with the architectural firm of Beyer, Blinder, Belle to increase the energy efficiency of the restaurant. The project was guided by both McDonald' Corporation and the New York State Thruway Authority, which owns the building. As part of the work, SWA analyzed methods to reduce the excess outside air in the facility. Three air-handling units condition the dining and great hall areas, bringing in continuously the design outside air (OA) rate. The restroom exhaust fan also operated day and night at full design rate, regardless of the number of people in the restrooms. Historically, the occupancy in the restaurant falls to less than half at night, and occasionally to as low as zero.

Figure 7.19 ▶ The McDonald's restaurant at Guilderland.

Several options to modulate the OA rate based on occupancy were studied with DOE-2.1 computer analyses. People counters showed the highest potential for savings ($4000/year). The next energy-efficient method involved scheduled outside air modulation ($1300/year). This method was selected because of its simplicity and low maintenance. The 3000 cfm exhaust fan in the restroom was retrofitted with a two-speed motor. The outside air dampers of three air-handling units received controls to simultaneously reduce the outside air rate to about 45% of the existing minimum. An electric time clock controls the operation, decreasing the outside air rates between 11 pm and 6 am. The manager can use an override twist switch to return the system to full OA/exhaust for a period of his or her choice, should an unex-plained influx of people increase occupancy to a level above 50% of design.

This conservative strategy has a payback below 4 years when including both "hard" costs and design costs.

The strategy has been retrofitted in 1996 to all McDonald's restaurants on the New York State Thruway. Lower paybacks are expected because of reduced design and installation costs related to volume work.

PRACTICAL CONSIDERATIONS FOR VENTILATION CONTROLS

Design
- Set minimum air exchange rates within a space to remove pollutants which may build up from building material and furnishing emissions.

- Ventilation control based on carbon dioxide concentration does not account for other indoor air pollutants. Industrial-grade VOC sensors can now analyze a much wider range of compounds. The cost of the equipment is also higher.
- Do not use CO_2 control systems as the exclusive means to modulate the outside air rates. Timers or EMCS scheduling are usually required to ensure proper air quality in the morning when few people may be present and the CO_2 buildup is slow.
- If the outside air rates are set to zero during unoccupied periods, it may be advisable to flush the building with outside air just before occupancy, to remove

accumulated emissions from building materials and furnishings. Morning air flushing may increase the energy use, but is worth considering for occupancies such as nursery schools, kindergartens, and schools.

Construction
- Install protective covers over sensors to prevent accidental damage.
- Locate the sensors in a representative position within the conditioned zone, in order to obtain accurate readings.
- Commission operation of ventilation controls.

Operation/Maintenance
- Calibrate sensors periodically (e.g., every 6 months) to ensure their continued accurate functioning.

OCCUPANCY-BASED VENTILATION CONTROLS ARE INCREASINGLY USED IN NONINDUSTRIAL APPLICATIONS

Occupant-Counting Systems
- Lechmere Stores, MA

Carbon Dioxide Systems
- Iona College, New Rochelle, NY
- Wesleyan University, Amherst, MA
- State District Court at the Detroit Madison Center, Detroit, MI
- Auditorium of Flakt Evaporator AB, Jonkoping, Sweden
- Tops Markets, Inc. Corporate Headquarters, Williamsville, NY
- Monticello High School, Albemarle County, VA

7.7 ▶ SPACE TEMPERATURE CONTROLS

Space temperature control is one of the most cost-effective means to adjust the thermal dynamics of a building, while reducing its energy use.

On the simplest level, thermostats may be set back or set up when a building is unoccupied, allowing the interior temperatures to float beyond the comfort range. More sophisticated controllers can also optimize HVAC equipment startup, and even schedule the various pieces of equipment.

Adaptive controllers can record operating patterns, "learn" to anticipate future events, and preadjust their thermal setpoints accordingly. Depending on the installation, they can be independent and local, or tied into a higher order energy monitoring and control system.

Occupancy sensors can also be used to turn on and off the HVAC system, lighting, and electrical equipment in buildings with intermittent occupancy, such as hotels, offices, etc.

7.7.1 ▶ Control Strategies for Efficient Space Temperature Management

Precise control of air temperature within buildings is often difficult to achieve. For example, temperatures tend to continue floating upward or downward even after space conditioning requirements have been satisfied, due to the time lag associated with running the system (thermostat to boiler, to pumps, to air handlers, etc.).

This thermal overshooting and undershooting often translates into energy inefficiencies of 10 to 20%. Strategies for greater precision in air temperature management can therefore save significant amounts of energy.

7.7.2 ▶ Control Applications for Space Temperature Management

ADAPTIVE PROGRAMMABLE THERMOSTATS

Programmable thermostats, thermostatic controllers, and programmable controllers can be used to manage local heating and cooling units and to provide night temperature setback, optimum startup time, operation scheduling, and in some cases, adaptive control of HVAC equipment.

Adaptive control means that the settings are automatically adjusted over time to optimize system performance based on recorded demand patterns (Fig. 7.20).

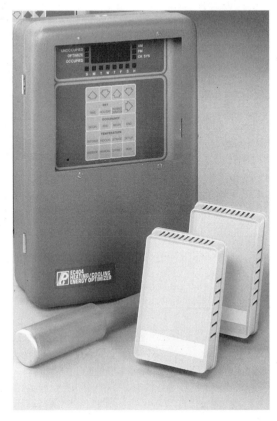

Figure 7.20 ▶ Wall-mounted controller can be programmed to record energy-demand patterns and to provide adaptive control (*courtesy Paragon Electric Company, Inc.*)

Adaptive programmable thermostats are generally appropriate for smaller commercial buildings or for local zone control within larger buildings.

Case Study: Municipal Buildings
In 1988, 43 municipal buildings in New York City were equipped with adaptive thermostatic controllers, at a cost of $588,000. The

controllers, which are tied into a central energy monitoring and control system, are estimated to be saving about $170,000 per year in energy costs.

Case Study: YMCA

A 75-year-old Boston area YMCA complex was equipped with programmable thermostats, to control the air temperature in its 200,000 ft^2 of conditioned space. The facility includes 357 residential rooms, offices, a gymnasium, and a restaurant.

Prior to the installation, the complex experienced uneven heating, which left many spaces either too hot or cold. Often, it became necessary to open some windows during the heating season to cool off overheated rooms. Energy savings attributable to the programmable thermostats were about 18%, or $140,000.

OCCUPANCY-BASED AIR TEMPERATURE CONTROL

In buildings where the occupancy changes in unpredictable patterns (e.g., hotels) occupancy sensors can be used to reduce energy use. As previously discussed with reference to lighting in Chap. 3, the sensors are typically small ultrasonic, infrared, or card key devices which sense the presence or absence of a guest or worker (Figs. 7.21 and 7.22).

The sensors are connected to thermostats, which are programmed with different temperature setpoints for occupied and unoccupied conditions. Commonly, these systems also turn off the lights and television when hotel rooms are empty.

Case Study: Hotel

The Radisson Maingate Hotel in Kissimmee, Florida, has been saving about $5000 per month on electricity after installing occupancy sensors. In each of its 56 rooms, when

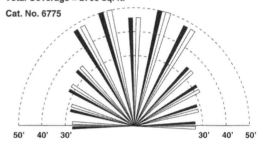

Horizontal field-of-view as seen from above.
Total Coverage = 2700 sq. ft.

Cat. No. 6775

Figure 7.21 ► Typical coverage patterns for occupancy sensors (*courtesy Leviton*).

a door is opened it trips a switch which activates an infrared motion sensor; if the sensor detects motion, it turns on the air-conditioning system. When the door is opened again, if no motion is detected for five minutes, the air conditioner is turned back off. Installation costs were about $120,000, which were projected to be recovered through energy savings in about two years.

Case Study: Office Park

The Otis Elevator Company installed 650 occupancy sensors in its 5 buildings around Farmington, CT, to reduce lighting costs. Efficient lamps and electronic ballasts were also retrofitted.

Additionally, 350 ultrasonic sensors save energy by turning off the water-source heat pumps when enclosed offices are unoccupied. Previously the two-ton heat pumps operated continuously. Ten to 15% of all the savings of the energy monitoring and control system are estimated to accrue due to the reduction in heat pump operation. The projected savings is $275,000 per year, with less than two years payback.

Figure 7.22 ▶ Infrared occupancy sensors may be wall or ceiling mounted (*courtesy Leviton*).

PRACTICAL CONSIDERATIONS FOR SPACE TEMPERATURE CONTROLS

Design

- Ensure that all programmable thermostats are equipped with a manual override to allow resetting for temporary scheduling changes.
- Consider space temperature recovery times when specifying occupancy sensor controls. It can take several minutes for a previously unconditioned space to reach design settings and during this time occupant comfort may be compromised. These systems, therefore, are not suitable for rooms where people are frequently going in and out.
- Carefully locate the sensors to avoid false readings of unoccupied space. This is especially important for infrared devices.
- Select sensing equipment with radio frequency shielding and electromagnetic protection to avoid electronic and electromagnetic interference. To this end use shielded cable for all sensing, signal, communications, and wiring.
- Refer also to Chap. 3 on occupancy sensors.

Construction

- Locate thermostats carefully so that they are in a representative place within each zone, and not in direct sunlight or in the path of a diffuser air flow.
- Install a protective cover over thermostats to prevent accidental damage and unauthorized tampering.

Operation/Maintenance

- Recheck the schedules on programmable thermostats periodically, to ensure that they are still appropriate.

7.8 ▶ WHOLE BUILDING CONTROLS

Thus far, this chapter has presented control strategies which improve the energy perfor-

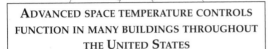

mance of specific HVAC components and systems within a building. However, some control measures, such as load shedding, affect the functioning of the entire building. In addition, comprehensive energy monitoring and control systems can be installed to provide building-wide optimization of all energy systems.

7.8.1 ► Energy-Efficient Control Strategies for the Entire Building

Synergic management of all energy-using systems in a building could save over 10% in electricity and fuel use, and could substantially reduce demand charges. This system integration is usually achieved with an energy monitoring and control system which is programmed to prioritize and optimize competing, and even conflicting, requests for energy.

Resolution of Conflicting Energy Use

Hospitals, for example, use large amounts of outside air. This air is preheated during cold periods. In mild weather economizers bring in 100% outside air. EMCS logic can determine if there is simultaneous heating and cooling or simultaneous preheat and economizer operation. This control strategy eliminates a wasteful (and common) problem. Another example of conflicting operation is a perimeter zone with baseboard heating and VAV cooling. During sunny days in late fall and early spring this zone may need cooling, yet the baseboards, operated with an outdoor air/water temperature reset, may deliver heat. Local or centralized controls can resolve this conflict and substantially reduce expenses.

Optimization of Energy Use

Building-wide controls can optimize the operation strategies of primary heating/cooling equipment, distribution systems (fans and pumps), and lighting. Optimum fan start/stop is discussed in Sec. 7.2.

If a space is allowed to attain high temperatures during unoccupied periods in summer, the fans will need to start early in the morning in order to reach comfortable conditions when people return to work. The savings in cooling may be canceled by increases in fan electricity use, unless the tradeoff is regulated by an energy monitoring and control system. The EMCS, for instance, could

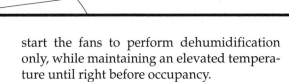

start the fans to perform dehumidification only, while maintaining an elevated temperature until right before occupancy.

Reduction of Energy Use and Demand

Finally, both energy use and demand can be reduced by cycling off equipment that is not essential during peak cooling demand. The sequence and duration of shutoff is generally determined through EMCS software.

The following section presents applications of EMCS functions and exemplifies the energy savings obtained through integration of systems in buildings.

7.8.2 ▶ Whole Building Control Applications

Modern commercial buildings can have complicated energy profiles. They are subject to widely varying internal and external loads from one zone to another, and with time of day, week, or season. Occupancies and uses often change radically as tenants and departments move in, out, and around. New heat-producing equipment and lighting may also be installed.

Under these circumstances, whole building control strategies offer the only practical method to closely match the needs of the lighting and HVAC systems. Often, these strategies are incorporated in energy monitoring and control systems. The following pages discuss the importance of EMCS for global energy conservation strategies, and then exemplify the use of such strategies by analyzing load shedding/demand limiting.

ENERGY MONITORING AND CONTROL SYSTEMS

Building-wide energy monitoring and control systems represent the highest order of energy control, and their use is becoming common in larger buildings.

The introduction of EMCS has been closely tied to the development of computerized building automation systems. In fact, energy management is often just one element controlled by an Integrated Building Automation System (IBAS), which may also regulate security, fire safety, and vertical transportation systems.

Energy monitoring and control systems gather sensor data, analyze them, and transform them into useful information to help operators make appropriate control decisions. More advanced IBAS incorporate logic for interaction between lighting, HVAC, and security. This way information obtained from automated occupancy count in different spaces can be used to adjust OA and temperature, turn off lights, or ensure that people are not left without elevator service if working late hours. Additionally, these systems can suggest when maintenance should be performed and provide alarms; they may even take automatic remedial action, if equipment fails, or if its performance deviates grossly from established norms (e.g., if a motor burns out or pipes rupture). Safeguards are typically built into the software to prevent destructive operator commands.

Often an EMCS presents the information in graphic form, either on a computer monitor or as hard-copy printout. In many systems, the output portrays energy performance by comparing actual energy use with historical data or theoretical goals.

Hourly energy-use graphs reveal the effectiveness of small operational changes. The monthly graph verifies whether the effect of any energy improvements is maintained over time, and detects gradual shifts in performance.

A typical EMCS is a computerized electronic network, with sensors and actuators at the bottom level, microprocessor controllers in the middle, and a PC computer at the top. A modem can also be connected to the PC, to allow remote monitoring and control of the system (Fig. 7.23).

In most energy monitoring and control systems, local controllers manage the operation of boilers, chillers, air handlers, pumps, gather data for reporting, and are capable of functioning independently from the central computer.

EMCS Functions

While every system is somewhat different, the main functions of most EMCS is to collect and display information on system performance (Fig. 7.24), to provide stand-alone, decentralized control of HVAC and lighting, and to enable centralized supervision of operating parameters (eg., temperature setpoints, load shedding limits, and equipment shutdown).

Advanced EMCS can serve building operators in ways beyond simply turning equipment on and off and carrying out preprogrammed control strategies. By storing, and more importantly, analyzing and displaying key energy, temperature, and flow data, and by drawing conclusions from these data, an EMCS can help the operator identify poorly performing control points and faulty equipment, and even suggest operational improvements, based on what it has learned from monitoring the equipment over time.

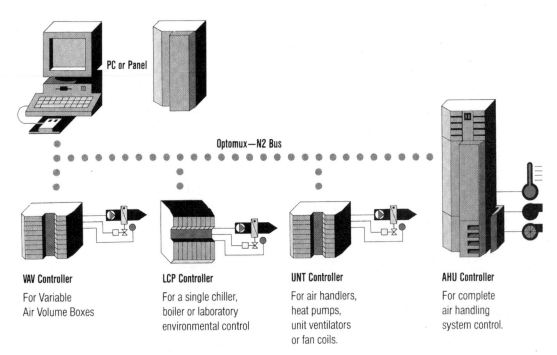

PC or Panel

Optomux—N2 Bus

VAV Controller
For Variable
Air Volume Boxes

LCP Controller
For a single chiller,
boiler or laboratory
environmental control

UNT Controller
For air handlers,
heat pumps,
unit ventilators
or fan coils.

AHU Controller
For complete
air handling
system control.

Figure 7.23 ► Energy monitoring and control system displays (*courtesy Andover Controls*).

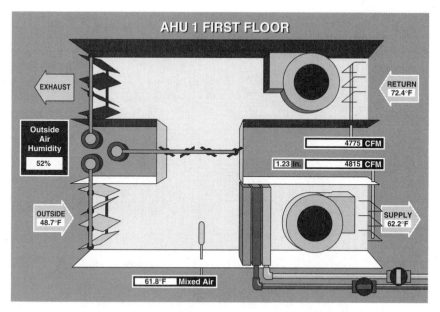

Figure 7.24 ▶ Diagram of components for typical energy monitoring and control system (*courtesy Johnson Controls*).

Case Study: Convention Center

A comprehensive energy monitoring and control system was installed in the Rochester Riverside Convention Center, in Rochester, NY (Fig. 7.25). This large system, with about 1300 data and control points, controls the HVAC, lighting, fire detection, and security system. Electricity cost is averaging from $20,000 to $25,000 per month, half of what it was prior to the EMCS installation.

Case Study: University

In 1988, Niagara University, located near Niagara Falls in New York State, installed an EMCS to improve the energy efficiency of its 28-building campus. Heating on the campus is provided by a central steam plant, while air conditioning is accomplished by local systems in the various buildings. Annual energy costs at the university total about $1.3 mil-

lion, or 5% of its entire operating budget, and the control system is expected to help keep these to a minimum.

Case Study: University

A comprehensive energy monitoring and control system was installed on the 40-acre campus of the University of Baltimore, in Maryland. This large complex includes some 33 buildings and 2.4 million ft² of occupied space. The system's $850,000 installation costs (including some improvements in the HVAC equipment) should be repaid through energy savings in about four years.

LOAD SHEDDING AND DEMAND LIMITING

The load-shedding and demand-limiting strategies belong in the larger family of global control strategies. Load-shedding strategies are

Figure 7.25 ▶ Atrium at the Rochester Riverside Convention Center, Rochester, NY (*courtesy Johnson Controls*).

enacted with the help of local control panels which monitor the electrical usage within buildings, and turn off noncritical equipment when predetermined demand levels are reached. When load-shedding strategies are used to reduce "spikes" in power demand (which can result in extra charges by the electrical utility) they are called *demand-control strategies.*

A basic load-shedding function could merely trigger a power disconnect when the electrical demand reaches a predetermined kw setpoint. The more sophisticated demand-limiting systems predict increases in power consumption based on past and current usage, and systematically turn off individual pieces of equipment *before* the critical moment, starting with the least

important device. Demand limiting can also include an optimal start procedure, which sequentially turns on mechanical equipment, to avoid high demand peaks at startup.

Load-shedding and demand-limiting strategies are usually part of an encompassing energy monitoring and control system, but can also be applied independently. These methods can be quite effective in the right applications which include:

1. demand-based electric billing
2. multiple pieces of equipment and systems that can be safely and conveniently cycled off and on
3. cooperation of occupants to avoid the overriding of demand-limiting controls

The type of control varies by application. The demand control can be based on a preset priority sequence (e.g., in a hospital). It can, alternately, disconnect circuits or equipment by rotation, with minimum and maximum periods for both on and off times. This could apply to a retail space served by multiple rooftop AC units. Demand control could also be temperature-driven, where a trend toward high electricity demand sets off a sequence which automatically raises the cooling setpoints, decreasing chiller energy use.

Finally, advanced demand control is adaptive, i.e., learns from the history of operation how to best anticipate the need for action and what sequence of control to implement.

Load shedders are effective in a variety of buildings, from large and complex to small commercial and retail buildings. Such small spaces still have numerous pieces of equipment and often oversized air conditioners that can be cycled on and off without creating comfort problems.

Since load shedding and demand limiting is usually just part of a larger energy control strategy, it is not always possible to isolate the precise energy savings, but the following example should help illustrate the savings potential.

Case Study: Office Building

The Boston Globe Newspaper uses a 250 point energy monitoring and control system which incorporates, among other functions, demand-limiting capabilities. The peak electric consumption was reduced by about 800 kw. The calculated payback for the entire EMCS is less than two years, given the fact that the local utility, Boston Edison Co., supported half the first cost.

PRACTICAL CONSIDERATIONS FOR WHOLE BUILDING CONTROLS

Design

- Identify all major energy users in a building before designing an EMCS. Include on the control list not only HVAC equipment and luminaires, but also office machinery and points that are likely to malfunction. For example, motorized dampers normally consume very little energy, but a malfunction could result in substantial energy waste. Exhaust fans are in the same category.

- Perform hourly energy analyses, using a program such as DOE-2.1, to properly capture the variation in energy uses and demands. The effectiveness of a particular EMCS strategy is highly dependent on the interplay of different equipment (lighting, HVAC, process) at different part-load conditions. Only a detailed computer model can simulate such conditions and can be used to realistically estimate the cost effectiveness of the EMCS.

- Design redundancy into the control system in case of equipment failure. Specifically, local controllers should be able to manage for a reasonable period of time if the EMCS central console malfunctions or needs servicing. Most local controllers should be able to operate using the last global information received, in case of failure of the communication bus line.

- Specify systems that provide operators with quick and clear information about system operation. Dynamic color graphic displays are an essential complement of numerical data. These displays provide a

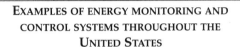

EXAMPLES OF ENERGY MONITORING AND CONTROL SYSTEMS THROUGHOUT THE UNITED STATES

- Lexington Medical Center, West Columbia, SC
- Brooklyn College, New York, NY
- 1300 Pennsylvania Ave., Washington, D.C.
- Latter-Day Saints Hospital, Salt Lake City, UT
- Harvard University, Cambridge, MA
- Alexandria Hospital, Alexandria, VA
- Koll Center, San Jose, CA
- Wayne State University, Detroit, MI
- World Bank Headquarters, Washington, D.C.
- Blue Cross/Blue Shield, Denver, CO
- Century Towers, New Haven, CT
- Pioneer Memorial Hospital, Prineville, OR
- Northwestern University, Evanston, IL
- Park Place, Fort Lauderdale, FL
- Shearson Lehman, New York, NY
- Central Trust Bank, Rochester, NY
- Good Samaritan Hospital, Lebanon, PA
- Manufacturers Hanover, Wilmington, DE
- Georgia State University, Atlanta, GA
- AT&T Windward, Alpharetta, GA

high level of systems diagnostics for the use of facility managers.

Construction
- Consider sharing EMCS wiring with the telephone system.

- Perform a thorough commissioning of all EMCS functions in peak cooling and peak heating modes, as well as in low-load conditions.

Operation/Maintenance
- Train operating staff thoroughly. If they do not fully understand the system, it cannot be used to best advantage. (Calls to outside maintenance personnel can be quite expensive.)
- Provide system upgrades when they become available, as enhancements are usually inexpensive relative to the advantages they bring.
- Purchase a maintenance contract if qualified in-house staff are not available, to ensure that the system continues to operate effectively over time.

7.9 ► DEVELOPMENTS ON THE HORIZON

The research and development activity in controls accelerates. Centralized controls evolve into more complex, yet simpler to use configurations; local controls receive more autonomy. Integration, a long-time goal, is now becoming a reality. The controls presented in this section exemplify the variety of developments currently underway.

EXPERT SYSTEMS AND ENERGY MONITORING AND CONTROL SYSTEMS

In the future, building energy controls are expected to make increasing use of *expert systems,* which incorporate algorithms to make *intelligent* operating decisions on the basis of stored and accumulated knowledge.

Expert systems are already being used in other fields. For example, in medicine they help physicians diagnose illnesses by analyzing a patient's symptoms. In buildings, integrated EMCS/Expert Systems will diagnose faults and inefficiencies of HVAC and lighting systems.

One key to the effectiveness of expert systems lies in their ability to learn from experience. When first installed, EMCS/Expert Systems would be programmed with background information on the building and its mechanical equipment. Over time, actual operating data would be recorded and added to these initial assumptions, thereby improving the diagnostic accuracy.

If a fault were detected, the EMCS/Expert System would inform the operator of the probable cause(s), suggest remedial action, and in the case of serious problems, directly initiate countermeasures.

For example, if a building interior air temperature began rising uncontrollably, the system would begin trying to establish the source of the problem by examining all of the relevant sensor inputs (e.g., cooling water flow and temperature, pump electricity use, airflow, temperature readings of nearby thermostats, etc.). Then, drawing upon its knowledge base, the EMCS/Expert System would predict the most likely cause(s) of the problem (e.g., 60% faulty pump, 28% pipe leakage, 12% faulty thermostat).

While EMCS/Expert Systems will never eliminate the need for human operators, they could facilitate quicker response to emergencies, and faster energy performance adjustments.

IAQ AND EMCS

Energy monitoring and control systems have been first used to reduce energy use and later to control temperature and lighting. A new function seems to have a good chance of incorporation in the future: Indoor Air Quality, or IAQ.

Industrial applications already use sensors to detect unwanted compounds, and controllers to evacuate the polluted air or fluid. Now these systems, designed for carbon monoxide, carbon dioxide, or for volatile organic compounds, have decreased in cost enough to be applicable to commercial, institutional, and educational buildings. Conference rooms, lounges, auditoriums, theaters, and cafeterias are first candidates.

At least one manufacturer of energy monitoring and control systems, with operations in both Europe and the United States, now offers the service.

Additionally, precise tracking of airflow and automatic IAQ sampling has been used for several years in the United States. These methods, generally based on tracer gas or similar nonreactive gases, are now employed in industrial facilities or for research purposes. With the cost being reduced to the $40,000 to $60,000 range, IAQ systems can be deployed in large facilities. The data obtained not only ensure better air quality, but can also confer greater accuracy in fine-tuning the operation of energy monitoring and control systems.

CHAPTER 8

TOOLS FOR ENERGY EFFICIENT DESIGN

8.1 ▶ DEVELOPMENT OF SOFTWARE FOR DESIGN

Computers are used to size HVAC equipment, predict energy consumption, visualize light distribution, and document physical layouts for buildings. Both computer-assisted calculations (sizing, lighting, and energy use) and computer-assisted drafting increase accuracy in design. However, the two processes are imperfectly linked; all too often they follow parallel paths, with substantial duplication of input and sizable chance for discrepancies.

Efforts are already underway to integrate lighting and energy. Recent trends in simulation software have strengthened the relationship between HVAC design and energy use predictions. The connection between accurate energy use analyses (typically developed with government funding) and HVAC equipment sizing (typically developed by equipment producers) is still tenuous, but the interest exists to incorporate better sizing routines into energy use packages.

The numerical input of energy packages can now be converted into plans and tridi-

mensional representations. The light patterns and intensities in a space can be visualized. Finally, the user interface has been progressing toward simplicity, in software for all stages of design.

8.2 ▶ TECHNICAL CHALLENGES FOR COMPUTER-ASSISTED, ENERGY-EFFICIENT DESIGN

DIFFICULTIES IN SOFTWARE INTEGRATION

The primary technical challenge for design software is to link computer-aided drafting, computer-aided HVAC sizing, computer-aided lighting design, and energy use predictions.

Currently, many buildings are designed with a Computer-Aided Design and Drafting (CADD) system. Then building dimensions are entered again in an HVAC sizing/energy analysis package, to select mechanical equipment and distribution systems. The building

Development of software for design

- Interactive, user-friendly software for energy-efficient schematic design of low-rise buildings is now available.
- Integration of high quality lighting and energy analysis has been made possible by tools sponsored by the U.S. Department of Energy.
- Specialized, easy-to-use software exists to visualize heat flows through complex building details and to calculate U-values and moisture condensation conditions.
- Expert systems, typically encountered in building operations management and in equipment manufacturing, are increasingly used for building design. Special applications already have such software, with more being developed.
- Input postprocessors have been developed for major energy simulation packages. Numerical entries can now be converted into plans and tridimensional representations of buildings.
- Full graphic input is still a few years away, but systematic work on this capability and on the linkage between drafting software and energy design/energy use packages is underway.
- All major energy use simulation programs have progressed in accuracy and range of applications. Pull-down menus, pop-up data screens, dialogue boxes, and use of graphic symbols have made this software much easier to use.

may also be reentered and resimulated on a dedicated energy analysis package, such as DOE-2. Lighting analyses are usually separate, on an entirely different software. Not all four steps are always taken, but the duplication in input occurs regularly, with a high incidence of errors. This situation was created in part by technical obstacles to software integration, and in part by the historical roots of the building software packages.

Four Software Families

The development of software for computer-aided, energy-efficient design was undertaken by four different sectors of the industry. The first CADD was conceived as an automated drafting tool which would increase speed and accuracy, particularly with repetitive tasks. CADD software was developed for the architecture profession. Its growth and refinement has been later guided by the needs of both architects and design engineers with little or no concern about energy use interfaces.

The second family of software, computer-assisted design of HVAC systems, was primarily intended to size and select equipment and distribution systems, such as boilers, chillers, pipes, fans, ducts, and VAV boxes.

Initially this software emphasized peak load calculations, but later it improved its algorithms for annual energy use simulations. Since the software focused on equipment, the building envelope received secondary consideration. There was no effort to provide graphic representations of the building (e.g., plans, elevations).

The third family of software helps designers visualize light intensity and patterns in space. The most evolved software has been government-sponsored.

The fourth family of software, computer-assisted energy use calculations, originated as a research tool for scientists. The software was not intended for widespread use. The computer programs were cumbersome and required hardware with large memory and storage. Currently, this category benefits from increased simplicity and reduced hardware constraints. Graphic interfaces now exist for the primary tool for large buildings, DOE-2. These interfaces convert numerical input into plans and building axonometrics. Other packages convert the output into graphs and charts. There are even elements of graphic input.

Problems with Software Interaction

The four types of software are often applied to the same building, without linkage to each other. The design process is time consuming and error prone.

The input to HVAC design and to energy simulation packages often contains trivial, yet potentially sizable errors: roofs placed over the wrong coordinates, walls longer by a factor of 10 because of a misplaced decimal point, windows missing, daylight sensors in the wrong spaces, etc. Until the recent advent of 3-D axonometrics created from computer code, the input was difficult to check. As a result, many errors in building geometry remained undetected.

Although the designer can now output an axonometric of the building coded in the computer, the opposite process, i.e., the creation of input from graphics, is in its incipient stages. It is still not possible to start with a CADD drawing and to directly create an energy or lighting analysis file. Two problems need to be solved: compatibility between software codes and a protocol for exchanging relevant information between graphic and calculation routines.

Compatibility among various software codes is an obstacle which can be surmounted. Some CADD software is written in the C language and could be readily interfaced with energy use programs. Other types of software can also be interfaced, even if with some additional effort.

However, not all *information* presented in the CADD software is pertinent to energy and sizing calculation procedures. The CADD input consists of multiple layers of drawings that depict in detail building elements, many of which are irrelevant to energy performance. For example, a floor plan drawn on CADD will describe interior partitions, piping layouts, luminaire layouts, flooring patterns, and other features important to building construction, but which have little or no bearing on energy analysis.

Other architectural features, such as complex facade shapes and multiple windows are fully described on CADD but are usually simplified for input to energy calculations. A facade with multiple small protrusions (Fig. 8.1) may be described by the analyst as a straight plane (Fig. 8.2). Several windows with the same orientation and in the same thermal zone (Fig. 8.3) may be combined as one big window (Fig. 8.4) to comply with memory limitations imposed by both software and hardware. Without such simplification procedures, the cost of energy analysis could be prohibitive for many buildings.

There are, of course, exceptions to this rule. Simplification is not recommended when light patterns are investigated. However, light studies are usually performed on a few representative spaces rather than on the

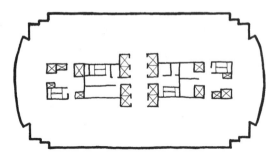

Figure 8.1 ▶ Building plan with multiple protrusions.

entire building, using specialized software, such as RADIANCE. The results are then transferred to an energy analysis tool which does employ simplified input.

Finally, simplifications need not be made if both the need and expertise exists to represent a building in great detail. Steven Winter Associates, Inc., for instance, simulated the energy use in the 800,000 ft² North Academic Center of the City College of New York using over 250 thermal zones on DOE-2.1E. This type of modeling is usually the province of specialized consulting firms performing in-depth energy studies.

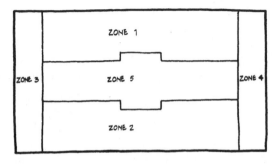

Figure 8.2 ▶ Computer input of building plan with multiple protrusions.

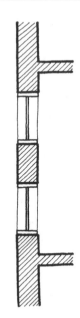

Figure 8.3 ▶ Zone with multiple windows.

Section 8.3 presents encouraging steps taken toward incorporating graphic representations of the building in the output of energy simulation programs. Section 8.4 outlines developments in the near- and more-distant future, including graphic-oriented input.

PROBLEMS WITH SOFTWARE FOR SCHEMATIC DESIGN

Computer-assisted energy analyses are routinely performed during the design development phase. By that time, however, major building characteristics, such as envelope geometry or ratio between fenestration area and opaque wall area, are already defined. Computer-software for schematic design should facilitate the initial decisions; however, such software is currently available only for low-rise buildings. (See discussion on ENERGY-10, SCHOOLSPEC, PEAR, and

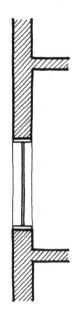

Figure 8.4 ▶ Computer input of zone with multiple windows (no daylight dimming).

RESEM that follows.) Simulations of high-rise or otherwise complex buildings are still difficult to undertake. Efforts made by Lawrence Berkeley Laboratory in the development of Power-DOE are now advancing the status of large-building software toward a more appropriate analysis technique for the schematic design phase.

One problem in developing schematic design software is caused by the lack of specificity inherent to the schematic design phase, which conflicts with the need for precise building dimensions and detailed operating schedules required for computer software. Describing a building at that level of specificity would be too time consuming and also irrelevant, since many original assumptions will change. Conversely, a too-sketchy description can give misleading results.

ENERGY-10 addresses this difficulty by providing libraries and a database with building defaults for almost any entry required. The libraries include thermal properties of materials and construction systems, as is typically done for most programs. However, ENERGY-10 goes a step further and for any construction type in its repertory it assigns default walls, roofs and windows. The defaults are based on typical construction practice. Defaults are also assigned for levels of lighting, equipment, schedules of building use, and even a simplified building geometry. This way, a simulation of a typical building can be immediately performed, with very few changes required. As more is known about the building, more specific information can be input to replace the defaults. The approach works well for low-rise, simpler buildings but has not yet been perfected for high-rise, complex buildings. For such buildings there is greater diversity of function and operation, of materials and systems, so the default-building process is more difficult by an order of magnitude.

Another set of problems pertains to the accuracy of algorithms. Highly simplified software executes fast but is approximate. On a typical building or on a large sample of buildings such software can give reasonable results. For a particular design the use of simplified software might create problems in adapting from the general, incipient stage (appropriate for simplified analysis) to a higher level of detail as the design progresses, especially if there are interactive phenomena such as daylighting and thermal mass. For this reason hourly simulations are desirable. However, detailed hourly simulations are sometimes (but not always) too lengthy for analysis of *large* buildings during this design phase, where dozens of scenarios need to be quickly explored. Fortunately, ongoing advances in computing power are removing the speed limitations.

Section 8.3 presents approaches used by schematic design software to solve these issues and to balance accuracy and simplicity.

8.3 ► ENERGY ANALYSIS SOFTWARE FOR SCHEMATIC DESIGN, DESIGN DEVELOPMENT, AND CONSTRUCTION DOCUMENTS

Concepts of energy efficiency are outlined during schematic design, fully explored during design development, and sometimes refined during the construction documents phase. Because each phase requires a very different level of detail in describing both the building and the energy conservation measures, each employs software with different capabilities.

During the past few years a promising start was made in computer programs for schematic design; enhancements were implemented in design development software, and many specialty packages were developed for construction documents.

Overall, the use of software for energy analyses has broadened, with rapid growth in applications for accurate tools. At the high-end, the interface between energy and lighting analysis has also strengthened.

SCHEMATIC DESIGN
The schematic design phase requires fast and reasonably accurate estimates of energy performance, to compare building designs and concepts. Shapes, construction systems, and materials are evaluated against each other; broadly different energy strategies and equipment types are assessed; and building operation scenarios are considered.

Currently, most designers of commercial buildings rely primarily on experience and manual calculation procedures, such as those included in ASHRAE publications (e.g., the *Handbook of Fundamentals* and the *Applications* volumes). However, software for several building types is already available.

Software
To integrate the goals of accuracy and simplicity, software developers restrict the range of applicability for their programs. For example, PEAR only applies to low-rise residences; RESEM only analyzes retrofits for schools and hospitals; ENERGY-10 currently accommodates only low-rise buildings.

Because of their focus, such programs provide complete building defaults and customized input screens, greatly reducing the time required for building description. Another essential requirement for schematic design software, fast run time, is achieved through three strategies:

- Some programs, such as PEAR and SCHOOLSPEC, are developed by compressing thousands of accurate, hourly simulations into look-up tables. The programs access these tables and interpolate between values.
- Other programs, such as ENERGY-10, perform very detailed simulations for specific applications. In this case only simpler, low-rise buildings can be simulated.

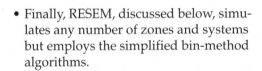

- Finally, RESEM, discussed below, simulates any number of zones and systems but employs the simplified bin-method algorithms.

One of the two current constraints on schematic design software—speed of execution—is becoming a nonissue with the exponential growth in computing speed. Within five years probably only the second constraint will remain a challenge—user interface. As will be shown later, ENERGY-10 has a promising approach to solving this problem, through extensive use of defaults, help screens, and interactive graphics.

Case Study: Residential Schematic Design

PEAR is a software package developed by Lawrence Berkeley Laboratory under U.S. Department of Energy sponsorship. It contains a combination of look-up table algorithms which access results from detailed hour-by-hour simulations with DOE-2.1. These simulations were performed in 45 U.S. locations, representative of all major weather areas. The results of these simulations are extended to about 900 locations using extrapolations based on weather characteristics. For the building types described (seven configurations of detached houses and townhouses) PEAR is accurate, fast, and user friendly (Fig. 8.5).

PEAR's range of applicability can grow only by adding more building types to the database. Multifamily housing information is currently available and could be added to the program next. No CADD linkage is available.

PEAR has been used by the U.S. Department of Energy to predict utility demand profiles, and by ASHRAE to derive compliance criteria for the 90.2 Standard *Energy-*

Efficient Design of New Low-Rise Residential Buildings.

Case Study: Schematic Design for Low-Rise Buildings

ENERGY-10 design software represents the most important advance in energy-efficient predesign tools. ENERGY-10 has been produced through a partnership of the U.S. Department of Energy's Office of Building Technology, the National Renewable Energy Laboratory, the Lawrence Berkeley National Laboratory, and the Passive Solar Industries Council (PSIC). Personnel from Steven Winter Associates, Inc., served on the PSIC technical committee charged with steering the project. Through this committee ENERGY-10 received input from architects, engineers, builders, and utility representatives. ENERGY-10 requires, for good performance, an IBM-compatible 486 DX2, Windows 3.1, and a minimum of 7 MB of hard disk space.

ENERGY-10 facilitates decision making early in the design process. It relies on a whole building approach and integrates daylighting, passive solar heating, and low energy cooling strategies with energy-efficient shell design and mechanical equipment.

ENERGY-10 shows the consequences of various design decisions. The evaluations are based on hour-by-hour calculations through all 8760 hours of the year. Weather data used are representative of typical (long-term) average conditions for a large selection of locations throughout the United States. Version 1 of the program (Fig. 8.6), released in 1996, evaluates a range of building types with one or two thermal zones. This could include, for instance, smaller commercial and institutional buildings such as schools, libraries, banks, government offices, warehouses, light

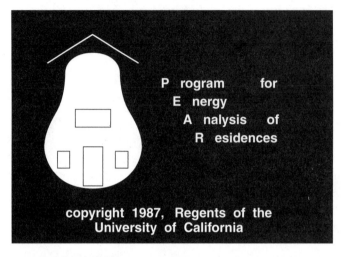

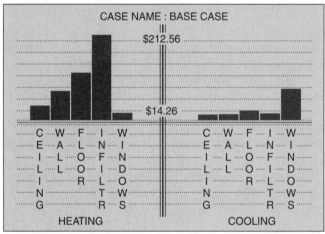

Press <End> to exit -->

Figure 8.5 ► **Examples of PEAR program screens (***courtesy Lawrence Berkeley National Laboratory***).**

industrial and low-rise residential buildings. The second version will expand the number of zones to simulate practically any configuration for low-rise buildings.

The time-consuming part of any building energy analysis is describing the building to the computer. This is particularly problematic if the building has not yet been designed and is therefore largely undefined. But this is exactly the time when energy analysis is most valuable. If a building is already designed, it is too late.

The ENERGY-10 procedure has developed a way to define and evaluate a building before it has been designed, using a process called *Autobuild*. The idea is that a *reference case* can be described by entering only a few inputs which are known during the pre-design phase of a project. Three of these choices are location (to determine the weather file), building size in ft², and building use category. Choices available are: assembly, education, grocery, lodging, mercantile and service, office, residential, restaurant, and warehouse. Also needed are the number of stories (1 or 2), type of HVAC sys-

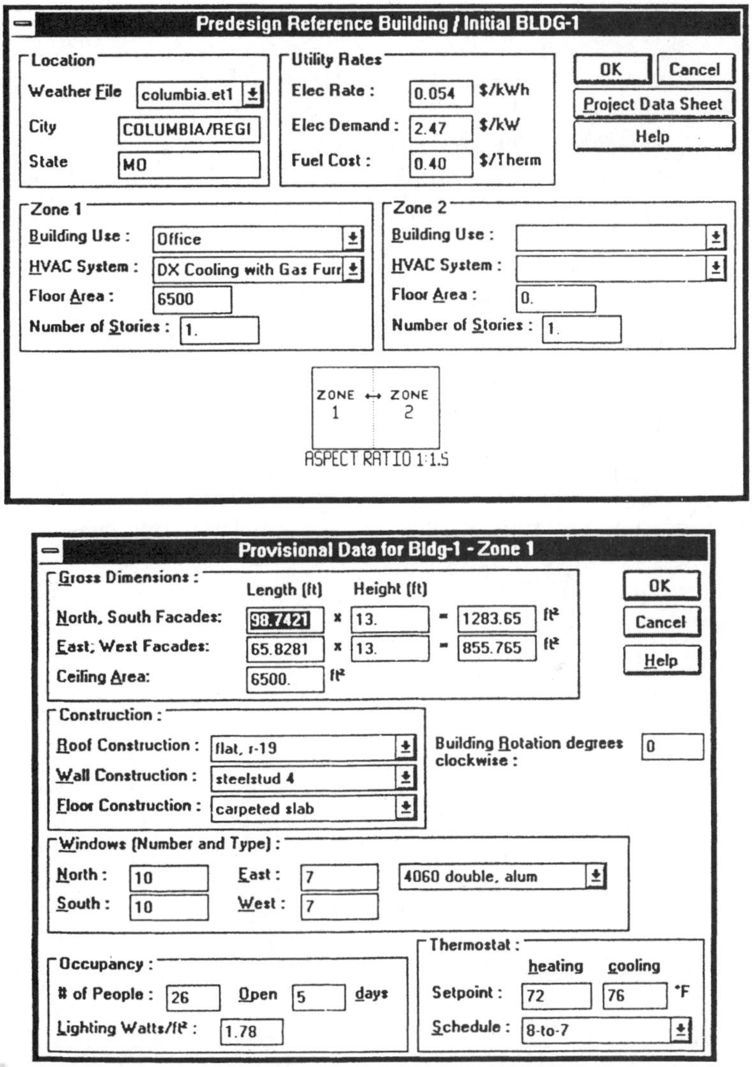

Figure 8.6 ▶ Screens of ENERGY-10 (*courtesy National Renewable Energy Laboratory*).

tem, and the utility rates. Starting with these inputs, ENERGY-10 can define and evaluate a simple "shoebox" building.

The building is called *reference case,* since it is intended to serve the same role as a reference book in the library. It is intended to represent typical design with typical energy efficiency. After performing an energy analysis on the reference case building, ENERGY-10 provides graphic results which indicate how energy is used (e.g., heating versus cooling versus lighting) and where the major opportunities for savings are. With this information, one is able to focus on the design areas with the maximum savings potential.

Autobuild goes one step further. It generates from the beginning not just one building description, but two. The second building is derived from the reference case. It is the same simple shoebox but with a variety of energy-efficient strategies which the designer applies. The purpose of this second building is to show what is the range of energy savings that can be expected for that specific building type in that specific climate. Energy-efficient strategies include additional insulation, efficient lights, daylighting, shading, improved glazing, passive solar heating with extra mass for heat storage and high-efficiency HVAC equipment. (The user selects the strategies from a menu.) This building is also evaluated, and the results for both buildings are illustrated in many graphic formats such as Annual Energy Use in thousands of Btus per ft^2 as shown in Fig. 8.7.

An additional feature of ENERGY-10 is called *rank. Rank* sequentially applies several energy-efficient strategies, evaluates their consequences, and orders the results by various indicators, such as annual energy savings and annual dollar savings. A brief discussion on a 6500 ft^2 bank in Columbia, MO, exempli-

fies the *rank* approach. ENERGY-10 calculates that high-efficiency HVAC equipment for heating and cooling ranks highest in energy savings, by reducing by about 18% the annual energy use. Insulation ranks second followed by HVAC controls and low-e glazing. A daylighting strategy which increases the fenestration area and dims the lamps might not save significant energy, because increases in heating and cooling energy offset much of the savings in lighting. Daylighting should not be discounted, however. In annual dollar savings daylighting ranks second, since it saves expensive electricity and reduces peak electrical demand.

The first set of results from ENERGY-10 illustrates the opportunity for energy savings, but the figures are based on a shoebox, while the building conceived by the designer is different. Now that the advantageous energy-efficient strategies have been identified, the shoebox can be easily modified to conform to the actual form, and to the characteristics of the actual building design, including actual window openings. The modifications are easy, since throughout ENERGY-10 everything is defaulted and everything can be edited. This saves time in setup, yet gives the flexibility in defining the building.

For example, the designer can edit the libraries (material properties, glazing properties, wall constructions, etc.) and save them for later use.

In another example, in the *shading geometry* dialog box, shading types for overhangs can be selected from a list of available choices, based on geometries that are usually advantageous for various latitudes. One can also define specific shading geometries for overhangs or fins using either dimensions or cut-off angles (Fig. 8.8).

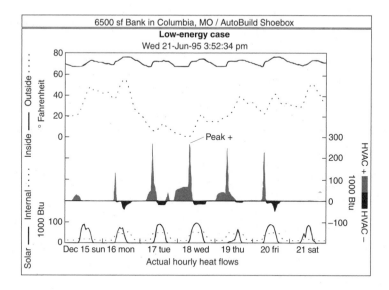

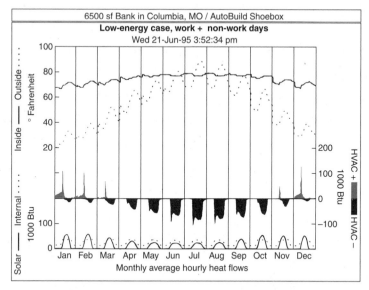

Figure 8.7 ▶ Graphic output of ENERGY-10 for a bank in Columbia, MO (*courtesy National Renewable Energy Laboratory*).

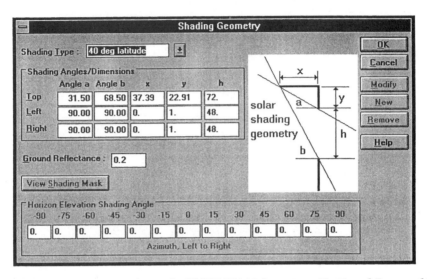

Figure 8.8 ▶ Shading geometry input in ENERGY-10 (*courtesy National Renewable Energy Laboratory*).

To sum up, the purpose of the ENERGY-10 software is to keep the evaluation of energy performance simple, allowing the user to easily incorporate these calculations into the design process of a small building. The analysis is greatly facilitated by the special ENERGY-10 features of *autobuild, apply,* and *rank.*

Case Study: Schools and Hospitals Schematic Design

RESEM was originally developed by Lawrence Berkeley Laboratory to provide estimates of retrofit savings, for the Institutional Conservation Program of the U.S. Department of Energy. Its thrust is to allow a quick evaluation of the potential for energy savings of a facility, before detailed, and expensive analyses are performed. This characteristic makes it also applicable to the schematic design phase in new buildings.

RESEM uses an ASHRAE modified bin-method to calculate the energy use in schools and hospitals. The bin-method does not simulate the building every hour; rather, it groups the outside air temperatures in a month in several bins: between 60°F and 65°F, between 65°F and 70°F, etc. The energy analyses are based on the number of hours comprised by each temperature bin for a given month. Because of this simplification, the bin-method runs much faster than hourly simulations. For buildings that do not use natural ventilation, solar strategies or significant thermal mass, and for HVAC equipment that does not have its performance greatly dependent on part-load conditions, the bin-method yields reasonably accurate results.

A useful feature of RESEM is that energy savings are based on actual utility bills paid by the facility.

RESEM automatically generates a complete building description for primary and secondary schools, universities, and hospitals. For these building types the user needs only to input the year of construction, building function, and floor area. The building description generated by RESEM (e.g., geometry, construction elements, HVAC, lighting, controls, etc.) can then be modified by the user.

RESEM has interactive input with pull-down menus, pop-up data screens, and dialogue boxes (Fig. 8.9). However, it does not provide output with plans or axonometric views.

RESEM has already been field-tested in the early 1990s.

Case Study: Modular and Relocatable Classroom Buildings—Schematic Design/Design Development

SCHOOLSPEC is an easy-to-use Windows™-based software package that can assist in the design of energy-efficient, environmentally-sensitive modular classrooms. The program provides a rigorous hour-by-hour energy analysis using a database created with DOE-2 simulations. Graphic displays are used for all aspects of the program including a real-time 3-D model of the building being simulated. SCHOOLSPEC was developed under the sponsorship of the U.S. Department of Energy by Steven Winter Associates, Inc.

SCHOOLSPEC can be used in all phases of the design process for modular classrooms, beginning with predesign and continuing through contract documents and specifications. SCHOOLSPEC provides two paths to satisfy users with different goals. One path is very easy and quick to use—it utilizes default values for most inputs. The other path allows for detailed data entry and customization. SCHOOLSPEC begins with the selection of a floor plan type from the graphic database, which contains single relocatable classrooms and buildings with 2, 4, 6, or 8 classrooms (Fig. 8.10). Plan dimensions can be modified

and a building roof type is selected (Fig. 8.11). After windows are also input, a 3-D model is automatically built by the program. This 3-D model can be rotated by the user to examine all geometric and layout features (Fig. 8.12). SCHOOLSPEC then provides default or "base case" values for the building's structure, finish materials, HVAC systems, lighting, and other design parameters—all editable.

The software facilitates the optimization of energy-efficient design including the application of the passive solar design strategies of Daylighting, Natural Ventilation, and the use of Solar Gain/Thermal Mass.

SCHOOLSPEC computes energy savings for these strategies and evaluates their cost effectiveness using the program's built-in cost database. Users can also define their thresholds for cost effectiveness and specify acceptable simple payback periods or life-cycle cost criteria. In a similar manner, SCHOOLSPEC allows users to evaluate insulation levels, improved glazings, more efficient lighting, and HVAC systems including their controls.

In the environmental area, SCHOOLSPEC facilitates the selection of construction materials for characteristics such as durability, acoustics, and a range of environmentally-sensitive issues. Detailed information and a rating scale is provided for concerns of indoor air quality, pollution during manufacture, product toxicity, recyclability and recycled content, and for the energy embodied during production. Once all of the materials have been selected, SCHOOLSPEC assembles the information into an outline specification of the classroom building that can assist in the bidding or procurement process.

DESIGN DEVELOPMENT
During design development the building geometry and construction systems are defined,

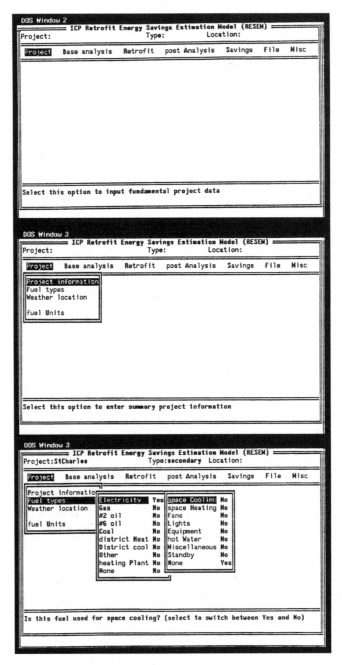

Figure 8.9 ▶ Screens of RESEM (*courtesy Lawrence Berkeley National Laboratory*).

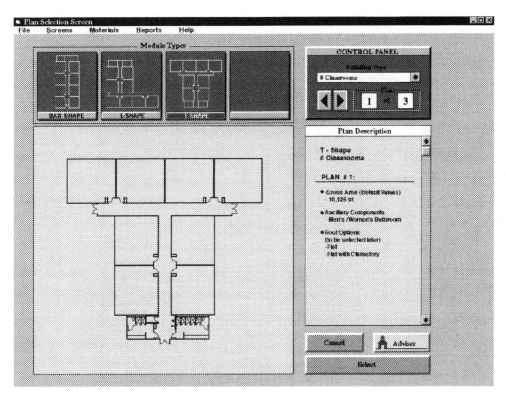

Figure 8.10 ▶ Plan selection screen in SCHOOLSPEC.

and the HVAC equipment is selected and sized. As a result most energy analysis work is concentrated in this phase.

The computer software is developed by diverse groups and organizations including the federal government, HVAC equipment manufacturers, utilities, trade associations, and professional firms.

Federal Government

The federal government has developed the most comprehensive and accurate energy simulation packages.

DOE-2.1 is wide-ranging and thoroughly validated, although by no means perfect. The DOE-2.1A version came into use in the early 1980s. Subsequent versions refined the algorithms for solar gain, daylighting, and control strategies, and increased the number of HVAC systems that can be simulated.

The HVAC equipment section comprises most configurations in wide use, including cogeneration, ice storage, and engine-driven chillers.

For analysis of large buildings, DOE-2 is the premier tool. The traditional DOE-2 input is very detailed and technical, using its own codified language. The output can be brief or exhaustive, according to need. In either case, the output is hard to interpret by persons without specific training.

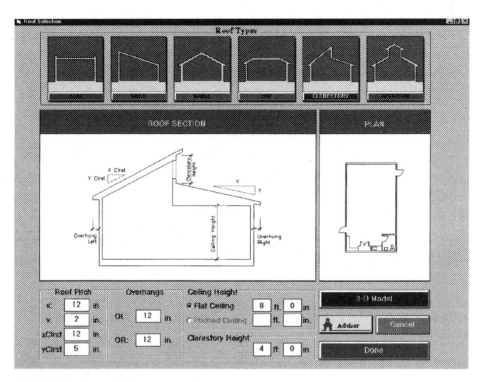

Figure 8.11 ▶ Roof selection screen in SCHOOLSPEC.

The new version of DOE-2, Power-DOE, brings screen-oriented input backed up by defaults. Other screen-oriented versions are also available, such as Vision DOE developed by Charles Eley and Associates. These versions are much easier to use by practitioners. It is probable that specialized consultants will employ both versions, the coded-language one to stretch the program into simulating assemblies and systems that are not prepackaged.

DOE-2 cannot be easily used to design distribution systems (e.g., ducts, pipes, VAV boxes). However, one positive development may greatly enhance the usability of this program: graphics software.

Graphics software serving to document the plans and volumetry of the building simulated is already available and continues to be improved. Fig. 8.13 shows the representation of a school simulated by Steven Winter Associates, Inc., using one of the 3-D input visualization packages on the market.

BLAST, developed at the National Institute of Standards and Technology, has also been widely validated. It is more accurate than DOE-2.1 in its simulation of thermal mass but is less detailed in modeling HVAC equipment. Like DOE-2.1, its input and output procedures are very complex and its use for HVAC design is limited. Graphic output is restricted to presentation of energy use patterns.

ASEAM, also federally sponsored, is considered to be a good tool for simulation of mechanical equipment. ASEAM is well suited for buildings with low mass and without very large glazed areas (such as atria). It has a good input structure for parametric runs. ASEAM is easier and faster to use than DOE-2, even if it is less accurate.

None of these government-sponsored packages interacts with CADD software. The sizes and locations of floors, roofs, walls, and openings are defined through extensive take-offs which entail a high risk of errors. However, the graphic representation of numeric input (available on DOE-2) represents a step forward.

HVAC Equipment Manufacturers
Software has been available for many years from producers of mechanical equipment. Several packages perform whole-building simulations and are used for *sizing* of both equipment and distribution systems, and for *prediction* of energy use. These computer programs are less exhaustive in their analysis of loads than the government-sponsored software, and as a result are less accurate in non-

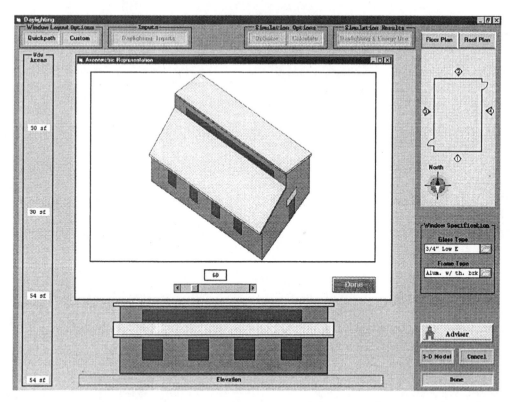

Figure 8.12 ▶ Daylighting screen of SCHOOLSPEC with 3-D mode pop-up screen in foreground.

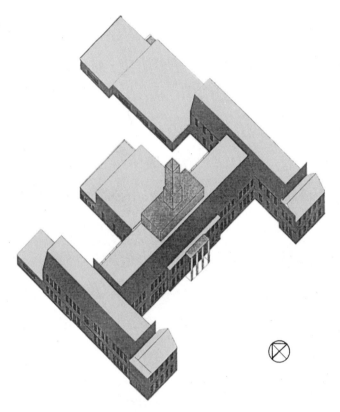

Figure 8.13 ► **Representation of building simulated with DOE-2.1 by Steven Winter Associates, Inc., using** *DrawBDL* **(***courtesy Joe Huang & Associates***).**

equipment areas such as envelope, shading, daylighting, and thermal mass.

Software is also available for design of specialized subsystems, including ice storage systems, cogeneration systems, and heat exchangers.

Generally, the programs do not interact with CADD software and do not echo the input in a graphic form.

One notable exception is software which interfaces CADD and duct/pipe design programs. The user sketches with a single line the distribution system on a CADD drawing. The interface program transports the sketch

data to the sizing routine, which dimensions the ducts or pipes. The results are then imported back to the CADD package, where the single-line sketch becomes an annotated, double-line drawing (Fig. 8.14).

Utilities

Utility companies supply software packages as part of demand-side management programs. Groups of utilities often share in the development and dissemination of software. Some of the programs are well developed and continuously updated (e.g., AXCESS which is now being merged into Power-DOE), while others have only local use or have such approximate calculation techniques that are bound to become obsolete.

Utility-developed programs lack graphic input and output routines or CADD linkages to represent buildings.

Trade Associations

Software has been developed by trade groups whose members install mechanical equipment or other HVAC components such as sheet metal ducts. These programs tend to be based on ASHRAE simplified calculation procedures, easy to use and reasonably accurate for uncomplicated situations. Their applicability is typically restricted to peak loads.

Professional Firms

Mechanical engineering firms sometimes develop their own proprietary software for design purposes. Often, ASHRAE simplified calculation procedures are combined with rules derived from experience. The accuracy of this software for energy consumption is typical of ASHRAE simplified algorithms. Enhancements vary from firm to firm and are rarely validated by outside sources.

Increased Use of Accurate Energy Analysis Software

For all their limitations, energy/sizing software packages are increasingly used to design buildings. As buildings became more complex, and as lighting and HVAC control strate-

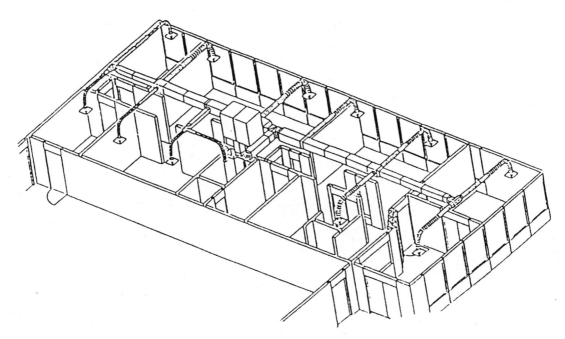

Figure 8.14 ▶ **Duct drawing using CADD/sizing interface (*courtesy Elite Software*).**

gies become more sophisticated, the need for accurate predictions of energy consumption grows. These tools give higher confidence in the selection of energy-saving components and systems.

Utility Demand-Side Management (DSM) has been relying, to a large extent, on energy software complemented by monitoring to predict savings. Better DSM programs, exemplified below, provide valuable education in energy efficiency to practicing architects and engineers.

Case Study: Northeast Utilities Energy Conscious Construction Program
The Energy Conscious Construction Program of Northeast Utilities started in 1989. Millions of ft^2 of new buildings in Connecticut and Massachusetts have been simulated using DOE-2, to determine the cost effectiveness of energy efficient strategies (see Fig. 8.15).

Offices, schools and universities, laboratories, medical facilities, prisons, retail centers, and central plants are among the projects analyzed. Energy-efficient strategies (EES) have

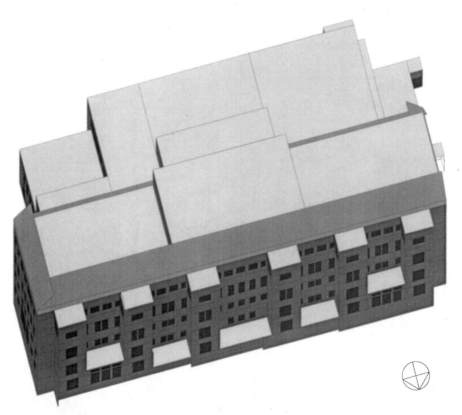

Figure 8.15 ▶ Axonometric representation of hospital generated from DOE-2.1E input (by Steven Winter Associates, Inc. using DrawBDL, for Northeast Utilities).

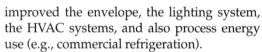

improved the envelope, the lighting system, the HVAC systems, and also process energy use (e.g., commercial refrigeration).

The Energy Conscious Construction Program has a significant effect on NU's 168,000 commercial customers. It has reduced the peak summer demand by thousands of Kw and the energy use by hundreds of megawatt-hours. It also decreased the electricity and fuel bills of NU's customers.

Another benefit is the heightened awareness of energy efficiency in the building design community. More architects and engineers have come to appreciate the advantage offered by accurate computer simulations in selecting and sizing building systems, and as important, in supporting design choices, such as higher quality fenestration, modular chiller plants, or DDC controls.

Case Study: Seattle City Light Simulations and Monitoring

From 1982 through 1988 Seattle City Light studied the energy consumption characteristics of commercial construction in its service area. As part of this program, seven buildings were monitored before and after energy conservation retrofits: two stores, two restaurants, two office buildings, and one grocery.

DOE-2.1B simulations predicted electricity savings of 14% for the entire group, and for all ECMs; the measured savings was 11%.

Although the agreement at group level was very good (Fig. 8.16) larger discrepancies were noted for specific EES in individual buildings. For example, the DOE-2.1B prediction of lighting EES was 97% of measured savings in the 90,000 ft^2 office building, but only 67% for the 15,000 ft^2 office building. Variation of actual versus assumed operation schedules was identified as a major factor in

such large discrepancies. For example, the exterior lights of the small office building were turned on only at dusk, and therefore the photocell controls could not achieve any savings.

Case Study: New England Power Corporation Design 2000 Program

The Design 2000 Program, sponsored by NEPC, has been basing its energy analyses on an enhanced ASEAM version. ASEAM is a bin-method program developed under the sponsorship of the U.S. Department of Energy. NEPC encourages energy efficiency in a wide range of new commercial, educational, and institutional buildings in Massachusetts. Large electricity users are the prime target.

Consolidated Edison Enlightened Energy Program

Consolidated Edison of New York Co., Inc., launched in 1991 a new component of the Enlightened Energy Program, to assign DSM incentives by accounting for the *dynamic interaction* of energy savings in new commercial buildings. DOE-2.1 simulations helped the utility decide how much it should pay for efficiency strategies such as daylighting, DDC controls, or chillers with good part-load performance. Figure 8.17 shows the 715,000 ft^2 GSA Federal Courthouse Building in Manhattan that has been analyzed using this process. (The architect for the building is Kohn, Pederson, Fox; the HVAC engineer is Consentini Associates.)

Steven Winter Associates, Inc., performed the DOE-2.1 energy analyses under subcontract to and in collaboration with Croxton Collaborative. Options examined included:

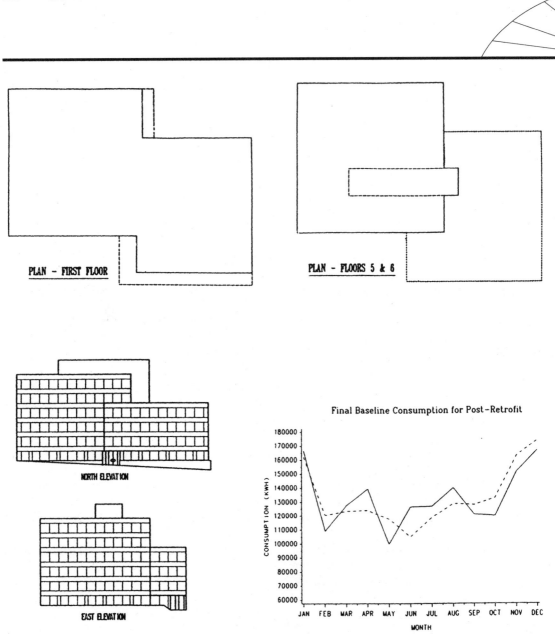

Figure 8.16 ► **Simulated versus measured energy use in Seattle office building** (*courtesy Seattle City Light*).

Figure 8.17 ▶ Federal Courthouse Building, Foley Square, Manhattan, New York City (*photograph courtesy Roy Wright*).

Envelope

- Several glazing types with different shading coefficients and U-values, but all maintaining a clear-glass appearance
- Air infiltration retarder

Lighting

- Efficient fluorescent lamps (e.g., 1.7 w/ft^2, 1.5 w/ft^2, 1.25 w/ft^2, 1.0 w/ft^2, and 0.75 w/ft^2) and electronic ballasts
- Occupancy sensors
- Continuous daylight dimming sensors with magnetic and electronic ballasts

HVAC

- Direct digital control for VAV boxes, connected into the occupancy sensor system
- Variable frequency drives for fans, hot water pumps, and chilled water pumps
- Efficient motors
- Enthalpy controls
- Higher efficiency electric chillers

The energy efficient strategies of the Courthouse were projected to save 3500 megawatt-hr per year and to reduce demand by 1350 kw.

CONSTRUCTION DOCUMENTS

Construction documents may use software for finalizing specific details. Typically, manufacturers of HVAC equipment offer programs for selecting energy-efficient configurations. Programs developed for envelope research are also used occasionally to improve the thermal integrity of fenestration, walls, roofs, and foundations.

The effect of energy simulation tools in the construction documents phase is limited, since all major decisions already have been taken.

HVAC Design

Optimization packages for heating and cooling coils balance the efficiency of heat trans-fer against fan and pump power during the selection of coil diameter and coil rows.

Computer programs for fans require input of design conditions to determine the most energy-efficient products.

Other software selects the type and size of coils in ice-storage applications. Equipment as diverse as cooling towers and vent hoods may also be refined during this phase.

Envelope Design

One computer program, FRAME, performs two-dimensional heat flow analyses on fenestration and opaque envelope details. FRAME stands out by its user-friendly interface. Figure 8.18 shows isothermal plots based on analyses performed by Steven Winter Associates, Inc., for a high-rise residential building. The work was performed for the Queens West Development Corporation and funded by the New York State Energy Office, whose functions are currently discharged by the New York State Energy Research and Development Authority (NYSERDA).

Sometimes two-dimensional computer analyses of heat flows are inadequate. For the Durst Office Tower in Times Square, New York City, Steven Winter Associates, Inc., modeled the heat flow at mullions, window sills and roof/wall junctions. The purpose of the work was to assist the architect, Fox and Fowle, select an energy-efficient curtain wall system, with reduced probability of moisture condensation, within the budget constraints of the project. A three-dimensional heat flow analysis program, HEATING-7, was used to perform the analyses. Figures 8.19 and 8.20 show the AutoCAD representation of two of the details considered for the project. The AutoCAD file was imported into HEATING-7, which was then used to evaluate construc-

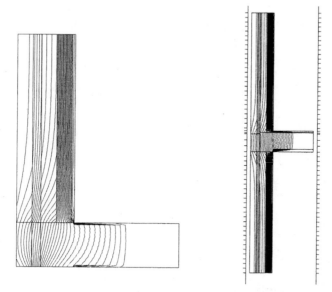

Figure 8.18 ▶ **Two-dimensional simulation tool for designing energy-efficient envelopes (FRAME) applied to masonry wall at junction with the floor slab, for Hunter's Point high-rise building, New York City (*Architect Cesar Pelli, HVAC engineer Cosentini Associates*).**

tion and insulation strategies. The work was funded by NYSERDA.

PRACTICAL CONSIDERATIONS FOR DESIGN SOFTWARE

Schematic Design
- Explore major design issues such as building geometry, percentage of glazed area, orientation, type of HVAC system (e.g., heat pumps versus chillers).
- Perform parametric runs to determine the *magnitude* of changes in energy use brought by energy conservation measures.

Any single result can be misleading because so many design decisions have not yet been made. However, parametric simulations will determine the relative importance of energy conservation measures (ECMs). These simulations will also show the range of condition over which the ECMs are effective.

For example, simulations may indicate that low-e glass in conjunction with daylighting strategies is more effective than reflective glass. Further, the parametric runs may identify the combinations of glazed area/shading coefficient over which daylighting remains effective (e.g., windows no larger than 35% of total wall area, with shading coefficient no higher than 0.6).

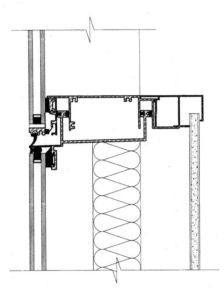

Figure 8.19 ► **Vertical section through curtain wall detail considered for Durst Office Building, New York City.**

Design Development

- Select the simulation package according to building type, energy efficient strategies examined, and accuracy required.

  For lightweight buildings where fenestration and daylighting ECMs are not considered, any major simulation package can be appropriate.

  If the building has significant thermal mass, large footprint, natural ventilation, or if fenestration or daylighting strategies are used, consider DOE-2 or BLAST. For detailed simulations of cooling and heating equipment, with analysis steps below one hour, consider the computer program TRNSYS.

- Assign at least as much time for debugging and corrections as for the description of the building.

- Develop procedures for input and checking.
- Verify results against empirical data.

Construction Documents

- Optimize subsystems whenever possible.
- Use 2-D and 3-D software to investigate the effect of thermal bridging in critical areas, especially if winter humidification (intentional or due to occupancy) is provided.
- Inquire with manufacturers about validation of their computer models.

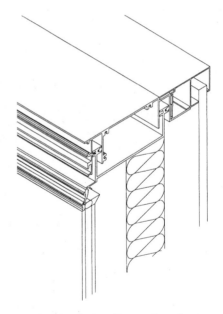

Figure 8.20 ► **Three-dimensional simulation tool for designing energy-efficient envelopes (HEATING-7) applied to curtain wall detail considered for the Durst Office Building (Architect Fox and Fowle, HVAC engineer Cosentini Associates).**

8.4 ▶ DEVELOPMENTS ON THE HORIZON

INTEGRATION

The most important software programs under development integrate CADD and HVAC design/energy analysis packages. The *output* of some software packages is already expressed in graphic form, albeit with numerous restrictions. It is likely that soon most major HVAC design/energy analysis programs will be able to output a graphic representation of the building that is simulated.

Next, the graphic input for schematic design will probably be perfected. Some small steps have already been taken with front-ends of software such as DOE-2. The simple building description of schematic design will make the task relatively easy.

ACCURATE DESIGN SOFTWARE FOR ENERGY EFFICIENCY IN COMMERCIAL BUILDINGS IS OFTEN USED IN THE UNITED STATES

Schematic Design
- Dozens of research greenhouses throughout the United States for the Agricultural Research Service of the U.S. Department of Agriculture, Greenbelt, MD
- Elementary and high schools in NY, VA

Design Development
- Hundreds of educational, institutional, and commercial buildings in California, Connecticut, Massachusetts, Oregon, Washington State under sponsorship of utilities
- Numerous schools, universities, and health care facilities under the Institutional Conservation Program of the U.S. Department of Energy
- Numerous major projects such as:
  —National Resource Defense Council, New York, NY
  —GSA Courthouse and Office Buildings, New York, NY
  —Maine School of Art, Portland, MA
  —Watson School of Science, Principia College, Elsah, IL
  —Monticello High School, Albemarle County, VA
  —Trump Riverside South High-Rise Residential Development, New York, NY

Construction Documents
- Envelope-related detailed analyses
  —Hunter's Point high-rise residences, Queens, NY
  —Nehemiah low-income development, Brooklyn, NY
  —Durst Office Building, Times Square, New York, NY
- Numerous analyses specific to HVAC equipment by practically all major engineering firms

Finally, links to existing CADD systems may be developed. Due to the complexity of such tools, it may be some time before they become available.

EXPERT SYSTEMS

Expert systems are computer programs that attempt to emulate the decision-making processes in the human mind. An expert system uses both numerical solutions *and* heuristic (experience-derived) rules. These rules are not always precise and may not yield a single result, but rather several results with varying certainties. This allows expert systems to function better than traditional software in many real-life situations, when data are missing or when numerical inputs alone cannot fully (or practically) describe the problem.

Currently most expert systems diagnose operation problems in process or in HVAC equipment. A cogeneration package, for example, detects irregular engine operation, power failure, or unacceptably high voltage output, and shuts down the unit. Another example is a

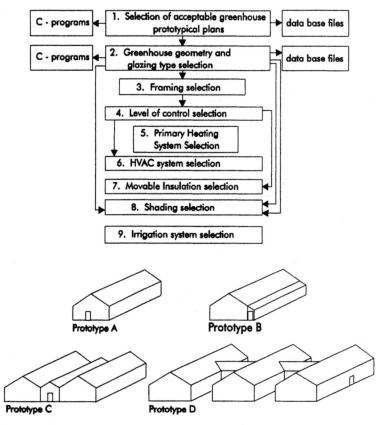

Figure 8.21 ► **Expert system for research greenhouses—building configurations.**

field expert system for chillers, which interprets noises during operation and predicts the likelihood of malfunctions or failures.

Although most of these expert systems are safety focused, energy is becoming a larger component.

The Expert Systems for Building Design

The U.S.D.A.'s Agricultural Research Service, for example, developed an expert system to define optimum configurations for research greenhouses. The expert system accesses a knowledge base of architecture, engineering, and heuristic rules, and uses a multiple-attribute analysis to weigh competing objectives in the decision-making process.

The selection process examines hundreds of options, including 46 greenhouse geometries, 4 structure types, 8 glazing types, and 11 HVAC characteristics (Fig. 8.21). Goals are ranked by the user on a scale of 1 to 10. For example, the goal "minimize first cost" in a greenhouse in Elmira, NY, may be ranked 9, and "minimize energy use" may be ranked 8. The other major goals include minimization of natural daylight during the heating season, and minimization of maintenance costs. Over 30 greenhouses have been built to date using this expert system.

Expert Systems for Building Operation

Energy monitoring and control systems collect consumption data for each major energy-using device in the building. Based on these data, expert systems can predict energy needs and can change building operations in anticipation.

Applications are currently limited to research centers, industrial settings, and large complexes, such as airports.

For example, the Joint Center for Energy Management at the University of Colorado is developing a neural network expert system to predict the energy use for the chiller plant serving a research office building owned by Hewlett-Packard. Based on these predictions, additional algorithms will optimize the chiller operation.

CONCLUSION

Energy efficiency is an ever-advancing field, just like all areas of sustained human interest. This book attempts to capture the more important developments of energy-efficient design and construction, but it could not be all-inclusive and equally-thorough in its treatment of topics. For example, geothermal heat pumps are not addressed, even though this technology is attractive from an energy, cost and environmental perspective in many situations. Applications of HVAC controls were merely illustrated, but many more exist, are used, and save energy every day in thousands of buildings.

Commissioning is mentioned in each chapter, under Practical Considerations; this subject could have occupied an independent section of its own. The most efficiently-designed building will give disappointing results if the execution of the envelope, of HVAC and lighting systems, and of controls diverges from the intentions of the building team. Quite often the errors are easily corrected: a fan positioned in reverse, controls misconnected, fire safing missing at the floor/wall junction. Also quite often, the consequences are major and the remedy, if it ever comes, too frequently is accompanied by a lawsuit.

Similar to commissioning, other themes are present throughout the book but are not treated separately. These include accuracy in energy analysis, comfort, indoor air quality, and environmental effects. All these are embraced by integrative design. Chapter 1 addressed the concept to some extent, but the catalog format of the book did not easily accommodate a sustained discussion. The purpose of the book is to immediately encourage applications of advances in one field, energy. The text is directed to the practitioner who wants to design an energy-efficient building. Excellence does require additional effort, as in anything we attempt. In this case, excellence requires integration of energy with issues of comfort, indoor air quality and the environment ("green").

The temptation to elaborate on criteria and methodology for excellence through integrative design was great. However, the case is often made that a 30% increase in the energy efficiency of most buildings has much greater effect than a 70%, or even 100%, increase in the energy-efficiency of a few. While it is also true that exceptional design and construction practice helps move the entire building profession by the power of example, this book focuses on the design with 30% improvement, achievable-here-and-now, and offers only glimpses of the emerging methods and techniques for integration of energy, IAQ and "green." Thirty percent improvement over current practice in energy efficiency is a significant achievement which requires sustained effort and focused design. Many practitioners who approach this range of better design will want to do more. We hope that this book laid foundations for the first leg of the journey and showed the direction for the last.

ABOUT THE LEAD AUTHOR

Adrian Tuluca, R.A., is a principal in charge of the
Energy/Environmental/IAQ at Steven Winter Associates, Inc., in Norwalk, Connecticut.